THE GOSPEL OF HERMES

Edited and Newly Translated from the
Greek and Latin Hermetica

BY
Duncan Greenlees, M. A. (Oxon.)

THE BOOK TREE
San Diego, California

Originally published
1949
by The Theosophical Publishing House
Adyar, Madras, India

New material, revisions and cover
© 2006
The Book Tree
All rights reserved

ISBN 978-1-58509-006-8

Cover layout and design
by Toni Villalas

Published by
The Book Tree
P.O. Box 16476
San Diego, CA 92176
www.thebooktree.com

We provide fascinating and educational products to help awaken the public to new ideas and information that would not be available otherwise.
Call 1 (800) 700-8733 for our *FREE BOOK TREE CATALOG*.

FOREWORD

Hermes was the god of wisdom in ancient Greece, Egypt and elsewhere. The various Hermetic books, although written anonymously, were all said to be inspired by this great god of wisdom, and the Hermetic teachings were a great source of wisdom for many in the ancient world. In this important book, Greenlees has collected together all of the most important Hermetic texts and put them together in one volume. He also does a great job in explaining what the teachings really mean, then closes the book by listing parallel passages, in columns, in order to compare Hermetic verses with those from the Gospels of China, Jesus, Islam, Zarathustra and the Mystic Christ.

Paul Tice

THE WORLD GOSPEL SERIES

Gather us in, Thou Love that fillest all,
Gather our rival faiths within Thy fold,
Rend each man's temple-veil and let it fall
That we may know that Thou hast been of old.
Gather us in; we worship only Thee:
In varied names we stretch a common hand;
In diverse forms a common Soul we see,
In many ships we seek one spirit-land.
Each sees one colour of Thy rainbow light,
Each looks upon one tint and calls it heaven:
Thou art the Fullness of our partial sight—
We are not perfect till we find the seven.

G. MATHESON

APART from a few scholars and devotees, the modern public are unwilling to spend time on reading through the whole of the lengthy Scriptures of the world. This little Series is planned to offer them in a cheap handy and attractive form the essence of each of the world's great Scriptures, translated and edited by one who has a deep and living sympathy for each of them.[1]

[1] Yet it is obvious that the writer does not thereby pronounce his own personal convictions.

It is based on the inevitable conclusion of any fair student that all the great Religions and their Scriptures come from one Divine Source, in varying degrees of purity of transmission, and according to the needs and capacities of those to whom they came—the authentic Word of God to man.

The Publishers hope to issue two volumes yearly, each of about 250 pages, with short notes or running commentary, and a brief introduction to point out the significance of the book in the history of world thought. This is Volume Three.

When the Series is completed, it will form a useful little reference library of the world's religious literature, which has done so much to mould the thought and culture of today, even though few individuals in each of the communities have perhaps been able to reach the ideal laid down in them.

DUNCAN GREENLEES

THE GOSPEL OF HERMES

THERE is one God, who alone is Good because He gives all things and Father because He makes all. He is eternally present everywhere, so all names are His, yet because He is infinitely above all no name can truly tell of Him. All things exist in Him as their Source and Life, so there is no death in all the universe; without Him nothing can exist, for He is in all as their essential being. God's activity is ceaseless, and this activity alone maintains the universe. All changes go on in Him, yet He Himself is changeless, immanent in all and yet transcending all. The whole universe is ruled by His divine Law and eternally tends to be a more faithful image of its Creator.

Himself eternally unmanifest, God through His reflections, the Universe and Man, yet reveals His goodness, wisdom, power to the Mind which He set in man to lead him to know and adore the Supreme. He has wonderfully designed the universe as a sevenfold Harmony under law, and He Himself pervades every atom of it, yet remains apart in His own Perfection. Mind constantly tends to soar upwards from this lower realm of Nature towards the pure transcendent Spirit, yet it has been trapped by desire in a body made of the matter of this lower Nature; being inwardly immortal, man can however escape to the higher life through love of the Eternal.

His earthly body is moulded at birth upon the soul, as a copy of the pattern set by destiny in the horoscope. His life here gives him a free choice of good or ill; if he turns to the senses he is sunk in vice and through many lives goes down deeper and deeper into the mire of misery. But if, led by Mind, the soul turns Godward, it is purified through pain, good deeds and adoration, until the body drops away and leaves it free; then it passes swiftly through the judgment by its own conscience into the higher realms of glory which are its real home. Higher and higher it soars into the Divine Life until it merges into the very Godhead. That is the aim of life; God made Man to know Him in His fullness and to love Him with all his heart and soul.

The ignorant are bound by destiny, but God saves His lovers from all such slavery. The only really mortal sin is a deliberate turning away from God, for the knowledge and love of God frees the soul from every kind of evil. The devotee is patient and gentle, silently adoring his Lord with all his being, whatever sorrows life may bring to him. Man's whole duty is to love God and do good to His creation, for by this he shares the harmony of the universe and fulfils His will. To accept help from above and pass it on to those below is the path to Perfection.

But in order to seek God, you must first despise the flesh and firmly renounce all worldly and sensual things that are not He, while you sincerely worship Him and do good to others. Then He reveals Himself to you as the One Reality and gives you the grace of love for Him, which draws you from outer sense to inner Spirit. There in the bliss of cosmic conciousness, yourself become the universe, you can adore Him in silent ecstasy.

By once knowing God as everywhere in His universe, you can become God in one swift act of omnidentity,[1] and then you see Him always in everything. Then you can come forth with power to teach other souls how to escape from the darkness of flesh to the light of God's Eternity.

---

[1] Dr. Bucke's word for the conscious awareness that the self is identical with the All.

THE GOSPEL OF HERMES

PREFACE

AND why Hermes? But that, as a personal question, would carry me back in memory to days of callow London studenthood, to a shop in Regent Street where Mead's big green volumes threw wide a magic door to a fragrant meadow whose fresh scents seemed to recall a long-forgotten age. In that meadow memory whispered strange beauties deeply buried in a portion of the mind never before laid open to the sunlight of the waking consciousness. It was an age of childlike trust in the Unseen, of daring exploration in the recesses of mind and universe, of reverence for the great starlike beings who, watching silently, guard our human race through these dangerous ages of its immaturity. One breath from that meadow—and the name of Hermes, the Thrice-Greatest one, became a bridge from London fogs and Oxford's "dreaming spires" to the kingdom of the deeper self, where dreams unveil Reality and past and present merge into the timeless "Now".

Years went by, and Petrie's little book opened a window on that meadow once again. More years, and then came Scott with his classical mind overbrimming with Plato and the Stoics, his clever restorations of the ancient text, his over-bold corrections to adjust it, Procrustes-wise, to the preconception. And so "The Gospel of Hermes" clamoured to be born, and has now to be introduced to the little growing family of the "World Gospel Series".[1]

I have used the method adopted for the Series in this volume also. Those who have struggled, even with lively sympathy and interest, through Mead's translation, and tried to piece together the Religion of the Mind from the untidy confusion into which time has plunged it, may welcome the comparative ease wherewith it may be followed here. I have used, in the main, Scott's text, save where his emendations seemed quite unneeded and due only to his inability to adopt the Hermetist's point of view.

There are scholars who ignore "contradictions", sailing among them with close-shut eyes, led on by their clear mental vision of the whole. There are scholars who see the "contradictions" and forget their context; they denounce the writer's inconsistency, or fly to an unwarranted guess of interpolation. I have tried to avoid both of these unscientific extremes; I have tried to find in every such "contradiction" the two sides of a single coin, the same truth from two opposing angles—both true but in different ways.

---

[1] I should like here to express my gratitude to Dr. G. Srinivasa Murti, the Hon. Director, Adyar Library, Madras, for his courtesy in permitting me to consult books even in this distant place. (Bimlipatam). D. G.

If I have been swayed by prepossessions in my work upon this Scripture, I may fairly claim them to have been that :

(i) The Hermetic books present a single consistent philosophical religion, based on real spiritual experience,

(ii) their writers were sincere men of clear intellect and noble purpose,

(iii) apparent differences of opinion herein can easily be reconciled by one who steps *inside* the system and views it from within. All religion is full of paradox, of apparent contradiction, for our words were never meant to define the Supernatural, but only to describe things of this lower world wherein our minds and bodies are for the time being held.

If any readers come to share these views after they have gone through this book, it is enough. Those who disbelieve in God and in His purpose in creation may get little out of it; but there are others, who by their own hearts or by the overwhelming evidences of past and present have been convinced that our lives are ruled by the Supernatural, by God, and these may find much of pleasure and of profit in reading what these grand old philosophers had to say of their experience. The choicest souls of Greece and Egypt they were; in them met the streams of the noblest thought of Europe and of Africa, and those who know of the agelong tradition of Yoga in India will see that Asia too has given of her best to swell that mighty twofold flood.

In this volume the running commentary has had to take a larger form than in the two earlier volumes of the

Series. The philosophy dives deeper than they and into obscurer modes of thought and speech, and what is almost a free paraphrase has seemed the best way to elucidate it to the reader. The Notes at the end will, I think, establish the claim of "Hermes" to teach what he has known for himself, because they show that what he has to say may be parallelled from many lands, among the writers of many creeds and many ages. This is a true religion; it speaks of realities that the reader may experience for himself, if he care to tread the path its authors have laid down.

Great has been the influence of "Hermes" on Western religion. It is impossible for an honest, unbiassed, reader to turn afterwards to the Christian mystics or even to our English hymns, without recognising the source of so many striking phrases, so many beautiful analogies, that have made religion real to millions in Europe all down these nineteen centuries. This is not to say that Christian theologians, mystical or dogmatic, have copied from the pagan writers. But many of the noblest Hermetists themselves—we need only name Dionysius the Syrian "Areopagite"—carried over into Christianity when converted the old theology and so enriched the new. They did not invent Hermetism, any more than the first Christians invented Christianity; they used the older truths, revealed in an earlier day, to explain, to beautify, the new-found revelation, and so made it acceptable to the great minds of the Alexandrian and Asiatic doctors of the Church. Nor can Islām deny the preparation of her field by the noble monotheism and devotion taught by "Hermes". Of course, it is easy to trace back St. Thomas Aquinas to St. Paul and to deny all pagan antecedents to this giant among scholastics. But St. Paul himself arose in a world rich with Hermetism; he spoke and wrote to men whose minds were ennobled by the concepts given by "Hermes" to the age; and, "being all things to all men", he thus doubtless won many of them into the Christian fold.

This book does not claim to try to replace Scott or Mead. Its aim is quite other. It seeks only to bring to the wider public of a war-harassed world the solution to life's problems reached long ago—perhaps while the Christ trod Palestinian lanes and fields—by men wholly devoted to the search of the One Reality. This age is shaken to its depths by the collapse of the optimistic materialism of a vanished generation; those who seek a new philosophy of life, those who can put away for awhile the bias of their own environment and religious ancestry, may see in their solution a glimmer of that Truth which can unite us all and bring back Paradise to a world washed clean of sin and passion, once more restored to purity and peace.

INTRODUCTION

1. Hermes and the Hermetists

Who was Hermes?

"HERMES" the supposed founder of the religious philosophy we shall study in this book, was not a man as the Buddha, the Prophet Muḥammed, Jesus, or Confucius were men. There was no special man who bore this name and who taught "the Religion of the Mind".

Hermes was the Greek God of the Mind, and so of Wisdom. Thus any writings held to be inspired by true Divine Wisdom might be, were, attributed to the God of Wisdom, and were said to be written by Hermes himself. This pseudonymity, usual in ancient days, had no motive of deceit in it—the book was written by "Hermes" (*i.e.* Wisdom) through the hand of a pupil of Wisdom, who saw no significance in his own share of the work that his unimportant personal name should be recorded. Disciples thus habitually wrote in the names of their teachers, humbly acknowledging a debt where it rightly belonged.

So we must first realise that all the writings from which our "Gospel of Hermes" is derived are really, in the modern and western sense, anonymous. This takes away nothing from their interest and value.

Mediterranean Hermes

In the last centuries before and the first centuries after the Christian Era began, the Mediterranean area was a welter of religions, philosophies, mystery cults, and salvation rites. The old State religions which had satisfied earlier generations had lost all meaning in an age newly awakening to the significance of the individual soul. A sense of sin, of separation from the Supreme Good, and a longing for reconciliation, together with a warm personal devotion to the Deity in various forms, had appeared in many individuals, and ever new attempts to solve these new problems of the heart were made by sectaries of many lands. The political unity created by the great Empires of Persia, Macedon, and Rome, led to attempts towards religious unity. The cults of Iraq, Persia, Syria, Anatolia, Greece, Egypt and the Jews found they shared so much of their essential groundwork that they might well merge into a single World Religion. It was only the swift State-aided rise of Christianity, far better organised and with a stronger personal appeal to average minds than its rivals, which ultimately stemmed the syncretic tide and killed the hope of such a development.

But in the meanwhile these other cults—of the Mother-Goddess Isis (under various names), the Victim-God Osiris (under various names), and the Wisdom God Hermes (under various names)—had spread far and wide, laying a strong foundation in the pagan mind for what was soon to follow and replace them all. Mead, in his first volume of the invaluable treatise *Thrice Greatest Hermes*, has given us a masterly account of the upwelling religious enthusiasm and enterprise of that age, and has shown well what part in it was played by the personal devotion offered to the Hellenistic God of Wisdom, Hermes. He translates from Dietrich and Reitzenstein, etc., several prayers to this deity which show many close parallels both with our " Gospel " and with ancient Egyptian hymns. Every student of the subject should make a thorough study of this volume, together with *Fragments of a Faith Forgotten*, by the same author, if he would find the truth, rather than merely confirm his own preconceived opinions.

Egyptian Hermes

Hermes, the God of Wisdom, reigned not only in Greece but also in Egypt and elsewhere. In the Nile Valley he was known under the ancient name of Thōut at his main seat of Chmūn, the " City of the Eight " (*i.e.* Ogdoad), or Hermopolis, at least 5000 years ago. There he played an important part in many myths, including those of the Creation; he was also the Recorder of the Gods, especially at the Judgment of the Dead— not that he was impartial, for he was a sort of pleader for the accused—and a Guide of the soul into the blissful paths of the other world. It was he who invented writing and wrote all the ancient scriptures, including the later *Book of Breathings*, which taught man how to become a god; under his supervision the laws were all drawn up and preserved in libraries; more than all this, he was himself the Divine Word from which creation all arose—the fount of the much later "Logos"-concept. As Lord of the Moon, he controlled the mysterious unseen world of night; he was also the Mind and the Speech of God, expressing and fulfilling the Eternal Will. Thus we meet with him in many ways associated with man's religious and spiritual life. It is impossible to study Boylan's scholarly treatise on *Thoth the Hermes of Egypt* without recognizing traces of the fictitious prophet " Hermes " of our " Gospel ".

The person of this ancient god, the teacher of Osiris, Isis (cf. KK 32), and many more, himself first taught by the " Good Spirit " or " Divine Mind " with whom he became one after his apotheosis, is taken over bodily and clothed in a very thin veil of the typical prophet then popular among Jewish Hellenistic circles. The same sort of ideal figure appears in the books : *Apocalypse of Baruch*, *4 Esdras*, and *2 Enoch*. The antecedents of our own " Hermes ", with his three chief disciples— Imuth the wise man of old, Ammon the type of all kings incarnating the god Amūn, and Tat the diminutive of Thōut who stands for the child of his teacher—are in the main Egyptian, though coloured by Jewish ideas of a religious teacher and by Platonic teaching methods through dialogue.

Mead gives us an interesting study of the old legends about the Books of Hermes preserved from " before the Flood " by being recorded on stone pillars in Egypt—

and disposes of the easy claim that these are forgeries and have no historic value. The scientist does not so carelessly dismiss evidences which correct his first hypotheses as our classicists have tried to invent a Pseudo-Philo and a Pseudo-Manetho to disprove the antiquity of the Hermetic teachings.

The Traditional Hermes

Scott gives us the legend as it was preserved by Vergicius, and it bears a family resemblance to Plutarch's story of the mission of Osiris in still more ancient days: "They say that this Hermes left his own country and travelled all over the world . . . ; and that he tried to teach men to revere and worship one God alone, the Demiurge and Genetor (begetter) of all things ; . . . and that he lived a very wise and pious life, occupied in intellectual contemplation and giving no heed to the gross things of the material world ; and that having returned to his own country, he wrote at that time many books of mystical philosophy and theology." (*Hermetica*, i, p. 33) But this is really no more than a summing up of the ideal laid down for men in the writings we are soon to study. The early Christian Fathers mostly held that Hermes lived before Moses, and was a pious and wise man whom God used to reveal truths which were later to be fully explained by Christianity.

The Hermetic Communities

Who then actually wrote the "Books of Hermes"? Men brought up in the immemorial Egyptian religious tradition, stirred to emulation by the then newly translated Hebrew scriptures and by the bold philosophies of the Greeks,—who came forward to offer the Egyptian version of the syncretistic religion, just as Philo pleaded for the Jewish version, and the Platonists and Stoics fought for a Greek version mainly based on Homer. These men were not merely Egyptian "patriots", who held all things of Egypt better than anything from other lands, but they firmly believed that they were themselves inspired by the Source of all truth, the very God of Wisdom Himself. Indeed, there are passages in their writings wherein even we, cut off by space and time from the occasion, can still almost hear the vibrant thrill of inspiration in their words, which, even in a language foreign to the writers, are full of beauty and of poetic rhythm, besides being instinct with noble thought and a marvellous sweep of mental vision.

They were men who, first of all, meant every word they said and wrote. Theirs is no literary concoction, made up in cold blood in some pedant's library; it is the expression of a passionate faith in men who staked their heart and soul upon its truth, who were ready to die for it and, as Ferguson reminds us, many of whom later did have the privilege of laying down their lives to witness to their faith and devotion.

They were men who loved God and fearlessly proclaimed that to love and serve God is the supreme end of human life, that it is man's highest privilege to worship, to draw near, to enter into the most intimate relationship with, the Supreme as the destined priest of living creatures, just as the High Priest alone could enter the Holy of Holies in Jerusalem on behalf of his fellow men.

They were men who had proved their sincerity by withdrawing from the lure and tinsel of worldly life into the solitudes of the deserts, there to spend their time in lonely contemplation, in silent worship, in fervent study, and in occasional joyful assembly with their fellows to adore the All-Holiest by hymn and prayer.

And then they were men whose love for other men subsisted wholly in this love for the Father and Giver of all, who is Himself the only Good, the Only Beautiful, the only Reality—to be seen in all; thus they served the world for His sake in no noisy tub-thumping but in secret prayers, in beautifying that little corner wherein they lived, by overcoming the passions of the flesh in their own persons, by cultivating the virtues with the aid of grace, and by unifying their minds and wills with that of the Supreme Beloved.

Petrie has made a clever study of these little communities of pagan monks and hermits, who gathered together in the deserts of Syria, Egypt and other lands; we can read of them also from eye-witnesses in Philo's *de Vitā Contemplativā* and in Josephus's account of the Essenes. They tell us of the monks' great attention to cleanliness, to their silence during meals, to a social exclusiveness like that maintained by the Christians in the 2nd c. " Clementine " books. In several minor details we find much that recalls the life led by early Buddhist monks in India and by the first Christian monks in

Egypt, as described by Palladius and in the Coptic tractates published by Zoega; these were in fact their spiritual descendents and many of them may well have been converted Hermetists themselves.

Mead and Scott both point out, in their different ways, that these true devotees of God swept into the rising Catholic Church in the 4th and later centuries and gave it great wealth of spiritual power, of personal conviction, of noble theology. They were among the "Gnōstics" of whom the learned Clement of Alexandria spoke so very highly, and the reader of this little "Gospel of Hermes", if familiar with the Fathers of the Eastern Churches, will not need to be shown how much Christian theology owes in its precision, in its inspiring vision, to these men who earlier explored the same fields of thought. Nor can he deny, if he study it with equal-minded sympathy, that the vigour of the presentation of God's Oneness in the *Qur'ān* was made possible largely because our unknown and nameless Hermetists had prepared the ground for it so well.

When Did They Write?

They wrote of God and the eternal verities of the human soul, a timeless reality, and from internal evidences we cannot possibly fix the exact dates of their writing. But the following facts must be given due weight if we would try to picture them accurately in time:

1. Cornelius Labeo, as we are told by Bousset and Ferguson, based some of his beliefs on these writings, and he died before A.D. 120.

2. Their teachings on the Logos or Word, and on the Aeon, are of a very early form when compared with those developed in the Fourth Gospel and in the 2nd c. Christian Gnōstics.

3. They nowhere show any clear signs of Christian influence.

4. The writers do not seem to have even heard of the doctrines of the Incarnation, Redemption, Resurrection—which could hardly have been possible in Egypt after the great Christian Gnōstics, Valentinus, Clement and the others had written and taught in Alexandria.

5. Plotinus in the 3rd c., shows great familiarity and affinity with the later elements in our writings.

6. Philo, the Jewish Gnōstic, early in the 1st c., is very close in his ideas of the Logos to those of " Hermes ", though slightly more developed.

7. In some writings, notably KK and St., the Egyptian framework stands uncontaminated by later ideas, which would suggest for these books a Ptolemaic date at the latest.

8. They show close affinity with the Petosiris-Nechepso literature of about B.C. 120.

9. The Christian Fathers often quoted them almost as Scripture, which argues a date of at least something B.C.

10. Affinities with Gnōsticism are mainly with the earlier non-Christian forms.

11. The legends preserved by Manetho (*ap.* Syncellus), Cicero in *de Natura Deorum*, 3 : 22, Ammianus, and Josephus (*Antiquities*, 1 : 2) trace the " Books of

Hermes" back to Egyptian inscriptions on secret temple walls—a parallel to which is the Memphite *Ptaḥ-document*, copied in the Ptolemaic age from a worn stone inscription, the original of which dates back to the Pyramid Age (3000 B.C.) as shown by Reitzenstein and Breasted.

12. Sanchuniathon's Phoenician Cosmogony claims to base itself on the Books of Thōut (Hermes), and is at latest early 1st c. A.D.

13. A Cosmogony in a poem of 1st c. B.C. (see Reitzenstein, *Zwei Religions-geschichtliche Fragen*: Strassburg, 1901) claims to be Hermetic and is very like the cosmogony given in our CH.

14. Though too much should not be made of this, the strongly conservative Egyptian spirit shown so forcibly in CH 16 : 1-2 and the quasi-historical allusions cited by Petrie do suggest a date several centuries B.C., for the original writing of these treatises.

Against this mass of evidence, to which Mead adds much more of equal weight, Scott (following the dogmatic assertions of older encyclopaedists whose main concern was to prove all valuable religious thought due to Christian influence or to European culture) puts up the following evidences :

1. The "Prophecy of Hermes" (our §§ 34-35) was fulfilled by the Syrian conquest in A.D. 269, and was therefore written shortly after that date. This is effectively refuted by Ferguson in the fourth of Scott's volumes.

2. "Hermes" is simply Platonism, modified here and there by Stoic ideas and occasionally coloured by a stray Egyptian phrase. But Reitzenstein had already shown that the Egyptian elements are fundamental, and I think the sentences quoted in our Notes, which could be indefinitely expanded, are enough to prove that "Hermes" deals with universal experience and is not a rehash of Platonic thought at all, as the Classicist would fancy.

Petrie may well be right in his claim that our texts were really Egyptian in the first place; not in the sense that they were translated into Greek from the Egyptian language, but that they were reinterpreted into Greek mode and idiom by men whose culture and mother-tongue were Egyptian, because Greek was then the language of international culture and the usual medium in the Schools of Alexandria.

The Spirit of Their Age

It was a tolerant age, wherein men sought with eager interest to find, in the scriptures of other lands, the truth they already knew from their own scriptures in other forms, yet still recognisable. The Ptolemies had encouraged scholars from all over the world to study in the great Library at Alexandria, where hundreds of scribes were always busy copying and translating the books written by prophets, poets and philosophers of all nations.

We find in "Hermes" none of that evil spirit of controversy and derogation which disgraced the theologians of the 4th and later centuries when Christian charity was lost in a mad hunt for heresies. Indeed only once does he speak strongly against a certain doctrine which, it seemed to him, blasphemed God's goodness, and that was the idea that a human soul could sink into the body of a beast (§ 32 : 1). Then in one passionate passage, (CH 16 : 1-2), he implores the King (Nekht-nebf, suggests Petrie) to see that these holy doctrines are not translated into Greek, because they would then become the prey of shallow-minded Greek pseudo-philosophers; this clearly seems to be a sincere protest and no archaistic pose.

The writers were content to seek God in their own way, and to leave others to seek Him in their own way. Their only concern was that the few who were gifted by God with the higher Mind to seek Him should not waste their lives in passions, in lower worldliness, or in fruitless controversy, but devote themselves earnestly to the immemorial Quest, and so fulfil the purpose of their own being and win eternal bliss in His Presence. In this, we find they have foreshadowed the purpose of our own "World Gospel Series", and salute them as our spiritual ancestors.

2. The Story of Our Texts

The Sources

Our "Gospel of Hermes" is derived from four main sources—the *Corpus Hermeticum* (CH), the excerpts from *Stobaeus* (St.), the *Perfect Sermon* or *The Aclepius*,

(PS), preserved in a Latin translation, and various short quotations and citations in other early writers (F). I have not included in the text passages from the Arabic *de Castigatione Animarum* (cited as DCA), an English version of which is given us by Scott, though much of this is probably a direct translation from early and genuine Greek Hermetica, lost to us in the original form. Nor have I used the so-called *Smaragdine Tablet*, said by Albertus Magnus to come from Phoenician, though it is easy to trace in this the fundamentals of our " Hermes " system : I append it here, for the student's convenience :

"I speak not fictitious things, but that which is certain and most true. What is below is like that which is above; and what is above is like that which is below—to accomplish the miracle of one thing. And as all things were produced by the One Word of One Being, so all things were produced from this one thing (*i.e.*, the universe-root) by adaptation. Its father is the Sun, its mother the Moon, the Wind carries it in its belly, its nurse is the Earth; it is the father of all perfection throughout the world. The power is vigorous if it be changed into earth; acting prudently and with judgment, separate the earth from the fire, the subtle from the gross. Ascend with the greatest sagacity from the earth to Heaven, and then again descend to the earth, and unite together the powers of things above and things below; thus you will obtain the glory of the whole world, and darkness

xxix

will fly away from you. This has more fortitude than ⸢fortitude itself, because it conquers every subtle thing and can penetrate every solid."
I shall leave the reader to find obvious parallels to every sentence of this " Tablet " in our " Gospel ".

The Corpus Hermeticum (CH)

We owe this valuable collection to the zeal of Psellus, a Byzantine scholar of the 11th c., but it is not quite certain how it fell into his hands. All our copies of the manuscript come from one copy, which is very corrupt, and there are signs that one or two tracts have fallen bodily out of the Corpus and so been lost. There would have been few copies in pagan days, as such books were kept in esoteric circles, and most of these must have perished during the 4th to 6th cc. while non-Christian religious literature was being systematically destroyed.

Ephraim Syrus shows that in A.D. 365 there were Hermetic books in Syria, perhaps already translated into Syriac, the Greek originals being kept in the Edessa Library. Scott has shown how at Harran, under the early Muslim rulers, a sect of Hermetists won toleration as " People of the Book " by claiming to be " Sabaeans " (cf. GI 28 : 3—Qur'ān, 5 : 69) using the writings of Hermes as their Holy Book, and giving the names of their Prophets as Idris or Enoch, and the Good Spirit (Agathodaimon : Akmon), whom they identified with Seth, the third son of Adam. From all this it is clear that in A.D. 830 there was a collection of Hermetica in

Syria, including some books now known to us only from fragments; Alkindi (d. cir. A.D. 873) says that Hermes taught his son "the unity of God" in the books accepted by the Harranians as their Scripture. In about A.D. 880 there was a clash at Harran between the Hermetists and the illiterate idolaters of the city, and the philosophers migrated to Baghdad, led by Thābit ibn Qurra, a great pagan writer, and their sect seems to have survived about two centuries in the Arab capital, until it was destroyed by the orthodox under Ghazali al Ashari. Yet as late as A.D. 1150 Shahrastani and Katibi quote teachings of the Harranians like our Hermeticism, and Suhrawardi, the mystic who died in 1191, agrees with much in both Plato and Hermes. The Arabic book *de Castigatione Animarum* is full of Hermetic thought, much of it clearly direct translation from Greek Hermetica.

Scott suggests that when, about A.D. 1050, the ban fell at Baghdad upon this pseudo-Sabaean philosophy, one of the faithful may well have fled with a copy of his sacred writings to Constantinople, then the Christian capital, and so those which still existed in the original Greek may have fallen into the hands of Psellus. The book soon travelled to Florence, and in due course it was printed at Ferrara in 1593 by Cardinal Patrizzi, who urged that it should replace Aristotle for study in the schools and monasteries. After great popularity in the Middle Ages, its dangerous resemblance to the Christian dogmas led to an almost total eclipse in the 18th c., and until Scott took it up no complete critical edition was attempted.

Plutarch (cir. A.D. 80) refers to Hermes the Thrice-Greatest, and Clement of Alexandria (210) says the Books of Hermes treat of Egyptian Religion (*Stromata*, 6 : 14), but does not quote from them; probably no copy was so early accessible to non-Hermetists. Tertullian (213) quotes a passage very like our Hermetica; Origen does not actually quote them though his own ideas are very close to theirs; Iamblichus asserts that these books were translated (interpreted?) from Egyptian by men acquainted with Platonic thought—which seems very near the truth. In his *Letter to Anebo*, Porphyry witnesses to these books, and Lactantius (311) quotes from them rather extensively; probably by that time converts had betrayed their old scripture to their new leaders. They were often referred to during the 4th c. Arian controversy.

As we have it 'now, the Corpus contains seventeen tractates, listed at the end of this volume on p. 236, there being no No. 15. Petrie and Scott differ widely in their estimates of their relative age, but CH 1, already quoted as Scripture in CH 13, will be among the earlier of the series, and CH 18, apparently by a professional orator of the closing 3rd c., is evidently the last. Petrie puts CH 12 as one of the earliest, dating it before B.C. 332, and CH 1 at about B.C. 200. Without analysing his reasons, Scott dismisses this with contempt. CH 7 is only a fragment, and two or three others are not quite complete, CH 17 being clearly only the conclusion of one almost wholly lost. CH 11 and CH 12 are each composed of two distinct treatises, probably by different authors.

Stobaeus (St)

We owe much to the interest of this early 6th c. student of pagan philosophers; he made four books of arranged extracts from their writings, and included among these three very long, and twenty-four short, extracts from Hermetic literature then extant and available to him. Many of these came from Sermons of Hermes to Tat and a few to Ammon. The books of Stobaeus were read by Photius, about A.D. 850, and later separated into two volumes, copied by different hands; the whole was later epitomized, and part of the epitome was lost. We are fortunate to have what survived.

For us the most important extracts are St. 23-24, the two books of *Kore Kosmou* (KK), St. 25-26, two fragments of a book or books wherein Isis is the teacher of Horus, her son, and St. 2 and St. 11, both of which seem to be complete tractates. The *Kore Kosmou* is purely Egyptian, save for a short Greek episode about Momus, (KK 28), as Petrie truly says; there is no trace of Jewish influence, so common at Alexandria after B.C. 100. Scott and Mead agree that it is really a unity, though Ferguson calls it " a botched compilation " of widely differing materials. It may be looked at in some ways almost as a parallel to Plutarch's book on Isis and Osiris, which he based on Manetho's work, about B.C. 280. From internal evidences, Petrie would date this work to the 5th c. B.C. in the main. The Isis-Horus books are slightly less purely Egyptian in tone, and Petrie would put them about B.C. 200. In his book

Poimandres, pp. 136-7, Reitzenstein shows that Isis was a teacher of the mysteries, herself taught by Hermes, in the Ptolemaic period, as in KK 32, and Lucian, in his *Gallus*, 18, tells us there were Books of Isis and Horus kept in the temple shrines in Egypt. The Isis-Stele of Kyme, Ptolemaic in date, is also in harmony with these indications. Some day we may admit that the *Kore Kosmou* is one of the most valuable surviving books of Egyptian myth and cosmology.

The Perfect Sermon (PS), known also as *The Asclepius*, is also of the utmost importance to students of Hermeticism. It is a free and very corrupt Latin translation of a lost Greek original, of which we have a few citations by Lactantius, Cyril, etc.; from these we can see how the translator added and deleted phrases at his will, and in places completely spoiled the meaning. Reitzenstein has shown how this book cannot therefore be used for dating the Hermetica until we know what was actually added by the translator on his own. There was an old tradition that this was the work of Apuleius, but though the style resembles his Reitzenstein rejects this view, holding the idiom to be later than A.D. 130; as it is Old Latin, it is presumably not later than 4th c. In A.D. 387, when he was still very near to Neoplatonic thought, St. Augustine, *Soliloquies*, quotes the Latin, but does not name the translator, who may have been, as Scott suggests, C. Marius Victorinus, a Hermetist (?) orator converted in A.D. 356 and died in A.D. 362.

Scott holds that PS consists of three separate tracts: (1) *PS 1-14a*, by a monist writer of late 2nd c., who had retired for contemplation and tillage; (ii) *PS 14b-16a*, by a dualist resembling Numenius and Hermogenes of the 3rd c. and (iii) *PS 16b-40*, by a Fayūm Egyptian (PS 27d), probably a priest, who approved of marriage and tolerated social life. In this third book he traces influences of Chaeremon and Posidonius, as rarely in CH. He holds that the three books were joined together, probably by the writer of CH 9 somewhere late in 3rd c., this editor adding the preface and epilogue we have used in GH §§9 and 43. Mead agrees that these two are later than most of the book PS.

Petrie finds signs that the book dates back to about B.C. 340, shortly after CH 16 with its anti-foreign diatribe; he notes the animal-worship deciding Egypt's districts and leading to wars (as in Juvenal, 1st c A.D.). Isis is still an angry goddess, and Egypt the most important land; he also says that the whole cosmology suggests some such early date, while there are no Aeon, Sophia or Logos doctrines as developed in Alexandria by B.C. 200. His points should be refuted, not ignored.

Fragments (F)

These are mostly preserved by Lactantius and Cyril of Alexandria, while a few are collected by Mead from (Pseudo)-Justin, Tertullian, Cyprian, Augustine, Suidas and Athenagoras. Several come from the same tractates as some of the excerpts by Stobaeus, and we have found some of value in reconstructing the story of Creation.

3. The Views of Modern Scholars

After mediaeval enthusiasm, the Hermetica had to face for nearly 150 years a bitter opposition, mainly because of the awkward results to Christian dogma which their acceptance as genuine independent works might entail. The general opinion during those years, never supported by any positive evidence, was that they were neo-Platonic or anti-Christian forgeries, of no value whatever to the history of religious thought. This notion dies hard; it is still trotted out by all who wish to dispose of " Hermes " in the usual hostile way.

The Encyclopaedias, such as Encyclopaedia Britannica, Encyclopaedia of Religion and Ethics, The American Encyclopaedia, etc., have generally, without adducing evidence, simply repeated this charge, alleging that the Hermetica are " a last effort of dying Paganism to resist a victorious Christianity ". The fact that they show no signs whatever of having heard of Christianity and make no attempt whatever to answer or refute any of its main doctrines, does not seem to have disturbed the smug complacency of these authorities in any way. The *Encyclopaedia Britannica* says they are of the early 3rd c. and syncretistic in nature—partly Oriental, partly an offshoot of Stoic and other Greek philosophies, with a mystical and gnōstic colouring, but presenting no one dogmatic system. We are left to wonder whether the author of this article ever read the Hermetica for himself. The *Hastings Encyclopaedia of Religion and Ethics* (1913), St. George Stock being the writer, says the books are mainly Platonist and apparently composed in Greek, but he has little of his own to contribute to the discussion beyond admitting that they teach a sort of pagan Gnōsticism and contain several striking parallels with the New Testament. Nor do any of the Encyclopaedias condescend to take real note of the work done by scholars expert in the subjects treated by the Hermetica; they are content with a parrot-like repetition of the dicta of retired Anglican clergymen who took their degrees at Oxford long long ago.

From Parthey to Mead

In 1854 Parthey first raised voice against the Neoplatonic forgery assumption. He believed that the Poimander (CH 1) at least was Egyptian in origin, and that we might well hope some day to find an Egyptian version of it in the demotic script current at the beginning of the Christian era. Four years later, *Artaud*, in 1858, held that the Hermetica teach the inner or esoteric side of Egyptian theology, as it was taught to initiates in the temples, and that they were definitely translated from Egyptian. The next big step forward was taken by *Ménard* in 1866, when he said that they stand to the Egyptian religious books much as Philo's work does to the Hebrew scriptures—as interpretative allegory and vision; he admitted that Christianity arose in an environment teeming with such theosophies, and is quoted by Mead (TGH i. p. 29) as saying: " Let us recognize in it the work of a beaten competitor and not of a plagiarist. Indeed the triumph of Christianity was prepared by those very men who thought themselves its rivals, but who were only its forerunners." He dated CH 1 and CH 13 a little before Basilides and Valentinus, say A.D. 90, about. In 1873, *Dévèria*, the Egyptologist, confirmed the views of Artaud with even greater assurance. But nothing moved the writers in Classical Dictionaries and the like. In 1896, *Aall* said the Hermetica must date to the 2nd c. B.C. and they are an offshoot from the source of the Logos-doctrine found in the Fourth Gospel, Jn. Then came, in 1904, the first really scientific study of a part of the Corpus; *Reitzenstein*, the philologist and expert on Hellenistic and West-Asian religion, published his *Poimandres*, wherein he clearly proved the Hermetica to be of mainly Hellenistic theology but strongly influenced by Egyptian tradition and contemporary with the New Testament books; he agrees in the main with Ménard's views, but denies any strong Jewish influence. He fixes the *terminus ad quem* for CH 1 at A.D. 100, and then shows that books of very similar type were current at Alexandria 250 years before that. He shows that the Petosiris in books of about B.C. 120 corresponds closely with our Asclepius, just as the Nechepso corresponds with Ammon (Note how close the name comes to that of Nekhtnebf, whom Petrie identifies with Ammon), and tells us how in that earlier literature Hermes reveals the wisdom to Asclepius and Anubis. At about A.D. 40, Vettius Valens tells us that Nechepso had direct knowledge of the "Inner Way" (Riess Frag, 1), quoting an "Apocalypse of Nechepso" in Greek, wherein the King left his body in ecstasy and heard a voice, which was a "substantial presence" (cf. § 1 : 1) guiding him; Seneca quotes from Posidonius (B.C. 135 to cir. 51) the same vision, saying it derives from Egypt. It is also noteworthy that Manetho (B.C. 280) translated Egyptian books into Greek, using the same Library of Rē' at Heliopolis where Plato is said to have studied; Plato tells us his wisdom came from the priests there; also Cicero (de Naturā Deorum, 3 : 22) says there were two Egyptian Hermes, the first of whom was too sacred for any name; so we have "the Good Spirit" as the teacher of our "Hermes". All this, and much more like it, cannot simply be brushed on one side unanswered because of prejudice. *Mead*, after a scholarly investigation of evidences, sums up: "The Wisdom of Egypt was the main source of our treatises without a doubt," (TGH, i. p. 8), which I believe is the correct statement of facts, though he unfortunately wastes much time on Marsham Adam's curious theories about the Great Pyramid and the "Book of the Dead", which no one knowing Egyptian could accept for a moment. We need not spend time on *Granger's* article of 1904 because he totally ignored what Reitzenstein, Bousset and so many others had proved; he stated that our writings were of Christian origin, dating about A.D. 190 but containing some earlier strata. We have already said enough of *Petrie's* and *Scott's* views.

To sum up, it must really be obvious to all who have the slightest knowledge of the Hermetica, of Gnōstic literature, and of Egyptian Religion, that the three are intimately linked, the Hermetica being mainly based upon certain ideas which might be traced back to the earliest strata of Egyptian thought; but the exact nature and extent of its reliance and dependence has yet to be worked out by men equipped with knowledge on both sides. But let it be said clearly once and for all that as Neo-platonism begins with Ammonius Saccas while our writings are certainly older than that, they cannot be any longer dubbed "Neo-platonic forgeries", and that as their teachings are demonstrably simpler, therefore earlier, than the Christian Gnōsis, it is equally absurd to consider them as attempts to bolster up a dying Paganism against a rising Christianity; the Christian Gnōsis was active before the writing of *1 Jn.* and *Rev.*,—probably, that is, by A.D. 92.

4. Their Influence on Later Thought

On the Christian Theologians

This book cannot attempt to enter on a history of Christian theology, nor is this the place or time for such an essay. But a perusal of the main writings of Clement of Alexandria, his *Stromata, Paedagogus, Exhortation* and *Outlines*, show many traces of influence by just such teachings as those we meet in our Hermetica. So also Origen, in A.D. 230, taught in his *Principles* much that could well have come from Hermetic teachers, and the influence was passed on to his illustrious and saintly pupils, Gregory of Neo-Caesarea, Pamphilus, Dionysius of Alexandria, Basil the Great, Gregory of Nazianzene, Gregory of Nyssa, Didymus, John of Jerusalem and Eusebius; Sts. Hilary of Poitiers, Ambrose the teacher of Augustine, Jerome and Athanasius himself, besides Vincent de Lerins, Victorinus, and Rufinus, may also be named among outstanding pupils of Origen, whose father was in all likelihood himself a Hermetist, and who stressed in all his writings just those elements of the Christian faith which came nearest to those of " Hermes ". From these, and their pupils, practically came the theology of the Christian schools today.

On the Western Mystics

Nor was the influence of this loftiest form of Western paganism less upon the so-called " Dionysius the Areopagite ", 6th c. Syrian father of the Christian mystics. Acting through the Saint Victors, the writer of the *Cloud of Unknowing*, Hilton's *Scale of Perfection*, Mother Julian of Norwich, Richard Rollo, Ruysbroeck, Henry Suso, and so even to the 16th century giants—Sts. Teresa and John of the Cross, the line has run unbroken down to our own day; Wordsworth, Carpenter, Blackwood are three writers whom the Hermetic schools might well have welcomed to their midst.

On the Sufis of Islam

And through the 9th c. " Sabaeans " of Baghdad the treasury of " Hermes " was shared further East with the followers of the Prophet of Arabia. It has often been thought that the rich outburst of Mysticism in Persia after the Muslim Conquest was due to something left behind by the dying Faith of Zarathushtra: yet there is little indeed in what we know of that Faith to confirm such an opinion. Rather it was the contact of broadminded Muslim theologians with the Plato of Harran on the one side and the Vedantins of India on the other that set fire to Rabi'a and her successors and gave Sind her Lal Shahbaz, her Shah Laṭif, and others.

5. Their Value to Our Day

And what has all this to do with us? As we go through this " Gospel of Hermes " in detail, I think the answer to this will be clear to many. We are now living in days of crass and impudent materialism, when what Hermes called "the greatest evil of men"— atheism, or wilful ignoring of the claims of God to our service and our love, is not only spreading everywhere but is set up as the sign of civilisation and of a truly advanced, liberal, and secular state. But the eternal truths behind this universe where we live are not in our hand, to alter as we will; the God whom we today thrust to one side is still the God who gives all, in whom alone all exist, as Hermes taught so long ago, and we shall find to our cost that we cannot stand apart from Him, nor can we leave Him out from our cabinets, our United Nations conferences. For its manly defence of true Religion in its strong stress upon the One God as the basis for all human thinking, Hermes is of eternal value to our world.

He taught a true religion. By that I do not lay claim to him as the founder of the one true faith, without which man cannot be saved. Our dogmas come and go; our cults rise and fall; our very gods change their names and forms. The downfall of Egypt's high creed foreseen in § 34 took place, and you cannot today find one man who will register as a Hermetist in any census. Yet the essentials of his doctrine stand as true for all time. He gave us a real road which we may follow all the way until it brings us to the very feet of God and merges us into His infinite glory. He teaches us that this universe wherein we live is not really an evil thing; it is the handiwork of an all-good God, who shows Himself to us through its beauties. We can find Him through the universe that He has made. C. S. Lewis, in his *Broadcast Talks*, rightly points out that just as we can know an artist better by his conversation than by his pictures, so we can know God better through the Moral Law, which is His voice in our hearts, than by looking at what He has made. But this is no real objection to the path laid down by Hermes, for the Moral Law is nothing outside the universe, but an essential part of it, without which there could have been no "Harmony" at all for us to study. It remains true that by identifying oneself with the all and seeking to serve, know and love God to the uttermost, resolutely turning away from the attractions of the lower things towards Him, we can drown our separate selves in Him and, as St. John of the Cross puts it, become window panes irradiate with His light. *Experientia docet*: he who tries it for himself will learn the efficacy of this method of spiritual yoga; it does not differ greatly from that taught in the Mystic schools of West and East alike today.

This Series does not try to point out defects in the various Religions that it studies. Hermetism failed to win the day and perished before Christianity probably because it was too lofty to draw or hold the love of ordinary men and women, and because it could not offer the glorious magnet of a living Christ. It were futile to deplore its disappearance from the world; the law of the survival of the fittest rules in religion as elsewhere, and there are great religions today which are dying because they do not adjust themselves to the changing needs of men and to the more vivid attractions of their rivals. The true religion must be that which is in accordance with the facts of the universe and therefore in harmony with the deepest needs of the human soul; such a religion must ultimately prevail, and it will be found to contain the highest and the noblest elements in all its forerunners, and something more and higher than their best. Let us look then at "Hermes", that we may find the richest treasures in his gift to humankind, knowing that these at least are true and will never fail us through the years.

6. Certain Technical Terms in this Gospel

NOUS, *Mind*. The Greak word is cognate with words meaning *think, understand, discern, notice, foresee, propose, plan, imply, sensible, thoughtful*. We have used it in our Gospel in two senses, distinguished by the use of a capital letter in one sense: 1. mind (*Skt.* **manas**), the thinking and perceiving and understanding power of all men, which distinguishes their actions from those of animals, which are purely instinctive because individuality has not yet developed in them; and, 2. Mind (*Skt.* **Atma-buddhi**), the Mind of God, the Supreme Mind which thought the universe into being with a word perfectly expressing Its Purpose. God puts this Divine Mind into the soul that strives through virtue and love to please Him; she is then able to perceive Him, to delight in Him, to become *one* with Him, because His Mind is in her, her will is united with His Will. This Mind is the eternal Reality of which the ordinary human mind is but a lower reflection in time and space. Hermetists called theirs the Religion of the Mind because it is through this gift of Divine Mind to certain men, Initiates, that they fulfilled the purpose of their creation and attained to bliss. So far were they from agreeing with the dictum that "the mind is slayer of the Real", that they actually called the Supreme Reality, God, by this very name—Mind.

LOGOS, *Word, Reason*. This word has many meanings in Greek, and it is sometimes hard to be sure of its exact sense in any particular context. It is derived from the verb **lego**, which has four main senses: (i) *lay down,* (ii) *arrange, select, choose,* (iii) *reckon up, count,* (iv) *tell, speak, say, mean.* So its general sense is selecting thoughts which have been arranged in order and then expressing them intelligibly. Thus **logos** has two main meanings: (*a*) word expressing thought, and (*b*) thought itself and the reasoning power which enables its expression, and a third rarer sense, specially in Hellenistic and Christian writing, which combines the Reason and the Divine Word, expressing it in one word. Under (*a*), the special meanings are *word* or *talk, saying* or *maxim, discussion, report, story, speech,* and under (*b*), *reason* or *reflection, consideration, proportion, reasonable grounds*; thus it is the source of our word *logical,* and of the *-logy* in *biology, geology* etc., and probably cognate with *legal, allege, legacy,* etc.

In our Gospel it is generally rendered as either *Word, Reason* or *Speech*; it is at times not quite certain which is the apposite word in a given context. In § 45 : 2, it is used in a peculiar sense as " the inner body which is pure Mind or Intuition's vehicle "; we may take it here to be almost the " Buddhic body " of Theosophical books.

GNOSIS, the source of our word *know* and cognate with Skt. **jnana**, probably derived from a root √ Ken, meaning *get*. Its original meanings are: (i) *judicial enquiry,* (ii) *knowledge* or *wisdom,* (iii) *recognition* or *acquaintance*; it is cognate with words meaning *judgment, opinion, prudence, resolve, will, discover, examine, understand, perceive, be acquainted with,* *friend*. But throughout the Hermetica it is used as in the Gnōstic books to signify a divinely guided enquiry into the nature of God, resulting in a perfect knowledge of Him and an identification with Him through the desire for union which we call love. Thus the " Gnōstic " is not a prattler of speculations about things ineffable, but the true **Brahma-jnani**, the Knower and Lover of God, who knows himself to be inseparate from the Divine All. Because God is the source, the giver, of all good, union with Him is total bliss, and separation from Him supreme misery, the fountain of all evil.

AGNOSIA, Ignorance, has the second meaning of *obscurity* or *darkness*. For he who does not know, seek for, God, looks away from the Light and is in darkness. In " Hermes " the word signifies not a mere non-knowing of the Real, which is misfortune but no sin, but a deliberate shutting of the eyes to it, a turning away from or rejection of God. This is the one truly unpardonable sin—the only sin meriting an agelong hell. For he who will not look up to God must inevitably be looking down, and then he will fall down, to hell.

THEOI, plural of the word which everywhere in " Hermes " means the one and only God. The word is cognate with Skt. **deva** and our word *divine*, which probably comes from the root $\sqrt{div}$, heaven. Thus the original meaning will be *those who live in heaven*, the *celestials*, the *stars*, and in our Gospel it often refers to the astrological Seven Planets, who rule the lives of all incarnate beings, as they circle round God's throne and obey His commands. But the second meaning corresponds to more Skt. **deva** as *Shining Ones*, and in this case it may best be rendered as *Angels*. In § 34 : 7 it is sharply opposed to obsessing demons who drive men into sin, and so seems equivalent to the Guardian Angel of Christianity. In Latin it is sometimes rendered as **numina**, awe-inspiring beings, or **divinitas**, the Divinity.

DAIMON is derived from the verb **daio** *kindle*, or *burn*; thus the "daimons" are really those who burn with God's wrath against sinners. It is cognate with words meaning *consuming, wretched, fate, fortune, god-inspired*, and thus *godlike;* but its usual senses are (i) *deity*, (ii) *fate, destiny* or *fortune*, (iii) *departed souls*, (iv) *evil spirits*. The third of these is that general in "Hermes", similar to the **daimon** who used to warn Sōkrates, though at times it signifies rather the avenger of sin.

HARMONIA comes from the word **harmos**, a joint; its meanings are (i) a *fitting together*, (ii) *union* or *covenant*, (iii) *ordinance, decree, fate*, (iv) *concord, harmony*, (v) *agreement*, and it is cognate with words meaning *bind, marriage, adapted to, yoked chariot, arrange, governor, agreeable*. In our text it has three meanings: (*a*) the horoscope, which shows how the planetary forces which work out destiny are coordinated and adjusted, (*b*) the created spheres, which are all under one great Law of destiny, (*c*) the loving sympathy which binds God, the angels and men in one chain of mutual service, and the understanding uniting the souls of the blessed in Heaven.

EUSEBEIA This word, which I have translated by Devotion or Piety, has the dictionary-meanings of a feeling of *awe* or *shame, fear, reverence, worship, piety, religion.* The adverbial prefix **eu,** parallel to Skt. **su,** conveys the meanings of *right, due,* and so *propitious.* Thus the Devotee is one who gives to God the reverence, service and worship that are His due, to which He has the right, and so it comes to mean nearly what the Hindu understands by **bhakta**—one who alone lives the truly propitious or happy course of life.

A BRIEF HERMETIC CATECHISM

1. *How did this Universe come into existence?*
   It was created by God.
2. *What is God?*
   He is the infinite and eternal Reality behind all phenomena, known to man as a Good Father in so far as He has revealed Himself through creation.
3. *How did God create the Universe?*
   He utters it as an active Word that perfectly expresses the eternal thought latent in His Mind, and it continues to create itself in accordance with His Will.
4. *Why does He utter this thought and so create?*
   His nature is perfect Goodness, so He must be always giving Himself.
5. *Does He desire anything for Himself through this activity?*
   No. As He eternally contains all things in Himself, there is nothing He can gain; nor can He ever lose, for there is nothing outside Himself.
6. *Is the Universe good?*
   As coming from, and yet remaining in, the One perfect Goodness, it cannot be evil; being

God's child, it shares His nature and immortality, but being a material body, it is subject to change and pain.

7. *What is Man?*

Man is the son of God's Mind, emanated by Him to enjoy eternal bliss in Heaven, but fallen into the material world in search of sensual pleasure. So he is dual in nature—part dwelling with God in Heaven, part enslaved to passions on earth.

8. *Why did God emanate Man?*

To share His own delight in the beauties of His universe, He willed a being endowed with reason to seek Him through these outer forms.

9. *How did Evil come into existence?*

God is all Light, but so as to enjoy the giving of Himself He willed that there should be another. This "other" has to be separate from Him, and separation from Him is total misery, darkness, evil. Thus appeared the Darkness, and in it all the opposites to God's good qualities.

10. *Why did God allow Evil to exist?*

As rusting is inherent in iron, so evil is inherent in matter. To give Man free will implies a free choice, which is only possible where there are pairs of opposites for him to choose between.

11. *Is Matter eternal?*

No. It forms itself out of the "Dark Principle" when that is "separated" from God; but it is relatively eternal in that it was always latent—with the whole Universe—in God's Mind.

12. *What is the origin of the individual Soul?*

It differentiates itself off from the Soul of the Universe, being deluded by the seeming separateness of forms and desirous of ensouling one of them.

13. *How did Man come to be imprisoned in flesh?*

Charmed by the Universe, he too desired to create like God, but seeing the attractions of physical matter he identified himself with that, and so was trapped in a body.

14. *How can he become free?*

By turning away from or conquering the desires of the body and straining upwards to the pure Spirit, wherein is his true home.

15. *Can he do this unaided?*

No, he must receive God's help.

16. *How does God help him?*

If he does his best, God Himself comes to him as Spiritual Mind, guards his senses from temptation, dwells in him, and leads him towards the Real.

17. *What is Man's duty on earth?*

To love and serve God, to beautify His creation and help it to fulfil His Will for it, to seek Him with all his heart and soul.

18. *What is the reward of righteousness?*

God's friendship in this life, a happy and peaceful death, and a swift passage through cleansing fires into God's presence, where the soul adores Him evermore together with the Angels.

19. *What happens to evil men?*

Being slaves to passion and vice, at death they are cast into a raging hell of stormy passion and misery until they fall into some physical body more degraded than before.

20. *Is there any protection from this danger?*

The only safety lies in devotion to God, for He saves His devotees from every kind of evil.

21. *Has Man the real power to choose?*

Man really belongs to Heaven and is above the control of destiny, but if he identifies himself with the lower desires he puts himself under its sway and loses the power to choose aright. But God restores this power to those who seek Him, and so Man is in fact absolutely free to choose.

22. *Why does not God give this help to all?*

Because then they would all be automata, pulled by His strings and so robbed of the merit of choosing Him instead of the narrow ego; thus they could no longer fulfil God's aim in creating them to seek Him behind all forms.

23. *Are Man's thoughts his own?*

No. His good thoughts come from God, his bad thoughts are suggested by evil spirits tempting him towards sensuality.

24. *Is Hermetism a dualist religion?*

No, and yes. It teaches only *one* God, in whom all exist, who exists as the eternal Life and Light in all, and it rejects the notions of independent evil and a personal devil. But it stresses the double nature of

Man—God and beast, the fight between which lasts as long as earthly life endures.

25. *Does it teach Reincarnation ?*

Man is in a physical body because, and as long as, he desires those sense-experiences which can only be had through a human physical body. As soon as he is free from such desires, reincarnation ceases. This is not a matter of time, nor is there any prescribed number of births to be endured.

26. *How does Man find God ?*

God can be seen in the whole Universe which He pervades, and so also in Man's own heart. By identifying himself with God in the whole Universe, Man can break out from the narrow prison of his body and enter the infinite Life and Light of the All—merging himself in God.

27. *Where is God ?*

He is everywhere and in all, and at the same time He is the ocean in which all have their being.

28. *Is there, then, no special Temple for Him ?*

This whole Universe is His body, the shrine wherein He dwells. But more especially He makes His home in the land, the human heart, that devotes herself to serve and worship Him, and such becomes a holy land, a saint.

29. *Can the true Gnōsis of God be given by another ?*

No. It arises in the heart as a pure gift of God's grace, when the heart is stainless and wholly dedicated to Him alone. But a child of God, himself already initiate in the Divine Wisdom, then takes form before the neophyte and awakens him to the knowledge and the love of God.

30. *Can you sum up this Religion in a few words?*

It is a path to loving union with the One God through the identification of a purified soul with the Universe, which is His image or His shadow.

SYNOPSIS

Chapter One: MIND THE SHEPHERD OF MEN. 1. "Hermes" sees in meditation a vision of creation; Mind shows him Darkness corrupting the infinite Divine Light. into chaos, until God's Word redeems the higher elements. 2. It is the beauty of Divine Mind that uplifts Nature and rules the universe through Destiny, differentiating spirit from matter. 3. God makes Man, immortal as Himself, and loves him as His own image; but desire draws man down into union with Nature and he is trapped in a material body. 4. It is this desire which becomes sex and populates the earth with bodies. Yet the real Man is still the child of Divine Mind, and he must return to eternal Life through the knowledge of immortal love, the love of God. 5. God helps good men to know and love Him, and so draws them from the senses to the Spirit, while the wicked are enslaved to sense and, rejecting the leading of the Mind, fall deeper into guilt and misery. 6. The way home to God is to surrender lower activities and to withdraw to the Inmost, where God is adored by the Immortals; they lead the soul into union with Him. 7. "Hermes" is led along this path by the inspirations of Divine Mind, and he adores God as the Ninefold Holy One, praying for the power to teach others. 8. Filled with that authority, he calls men away from sense-life to God, urging them to take a guide to Eternal Life. Many scoff at him, but some are drawn to the love of God and become his disciples.

Chapter Two: THE GOOD FATHER. 9. "Hermes" begins his detailed teaching of his disciples. He tells them how impossible it is really to understand Infinite God, who is above all we finite beings can say or think of Him ; He is all that, and more ; no words can limit Him.   10. We should give to Him only the greatest, most glorious of names, such as " Father " because He makes all things, and " the Good ", because He gives all ; such names none but He can bear. 11. He is the Source of every good and perfect thing ; He alone is truly self-sufficient, lacking nothing. All embodied beings are subject to change, to gain and loss, so they can give no good, for the real Good can only be in the Eternal and Changeless Reality. 12. All the Beauty and Goodness are in God alone, and He is to be found through Knowledge and Devotion. 13. This whole universe exists in God ; He is the Model of all forms there are, while He Himself remains unlimited by Form. 14. All changes go on within the Unchanging God whose real Being is unknown, and they in part reveal Him to His children. 15. He is the ultimate Source of all, who eternally pervades and surrounds the Mind, the Soul, the Body. 16. All things come from God, and His Word breathes into them His glory, so that they may seek and find Him. Through Nature, the image of His Beauty, the whole universe came into being, and it is ruled by unfailing laws.

Chapter Three: **GOD'S COSMIC IMAGE**. 17. The whole universe obeys God's laws, and it is for man also to glorify God by fulfilling His Will on earth. 18. In Man and in the Universe thought and feeling are interdependent and reflect God's thought and feeling. Through them Man may reach God, for all exist in Him ; mind is led awhile by reason and then it becomes the guide to God. 19. Nothing is void, for all contain the unseen, which is cognate with God, the only Reality. 20. Nothing could exist without God within, and as God is Life, there is no dead thing in the universe ; everywhere is God, Eternal Life and Light. 21. This beautiful universe is ever young, though ever born and dying ; the whole is governed by one Law, which proclaims one Lawgiver, 22, who is always at work making all things like Himself, for if He ceased activity, all would cease to be. He is other than His creation, for He is its source; yet He would not be God if He were not ever giving Himself out in creation. 23. The Unmanifest generously reveals Himself by creative thinking; He may be seen in the wonders of the universe, whose very existence proves the Artist behind and in it all. 24. He is above all our praises, for He is Himself the All, free of Space and Time, and beyond every limitation of our thought or speech.

Chapter Four: **MAN IN THE UNIVERSE.** 25. The horoscope of a new life's destiny moulds the body to match an incoming soul, and draws the soul into the unwelcome prison of flesh. 26. Sex-love is a mighty force, for it reflects God's creative power, made attractive so that new bodies may be formed and men taught love. 27. Death is only the breaking of a painful link between the soul and a worn-out body; the soul is set free into the inner worlds, where it is purified in its subtle body of light. 28. All souls are at once seen as they really are; the remorse of a seared conscience sends the evil into hellish planes, while God's Light glorifies the virtuous with all nobility and leads them into His eternal Presence. 29. Souls are alike in nature but vary in rank, the higher grade being silent and reserved. Mind exalts the soul through pain, and so leads it to know God, guiding it after death to the plane suited to its own rank and nature. Helped by those above, each soul can also help those below; if it deliberately turns to evil, it will fall into hell, but sins of frailty and ignorance are easily atoned and forgiven. 30. The ignorant masses are swayed by destiny and the "stars", but God saves the Mind-led from such slavery, for He is above destiny and is our only way to Freedom. 31. God can only be sought, and true knowledge caused to suffuse the mind, by turning away from sense-attractions; this conquest of the body is not easy, but it leads to ever-increasing joy. 32. The miserable result of a lack of devotion to God is to fall back again into a physical body built by Nature to express the soul's destiny on earth. 33. The noblest of souls is a King, God's representative on earth, whose very name or image can establish righteousness and peace. 34. The eclipse of this noble Religion will plunge the whole world into ignorance, crime and misery, Egypt's holy land becoming a filthy corpse while men sink into the folly of materialism; when faith disappears the Gods withdraw and evil spirits take their place; the world falls into ruin. 35. At the darkest hour God Himself will restore things to their early state of blessedness; a new Golden Age will then begin. 36. God made Man to love and worship Him, and to tend His world; He lives in Man as the enlightened Mind. Thus Man is higher even than the Angels, for through Mind he rules the universe, and he is the link uniting Godhead to the lower planes. 37. When he knows God through the Divine Mind in himself, Man can attain perfection and be made one with God; it is only those who are sunk in ignorance of God who fall into the snare of sense and body.

Chapter Five: THE WAY TO GOD. 38. Devotion is the knowledge and love of God and His universe, and this is a man's highest privilege, being God's gift to beings endowed with Mind to worship Him. 39. He who knows God loves God, and is patient amid all injustice from his fellows, for his link with God is the final remedy for all evil. 40. The Real, the one absolute Truth, is only what is eternal, changeless, limitless—that is, God's own formless Beauty. It can only be found by turning away from the temporal, the world of sense, which shakes the silence wherein Grace, through the dawning spiritual sense of cosmic life, reveals the Truth behind phenomena. 41. Only the soul can know the Divine; through the Mind alone the Beautiful and Good can be seen, while the inner powers grow until the dawn of ecstasy deifies the human soul and blinds it to all lower things. 42. God can only be known by becoming God, realising by an act of will His omnipresence in His universe. That realisation will then be known everywhere and always. 43. "Hermes" ends his long sermon by leading the disciples in thanking God for His gift of the knowledge and love of Him. He warns them against the use of ritual instead of spiritual adoration.

Chapter Six: **THE REBIRTH OF TAT.** 44. "Hermes" privately teaches Tat how, when the seeker for God has put away the world he is initiated into the highest Mystery, which brings God to birth in his heart. 45. Having renounced all lower things, Tat enters into the Silence, and God's grace transforms his being into the Universal Soul. 46. The Reborn has now the power worthily to glorify God and so fulfil the purpose of his creation. 47. His whole being, with all its powers, is devoted to the adoration of God, wherein he joins the harmony of all Nature's worship. 48. God is worshipped through the Mind and Reason, and that worship naturally takes the form of a joyous paean, which is the first fruit of initiation. 49. This sublime teaching of how to find God through contemplating His universe is only to be given to the few who may be worthy; it is to be guarded in silence as the heart's greatest treasure.

CONTENTS

	PAGE
The Gospel of Hermes	vii
Preface	xi
Introduction: Hermes and the Hermetists, The Story of Our Texts, The Views of Modern Scholars, Their Influence on Later Thought, Their Value to Our Days, The Significance of Certain Hermetic Terms	xvi
A Brief Hermetic Catechism	xlix
Synopsis	lv

CHAPTER ONE: MIND, THE SHEPHERD OF MEN

1. A Vision of the Beginnings, 2. Nature Brings Forth, 3. Man, the Child of Earth and Heaven, 4. Ignorance is Bondage, 5. Knowledge is Liberation, 6. The Upward Way, 7. The Thanksgiving of "Hermes", 8. The Mission of "Hermes" 1

CHAPTER TWO: THE GOOD FATHER

9. God Transcendent, 10. God's Great Names, 11. Good is Only in God, 12. God the Beautiful,

	PAGE

13. Has God Form? 14. God Reveals Himself, 15. God and His Universe, 16. The Making of the Universe 26

CHAPTER THREE: GOD'S COSMIC IMAGE

17. Man and the Universe, 18. Thought and Feeling, 19. The Content of Space, 20. The Immortal God is in All, 21. One God Made the Universe, 22. God the Universal Worker, 23. God Unmanifest made Manifest, 24. A Hymn to the Supreme God 52

CHAPTER FOUR: MAN IN THE UNIVERSE

25. Man Comes into the World, 26. Human Love, 27. Death, and After, 28. The Judgment of Souls, 29. The Path of Souls, 30. Providence and Destiny, 31. The Vital Choice, 32. Reincarnation, 33. The Ideal King of Men, 34. The Age of Darkness, 35. The Restoration of All Things, 36. The Nobility of Man, 37. The Chalice of Divine Mind 78

CHAPTER FIVE: THE WAY TO GOD

38. Man's Fullest Glory, 39. Devotion and the Devotee, 40. The Truth and the Way,

PAGE

41. The Divine Ecstasy, 42. The Yoga of Egypt,
43. Thanksgiving for the Gnōsis 132

CHAPTER SIX: THE REBIRTH OF TAT

44. Where, When, and How? 45. Initiation,
46. Preparation for the Secret Hymnody, 47. The
Secret Universal Hymnody, 48. The Neophyte's
Joy, 49. The Last Words of "Hermes" . . 156

Notes 175
Sources of "The Gospel of Hermes" . .
Index 241
Books on the Hermetica and Other Books
    Referred to 248
Parallels with The Gospels of Islām, China, Jesus,
    Zarathustra and the Mystic Christ . . . 254
The World Gospel Series 261

CHAPTER ONE

MIND, THE SHEPHERD OF MEN

I have chosen to keep this first chapter as an almost intact translation of the " Poimandres " (CH 1), which is the best known of the surviving Hermetica and a striking example of the apocalyptic which was no doubt prominent among the scriptures used in the Hermetic schools and āshrams. It was already quoted as authentic scripture by the writers of CH 10 and 16, and as it is a coherent unit any attempt to analyse or rearrange its material would serve only to confuse our view of the noble religion which in Egypt, and later in Syria, stood for a time as a rival to the nascent Christian doctrine.

It seems clear that the book is a sincere, a true, report of an actual vision enjoyed by the seer who wrote it down. It is a piece of autobiography. We shall never know the author's name, but those who adhered to his religion gave him the generic name of " Hermes ", and the fiction will serve our purpose very well. Illumined, taught, by the Universal Mind, the seer indeed became the god of wisdom for his people, a true prophet, a mediator between God and Man. Having thus learned the true nature of God and His creation, " Hermes " goes out to share his wisdom with his fellows ; like Muhammed, Confucius, Jesus—all real prophets—he finds some to listen, and some to sneer and turn away, preferring their own darkness and folly to the redeeming light of Truth.

1. A Vision of the Beginnings

1. Once, having begun to think about existent things, and my mind having eagerly soared to a great height while my bodily senses were held back just as in those who are heavy with sleep,[1] . . . I seemed to meet a vast and infinitely great Being, who called me by name and asked me, "What would you hear and see, and learn and know by meditation?" I said, "Who art Thou?"—and He replied, "I am Poimandres,[2] the Supreme Mind."—I answered Him, "I desire to learn the things that are and to understand their nature, and to know God; about these things," said I, "I long to hear."—He spoke to me again, "I know what you desire, for indeed I am with you everywhere.[3] Hold in your mind whatever you would learn, and I will teach you." (CH 1 : 1-3)

2. As soon as He had said this, immediately everything changed in aspect before me and

[1] Numbers refer the Notes at the end of the Book.

was opened out in a flash. And I saw a boundless Vision; and all became Light, soft and joyous; and I loved it at sight. But after a while a terrible and gloomy darkness had come settling down in one part, twisting in coils like a serpent. Then I saw the darkness change into a sort of moistness,[4] tossed about unspeakably and pouring out smoke as from a fire; and I heard it giving out an indescribable sound of wailing, for an inarticulate cry was sent out of it. (CH 1 : 4)

3. But out of the Light came forth a holy Word and stood upon the moistness, seeming to me the voice of Light. And pure Fire sprang forth out of the moistness and up to the heights—radiant it was, and swift and active. Thereupon Air also, being light, followed the Fire, rising up . . . so that it seemed to hang down from it. . . . But Earth and Water stayed apart, so mingled together that the earth could not be seen, yet they were kept moving by reason of the breath-like Word stirring over them. (CH 1 : 5)

With single heart and mind, "Hermes" seeks God in an eager thirst for truth. So intent is he that the senses of the body are suspended, his whole mind leaps forth, and he enters into ecstasy. God, the Mind of the

Universe, of whom his own little mind is but an image, a reflection, manifests to him as an Infinite Being ready to pour light into his aspiring mind.

He sees the dawn of all things, the timeless eternal Source of all creation. All is pure and blissful Light at first, the one infinitely lovable Divine Fount of everything. Willing to create, to express Itself as manifold Good and Beauty, to give Itself, the Light seems to divide into the first pair of opposites—Light and Darkness, Darkness the parent of change, of pain, of evil, of death. The Darkness swiftly condenses into a slimy serpent-like wetness, which coils and twists and heaves itself about as though in agony, groaning after the perfection which belongs to God alone.

But even the prayer of this inchoate horror is heard by God. Its cry for Divine aid calls forth the First Divine Mission or Emanation—the Word of God. The unchanging First Cause is manifested as Creative Wisdom and dominates the lower forces which have themselves come forth from His Will and Thought. The power of Wisdom separates the deipetal, upward-striving, elements of Fire and Air—Will and Intellect—from the "heavier" deifugal elements of Water and Earth— Emotion and Bodily Desires—which were latent in this primeval archetype of Matter. Over these latter the Divine Word, the "Spirit of God" in the ancient Chaldean narrative of Genesis (1 : 2), brooded in creative silence. The stage is set for a new Cosmic Day.

2. Nature Brings Forth

1. Poimandres spoke to me audibly, "Have you understood the meaning of this Vision?"—"(Tell me, Thou,) and I shall

know," said I.—He said, "That Light am I, Mind, the First God, who am before the moistness which appeared out of darkness; and the radiant Word from Mind is God's Son. . . . What sees and hears in you (is) the Lord's Word, and Mind is (its) father, for they are not separate[5] from one another, and the union of these is life. . . . Now concentrate upon the Light, and recognize it." (CH 1 : 6)

2. Saying such things, He gazed straight into my eyes for a long time, so that I trembled at His aspect. But looking up again I beheld in my mind that the Light consisted of unnumbered Powers[6] and had become a boundless universe. This I perceived, seeing by means of the word of Poimandres. (CH 1 : 7)

3. Then as I was amazed He spoke to me again, " You have seen in the mind the Archetypal Form which is before the beginning and is endless." . . . " Then," said I, " whence did the elements of Nature draw their being ?" —He answered this, " From God's Will; seeing the beautiful universe, she copied it, making herself a Universe by means of

elements arising from her and the births of souls. (CH 1 : 8)

4. "Then the First Mind, being Life and Light, male-female, brought forth another, a Creative Mind which, being the Second, created out of Fire and Wind seven Rulers circling round the sensible universe, and their government is Destiny. Immediately the Word of God sprang up[7] from the downward-tending elements of Nature into the pure creation, and was united with the Creative Mind, for it was of the same substance. Thus the downward-tending elements of Nature were left reasonless, so as to be mere matter. (CH 1 : 9-10)

5. "Next the Creative Mind, together with the Word, going round the orbits (of the Rulers) and whirling them with a rustling sound, set His creations in revolution and let them revolve from an infinite beginning to a boundless end—for their orbit begins where it ends. (And Nature), as Mind willed, brought forth reasonless animals[8] out of the downward-tending elements, for she no longer had the Word; Air brought forth birds, and the Water swimmers—for the Earth and the Water had parted from each other—and (the Earth)

brought forth quadrupeds (and) creeping things, beasts wild and tame. (CH 1 : 11)

God, Mind, now explains the relationship between the seer and the seen. It is the spark of divine light in himself that enables him to see its source, the Light Infinite ; it is the reason, the mind, in himself that lets him hear the Word of God, which perfectly expresses the Perfect Mind while mystically still inseparate therefrom : "The Heavenly Word, proceeding forth yet leaving not the Father's side", as St. Thomas Aquinas has it. For Mind, and Thought its child, are one ; without this dual unity no life can be. The Father and the Son are one, to use the later Christian idiom.

The seer must now learn more of God's nature. Emboldened by the Divine Teacher's initiatory gaze to face the soft glory of that adorable Radiance, he perceives that It is made up of infinite lesser lights, the sparks of a boundless Flame, the worlds of a limitless universe, the powers of eternal Life, God's very Being. This is the "higher life", the "noetic cosmos", the Ideal World-Order, whereof the Platonists speak ; it is the soul's "true native land", the one unchanging Reality from whom we came, to whom we shall return. From this supernal Truth, as in a mirror, our sense-world has borrowed its countless beauties, its amazing harmony and order ; it is but a shadow-world, a "looking-glass land", reflecting God's glory and moulded out of crude matter by Nature's laws under the creative Will of God.

God is Himself both Light the Father and Life the Mother ; He now emanates the Second Mission, Creative Mind, to bring the natural universe into harmony with the Eternal Being. He forms seven spiritual Planetary Lords to govern the new creation as rulers of Destiny and to administer the Divine Law in the lives evolving through material forms. The spiritual elements in cosmos and in man—for all this is a macrocosmic story of what goes on in every human soul awakened by God's touch—leap upwards to unite with God's Formative Mind, leaving inert matter to itself, just as the soaring mind of "Hermes" has left his body a senseless mass of clay.

Wisdom and Order, having met in the midst, then together set the whole vast cycle of our universe in ceaseless motion under the Divine laws of purpose and reason through unending time. Blind Nature, deserted by the upward-soaring Mind or Word, produced her brood of mindless creatures, plants and animals. Age follows age upon the solidifying earth, while race succeeds to race; the great lizards give way at last to mammals, and the theatre is prepared for Man, their destined sovereign.

3. Man, the Child of Earth and Heaven

1. "But Mind, the Father of all, He who is Life and Light, gave birth [9] to Man, one like* Himself [10], with whom He fell in love as being His own Child; for he was most beautiful having the likeness of the Father, so naturally the Father fell in love [11] with His own Form. And He entrusted to him all creation. Then, taking his place in the sphere of creation, Man observed what his Brother had created, and he too willed to create. Then the Father gave him leave,[12] having in him all the energy of the Rulers. (CH 1 : 12-13)

* *Or* : equal to.

2. "These fell in love with him, and each one gave a share of his own **nature**.[13] Then, having gained full knowledge of their being and shared in their nature, he willed to break through the circumference of the orbits and to wear down their might. So he looked down through the Harmony ... and showed to the downward-tending Nature the beautiful Form of God. (CH 1 : 13-14)

3. "She, seeing the beauty of God's Form, smiled with insatiable love of Man, catching a reflection of that most lovely form in the water and a shadow upon the earth; while he, seeing the form like his own which was in the water, loved it and willed to dwell therein. Along with the willing came the power to act, and he occupied the reasonless **matter**.* Then Nature took hold of her beloved and twined herself closely round him, and they mingled together, because they loved each other. (CH 1 : 14)

4. "And this is why man, unlike all (other) living things on earth, is twofold—mortal because of the body, and immortal [14] because of the essential Man. He is immortal and has

* *Or*: Form.

all things in his power, and yet he suffers mortality because he is subject to destiny. Being above the Harmony, he has become a slave within the Harmony. Though he is male-female [15] from a male-female Father, and sleepless from an unsleeping Father, yet he is overcome (by passionate desire and forgetfulness). (CH 1 : 15)

5. "This is the mystery which has been kept hidden until this day: Nature, having mingled with Man, brought forth the most marvellous wonder. For inasmuch as he had (from) the Harmony the nature of the seven (Rulers), who as I told you (were made of) fire and wind, Nature did not delay but immediately gave birth to seven Men in accordance with the natures of the Seven Rulers, male-female and air-floating. . . . The birth of these seven took place in this way: Nature brought forth the bodies—earth was the female and water the male; she took ripeness from fire and breath from **air**; (but their bodiless part came into being) in accordance with the form of Man. So Man changed from Life and Light into soul and mind; all things (continued so) until the

end of a period and the beginnings of births. (CH 1 : 16-17)

Man, with God and Universe the Third Person of the Hermetic Trinity, is not the handiwork of any Demiurge but the very Son of the Supreme, born of His substance and bound to Him by eternal ties of love based on that identity of Being. Man takes his rightful place in the Eighth Sphere, above the Seven Rulers, as the lord of all creation—pure Mind immaculate, unstained by matter. This is Adam, the Ideal Man of many myths, especially among the Gnōstics—Man as he came forth from God, sinless and divine before his "fall" into darkness and evil. In his turn, Man willed to use his divine prerogative of creation; being free, entitled to use his powers as he would, his desire was expressed in action.

Coming from the same Source as they, he bore within himself the nature of each of the Seven Rulers, and with their aid he broke through the upward limits of Fate's realm and so came into contact with that same blind Nature who was building form after form until one could be a vehicle for Mind. Man was the predestined redeemer for blind and mindless Matter; he must come down, so as later to lift it up again into the fullness of God's eternal Light.

Enamoured of the beauty of this Mind-endowed being, Nature, the primal Eve, lured him down into her fascinating world of sense, so as to entangle him in the worthy vehicle she had now prepared. By many devious ways God's plan works through ! Man found that image good to look upon, for it was a shadow-reflection of his own form in the noetic world from which he came. Sight, admiration, desire, possession. He entered the body, and was caught in the toils of that flesh which he had found so charming from afar. It is the old old tale of the Fall of Man, found in a hundred forms in myth and legend, perhaps most beautifully told in the Gnōstic history of the Sophia.

So man is dual. In himself divine and a heaven-dweller, he is yet to outward seeming a mere mortal bound in flesh. Though born God's child, heir to the universe, he has chosen to suffer as the slave of Fate, captive under the laws of Matter. Though he is really passionless, eternally aware of his own divine Being, as in the Vedānta, he has embraced a life of passion and oblivion. He has drunk of Lēthē's waters, and now sleeps " near the hard-breathing serpent " in the " Egypt " of the body. He awaits his saviour, the message from on high, to recall him to his glory in his Father's home ; but still, a prodigal, he feeds upon the husks of swine.

"Hermes" now sees the first incarnate men, in seven races, to correspond with the Seven Rulers ; as in the *Secret Doctrine* these are hermaphrodite, with bodies so light and subtle that they float above the surface of the earth. Ages pass away before the sexes at last are separated, while gradually higher types of human soul descend into the gradually evolving higher types of body. The bisexual stage in embryology seems a faint relic of such a primal type of man.

4. Ignorance is Bondage

1. " When the period came to an end, the chain binding all together was loosened by God's Will; for all living creatures being bisexual were parted asunder,[16] together with man, and there came to be males in part and likewise females. God immediately spoke in a holy word : ' Increase exceedingly and multiply

abundantly all creatures and creations."[17] And let the man with mind in him recall that he is immortal and that carnal love is the cause of death ; (and he who has come to know himself again enters into the Good).' (CH 1 : 18)

2. "When He had said this, Providence by means of Destiny and the Harmony brought about the couplings and set births in train ; and all things were multiplied according to their kind. And he who has recognized himself has already come into the transcendent Good, while he who has dearly loved the body, being led astray by carnal desire, continues to wander in the darkness of sense-life, suffering the lot of death." (CH 1 : 19)

3. "But how have the ignorant sinned so greatly," I asked, "that they should be deprived of immortality?" ... "If you have understood," (said Poimandres), "tell me why those who are in ignorance deserve death."— "Because the gloomy Darkness is the original source of the body they inhabit, whence came the moistness of which the body is composed, (so those who love the body are captives) in the sense-world whence death is quaffed." (CH 1 : 20)

4. "You have rightly understood, O man. But how does the one who has recognized himself enter into Him, as God's word has it?"—I answered, "Because from Light and Life is made up the Father of all from whom Man has sprung."—"You are quite right; if then, being composed of Life and Light, you learn that you happen to be out of them, then you will enter again into Life and Light." [18] These things said Poimandres. (CH 1 : 21)

At last the sexes are divided; plants and animals, men and women, give birth to offspring. God wills that many should be born on earth as vehicles for descending souls who shall later people Heaven. He makes a covenant whith human beings: "Love for the body, a craving for sensation, enslaves you to Matter, makes you captives in exile and prisoners of death; love for the mind or spirit, the knowledge of your real divine Self, leads to the love of God and draws you upward into Life and Light. Now choose your path."

And so the great wheel of birth and death was set a-rolling, the only escape from which is Self-Realization, which is itself the very act of merging into God even while the body is alive, the state of Jivanmukti. Those who turn from this to sense-allurements are lost in weary wanderings through the woes of gloomy ignorance and death.

This is no arbitrary decree of a tyrant, but a natural law of justice, of cause and effect: the sense-world itself arises from the coiling Darkness that blotted out a part of Light's realm (§ 1 : 2), and is the natural home of ignorance, pain and death; while Man in his higher part belongs to the Light Itself and has but to recognize his real nature to enter at once upon his heritage. As Māni* tells us, to know this duality is the first step on the path that leads us upward to our eternal fatherland.

5. Knowledge is Liberation

1. "But tell me this also," (said) I; "God said, 'Let the man who has mind in him recognize himself'; then have not all men mind?"[19]—Mind answered me, "... I, Mind, come to such men as are good and pure and merciful, (and) to the pious; and My presence becomes a support (to them), so they immediately come to know all. Then they win the Father's grace by their loving deeds, and they give Him thanks, praising and singing hymns in order before Him with deep affection. (CH 1 : 21-22)

2. "Even before they give up the body to its natural death, they loathe the senses, knowing their activities; or rather it is I, Mind, who will not let the hostile forces of the body take full effect; (for) being guardian of the gates I Myself will bar the entries, cutting off the designs of evil and base activities. (CH 1 : 22)

* See *Journal Asiatique* XI series I (1913).

3. "But I keep far away from the foolish and evil and wicked, the envious and greedy, the slayers and impious, yielding place to the avenging spirit. And he brings upon **such a man** the fierceness of fire [20] and tortures (him), tossing him about through the senses, nay even makes him more ready for lawless deeds so that he may incur the greater punishment. Yet he does not cease from blind struggling . . ., holding excessively [21] to desire, and so by his own doing he increases the fire yet more." (CH 1 : 23)

True Mind, or Spiritual Insight, which is the one link between fallen man and God his Father, can only rest in those who try to do God's Will, who love and worship Him and show kindness to their fellow creatures. God comes to such; He strengthens them, and enlightens them with all true knowledge—best of all, as they come to know Him well their love and adoration grow more fervent. Even while still in the body, they are helped by God to turn away from the world's enticements, the temptations of the flesh; He Himself plays watchman over the open gates of their senses to keep away all lurking evil that would enter to disturb their contemplation.

But how can even God help those who wilfully prefer a life of vice, and make themselves the slaves of passion and desire? Instead of this Divine protector comes an avenging demon, who drives the unhappy wretches deeper and deeper into the mire of sensuality and sin, burning them in every kind of agony, which only urges them on to greater recklessness of evil. The soul cannot stand still; it must either climb up to Heaven, or fall into the depths of Hell.

6. The Upward Way

1. " Now tell me further," (said I) "(about) the present Way Up, how I shall enter into Life."—To this Poimandres replied, " Well, first at the dissolution of the material body you give up the body itself to be changed, and the form which you had becomes invisible; the **vital breath** you hand over, devitalized, to the **air**, and the bodily senses pass back into their own sources, becoming parts (of the world) and again combining into (other) workings. (CH 1 : 24)

2. "And this is how man speeds on his way up through the Harmony: to the first zone he gives up the force that works growth and decrease, to the second the scheming of evil cunning; to the third the fraud of desire, to the fourth domineering arrogance, to the fifth unholy daring and rash audacity, to the sixth evil strivings for wealth, and to the seventh the lie that waits in ambush. (CH 1 : 25)

3. "And then, when he has been stripped bare [22] of all the workings of the Harmony, he attains to the nature of the Eighth (Sphere), being in possession of his own proper Power. Together with those who are (there), he hymns the Father, while those who are present rejoice [23] with him over his coming. Next, having been made like his companions, he also hears the Powers who sway the nature of the Eighth [24] singing hymns to God in a certain language of their own. And then they return in order to the Father; they give themselves up to (the) Powers, and becoming themselves Powers they come to be in God. (CH 1 : 26)

4. "This is the good End for those who have attained to Gnōsis—to be made God. And now, why do you delay? Having received all, must you not become a guide for the worthy, so that through you the race of humankind may be saved by God?" (CH 1 : 26)

The Way Home to God is analogous to that taken by every soul at the body's death. Its gross matter is left for Nature to disintegrate into material for new bodies, and the soul stands free in her inner subtle body; her life flows back into the general atmosphere, while her senses retreat into the great ocean of subconscious sense whence they derived.

She passes swiftly through the seven inner zones of emotion, (the purgative Astral Plane?) yielding up in each the evil quality there assumed during her descent, these qualities corresponding to the lower influences of the seven planets in the "horoscope" of her now-closing life. Freed from all veils of sense and matter, liberated from the passions that reign therein—for purgation must ever precede illumination and union—she stands "naked", mystically speaking, in the Ogdoad, that Eighth Sphere from which Man first came down, his true home. She takes her rightful place among the Powers of the Light, who welcome her to inmost fellowship with songs and robes of glory, like the returning prodigal of Bardaisan's hymn.

With these lofty spiritual "Powers", who compose God's "substance" of Light, she proceeds in adoring love to merge herself into God's very Being. This is our destined goal—to go home rejoicing to God, to be made one with Him, to become ourselves Divine. It is taught by the mystics and yogis of every creed, though its ineffable bliss can be known only by experience; those born blind cannot distinguish colours from their mere names. Having glimpsed this glory that God has planned for every human soul, we cannot but be filled with apostolic zeal to awaken our sleeping brothers to the effort needed to attain it. Thus "Hermes" is called to be a Prophet, a missionary of the glorious truth.

7. The Thanksgiving of "Hermes"

1. Having said this to me, Poimandres merged into the Powers,[25] (CH 1 : 26) while I wrote down **his** kindness in my heart; I was overwhelmed with joy, being filled with all that I desired. The sleep of the body had

become a waking of the soul; the closing of the eyes, true vision; my silence, pregnant with the Good; and the suppression of speech, a brood of good things. And this came to me because I had received from Poimandres, that is, from the Supreme Mind, the teaching (whereby) I had become inspired and attained to (the Plain of) Truth.[26] For this reason I give with all my soul and strength praise unto God the Father: (CH 1 : 30)

2. "Accept the reasonable offerings from a soul and heart uplifted to Thee, O Thou unutterable, ineffable, whom (only) silence can declare! Holy is (the God who) has revealed to me a glimpse of Life and (Light) derived from the Mind! For this cause I believe and bear witness (that) I advance to Life and Light. Blessed art Thou, O Father! Thy Man would share Thy holiness, even as Thou hast given him the full authority (to do). I implore for myself that I may never fall away from the Gnōsis which is in keeping with our being; grant my prayer, and fill me with the power of this grace; (and then) I will enlighten those of the Race (who are) in ignorance, my brothers and Thy sons! (CH 1 : 31-32)

3. "Holy is God, the Father of all, (who is before) the origin! Holy is God, whose Will is fulfilled by His own Powers! Holy is God, who wills to be known [27] and is known by His own! Holy art Thou who by a word hast constructed what exists! Holy art Thou of whom all Nature is an image! Holy art Thou whom Nature has not obscured! Holy art Thou, more mighty than all power! Holy art Thou, greater than all pre-eminence! Holy art Thou, surpassing all (our) praises!"[28]—(CH 1 : 31)

Most of this section was anciently transferred to the end of the booklet "Poimandres", so as to close it appropriately with a hymn of praise, but it certainly reads better when restored to its natural position here.

Having received the Gnōsis—the knowledge that unites the soul with God in love—from his Divine Teacher, "Hermes" has first to give his thanks, and then to try to pass it on to others. Scott (S) thinks the existing Ninefold Hymn (here retained in para. 3) was a slightly later expansion of one sentence in para. 2 which he restored from indications in a later copy. I have accepted this suggestion.

The Divine Mind is now formed in the initiated "Hermes", so He ceases to manifest outside him— Poimandres disappears. The seer now finds that his whole life, sleeping or awake, is henceforth illumined by the inner Light from God; the Path meets his eyes in everything (cf. § 42 : 5), especially when he silently looks into his own heart. He is now empowered to advance swiftly to perfection until he attains to full union with the Father.

His little prayer is a noble one. Thanking the All-Good for this revelation of the Truth, "Hermes" asks that he may never be cut off from the life of grace but helped to share it with his fellow men; he declares his faith in the Inner Guide, and asks to become as holy as the all-holy God Himself. (cf. § 43 : 3-5 and Mt. 5 : 48) The Ninefold Hymn to God's infinite glory seems to have been used in the 4th century by some Christian in his own private worship.

8. The Mission of "Hermes"

1. Then I . . . was sent forth by **God**, having been filled with power and taught the nature of the All and the supreme vision. So I began to proclaim to men the beauty of devotion and of Gnōsis. (Ch 1 : 27)

2. (This is what I said :) "O people, earth-born folk who have given yourselves over to a drunken[29] sleep[30] in the ignorance of God (CH 1 : 27), whither are you being swept away, . . . you drunkards who have sopped up the strong drink of ignorance?[31] (CH 7 : 1) Become sober now,[32] and cease to be intoxicated and spellbound by irrational sleep! (CH 1 : 27) Look up with the eyes of the heart —if you cannot all do this, at least those who can, for this evil of ignorance floods all the earth and **sweeps along** the soul which is

shut up in the body, not letting it anchor in the havens of Salvation." (CH 7 : 1)

3. When they had heard this, they came together with one accord round me. Then I said, "O men, (CH 1 : 28) do not let yourselves be carried off by the strong current, but make use of a back-flow, you who can, and gain the harbour, to drop your anchor there!" (CH 7 : 1) (I went on), "Why have you given yourselves up to death when you have the power[33] to share in immortality? Repent, you who have made Error your travel-companion and have shared your plate with Ignorance! Put away the (body of) darkness; lay hold upon the light of immortality, abandoning corruption. (CH 1 : 28) Look for one to lead you by the hand and guide you[34] up to the gates of Gnōsis, where shines the clear light pure from darkness, where not even one is drunken but all are sober, gazing steadily with the heart on Him, who wills (thus) to be seen!" (CH 7 : 2)

4. Now some of them went off mocking, having given themselves up to the way of death, but others threw themselves at my feet and begged to be taught. So I, lifting them

up, became a guide of the Race, teaching the doctrines of how and in what way they could be saved. And I sowed (in) them the words of wisdom,[35] and (the seed) was watered with ambrosial water.[36] Then, when evening had come and the sun's light was beginning to go down, I told them all to give thanks to God, and when they had fully ended their thanksgiving they went away, each one to his own resting-place. (CH 1 : 29)

In the main, this "Religion of the Mind" was a philosophy, a yoga, a devotion for the select few who gave themselves to God in silent contemplation. But we see both here and in § 37 : 3-5 that it also to some extent preached in public, like some of the Christian Gnōstics; there is no need, however, to imagine with S that such propaganda was intended to answer the Christians; Jews and others had preached their religions in public long before: the Buddha in India is an example! Nor need we find Plato in everything Hermetic; drunkenness can be so obvious a metaphor for ignorance and sin that it must have occurred to many. The Egyptian legend of the "Destruction of Men" associates drink with violence and anger.

In a brief but powerful sermon "Hermes", or the Hermetist we have agreed to give that name, appeals to his neighbours to awaken to their danger as they drift to spiritual death like men in a boat swept away by the flooded Nile. It is ignorance, that is, estrangement from God, that leads to ruin; if they will but put off the dark prison of the body and its senses, they will soon find the spiritual Guide to lead them to Self-Realization.

MIND, THE SHEPHERD OF MEN

Thus they will find the God of their salvation, seeing Him clearly when they look away from all else (the full meaning of the Greek word: *aphorao*). This is how "Hermes" uses his God-given authority to teach men.

His experience is like that of most Prophets (cf. GI 34, 36); many turn away with jests on their lips, preferring their own ruin to the Way of Life he came to teach. But some took him humbly and gratefully as their teacher; his words were made fruitful by God's grace, and they gave God thanks for enlightening them by His loving mercy.

CHAPTER TWO

THE GOOD FATHER

I have used the literary fiction employed by the compiler of the " Perfect Sermon " (PS) as a framework for his own book, to provide an imaginary background for our next four chapters. " Hermes " here appears as the teacher of a small group of his disciples and conveys by word of mouth the whole philosophy of his school, as I have arranged it here in extracts from nearly fifty different books and sermons.

So from §9 to §43 we may picture the little group seated in the small shrine-room of the teacher's hermitage—" Hermes " himself inspired by the God of Truth and Light as he unveils the Divine glories before his pupils: Tat, the beloved son, heir to his spiritual father's wisdom; Imouth-Asclepius, the learned scholar; and Ammon the King, type of all disciples living in the outer world. We shall see later, in Chapter 6, how this oral instruction is followed for Tat by the actual experience of Divine Reality, so that he identifies himself with the Universal Life and becomes a teacher in his turn.

This Second Chapter tries to describe the Supreme God, Unmanifest, and yet revealed through His creation. We shall find in it much of the sublime, such as is rarely found in the recognized scriptures, much that recalls Plotinus and the other followers of the immortal Plato; but nothing here is exclusively Platonic, and many passages are closely parallel to *The Divine Names* of the Areopagite, 6th. century father of all Catholic mystics. God is One, in all religions, whatever be His many names in different tongues; and man is one, the experience of Reality by man is one, the mystic life is one, in all lands and in all ages.

9. God Transcendent

1. " God, God has led you to us, Asclepius, so that you may be present for a divine teaching ; . . . but go forth just for a moment and call Tat to join us," (said " Hermes "). When **Tat** had entered, Asclepius suggested that Ammon also should be present. The Thrice-greatest said, " No ill will keeps Ammon from us, . . . but you should not call anyone else besides, lest a most sacred teaching on so vast a subject be profaned by the entry and presence of many people." . . . When Ammon also had entered the sanctuary, the place was made holy by the reverence of the four men, and was filled with the Divine Presence ; the listeners attended in respectful silence, the hearts and minds of all hanging (on the words), as the divine Desire-for-God began to speak from the mouth of " Hermes " in this way : (PS 1 : 1)

2. "To understand God is difficult, to declare Him impossible [1] even for one able to understand; for it is not **easy** for the Perfect to be grasped by the imperfect, or the Invisible by the visible, and it is hard for the Eternal to company with the ephemeral. . . . It is the distance between these (two) which dims the vision of the Beautiful.[2] . . . I imagine, I imagine that what it is impossible to tell out is God. (St. 1 : 1-2)

3. Whether God be called Father, or the Lord of all, or by any other name which is used among us to convey our meaning, He ought to be hallowed by men with deeper sanctity and reverence by contemplation on so great a Divinity; for we can correctly define Him by none of these names.[3] (PS 20 : 1)

4. God is One. And the One needs no name; the One is nameless, for He has no need of a name, being alone. (F 3) Indeed, I have no hope [4] that the Creator of all greatness and the Father or Lord of all things can be named by one name, even though it were made of many. I hold that He is nameless, or rather is all-named [5], since He is One and All; so that we must either call everything

by His name, or Him by the names of all. (PS 20 : 2)

It is God who chooses those who are to enter the mysteries of His wisdom. Here we get our first hint that the "pearls" of this teaching must not be "cast before swine", but kept for those who may be worthy. Yoga should not be spoken of before a crowd, or holy things may be exposed to the ridicule of the ignorant and foolish. Mead (M) notes how "Hermes" has three main disciples, as Jesus had his Peter, James and John.

The first sentence of this teaching is the one most quoted of all Hermetic sayings in ancient times; it probably stood at the beginning of the collection of books used by Stobaeus. God is infinite, so His nature must ever be ineffable to finite man. He can be known only by one who becomes like His Divinity, and for all others He is the God who "dwells in thick darkness", veiled in a silence naught can break. The infinite distance between the Creator's absolute self-sufficiency and the creature's nothingness prevents him from seeing God as He truly is. Only when His grace annihilates that difference and takes us up into Himself can we know and love Him as He deserves.

Though in our silent contemplation we need no name for Him, when we speak of Him to others we must use words. Not that these words can do anything but distort our thought of Him, but we have to choose names for Him in speech. So we choose those names which are most loved and honoured. We call God Father and think of His love and goodness, King and think of His power and justice, Mother and think of His tender heart. And so by using noble names for Him in our loving prayer and conversation we deepen our awe and love for Him who is all in all. Indeed, it is our reverence which can hallow any name we use and make it worthy of our Lord.

He alone *is*; outside of Him is nothing. So we really need no name for Him at all. Any name that we can take is a name for Him, in part; for all things exist only in Him and reflect a tiny shadow of His infinite beauty and generous goodness. All names are His, in part; but no name can be really His, for He is infinite even beyond the very meaning of the word "infinite", and nothing can define Him. He is ineffable; His true Name can be uttered only by the deepest silence.

10. God's Great Names

1. The source and limit and connecting link of all things is God, (CH 8 : 5) and the other appellation (of God) is that of "Father"[6] as being the Maker of all, for the father's (work) is to make. (CH 2 : 17) Now what is sweeter (to a son) than his true father? ... Well, is it right to assign to Him only the name of "God", or that of the "Maker", or that of the "Father"? No, even all the three—"God" for His power, "Maker" for His activity, and "Father" for His goodness. (CH 14 : 4).

2. Now the Good is one who gives all things and takes nothing; God gives all[7] and takes nought; so God is the Good, and the Good is God. (CH 2 : 16) And so we should worship God in these two names, which belong

to Him alone and to no one else. For none of the others who are called gods, nor men, nor spirits, can in even any degree be good, save only God;[8] everything else is far from the nature of the Good. . . . So never call anything else good, or you will be impious; nor ever call God anything but only the Good, or again you will be impious. (CH 2 : 14-15)

3. The Good is spoken of by all in words, but what it is is never understood by all. . . . Ignorantly they name the gods and certain men as "good", though never can they be or become such. For (to these the Good) is wholly foreign, but (it is) inseparable from God, for God Himself is that. All the other immortals (are called) gods, being honoured by God's name; but God (is called) the Good not by courtesy but by very nature. For God's nature is one with that of the Good. (CH 2 : 16) Who then is He, and how shall we come to know Him? (CH 14 : 4)

"Hermes" now takes up three popular names for God, honouring His power, His activity, and His generosity. Only God is good, for "goodness" means absolute generosity, ceaseless giving, and none but God, who *is* all, can give all, by giving Himself to men. To call others, who take as well as give, " good " is impiety to God; to call God's absolute and unconditioned goodness in question is to blaspheme.

The word "good" may easily be used without thought of its real meaning, so many people give the name to things and persons incorrectly, as though such could ever be totally self-sufficient like God. It is only by courtesy that lesser beings receive this epithet, but only the Supreme Source of all has any right to it, for He contains all things in His own eternal Being and is ever giving them out in ceaseless acts of creation.

11. Good is Only in God

1. Now whatever supplies is called good, but (the) Good is one thing, source of all, (supplying) everything and always; and this pertains to none save God alone. For He lacks nothing so that He should become bad in longing to obtain it;[9] nor does anything exist which He could lose, that He might be grieved on the loss of it; nor is there anything stronger than Himself, by which war might be waged on Him; nor has He any consort[10] by whom He might be infatuated; nor is there a rebel[11] by whom He might be annoyed, nor (anyone) wiser (than He) to make Him jealous. (CH. 6:1)

2. Since not one of these exists in His Being, what is left but only the Good? Now

just as there (are) no (evils) in such a Being, so will the Good be found in no other. . . . Things that come into being are full of passions, seeing that the very process of birth (itself) is liable to pain ; now wherever there is passion good can nowhere be, and wherever the Good is not even one passion can ever be. Hence it is impossible for the Good to be in birth, but solely in the unborn."[12] (CH 6 : 1-2) All that comes into being is imperfect, subject to both growth and decrease ; but to the **unborn** * neither of these things happens. (CH 4 : 11)

3. The universe is good in so far as it also makes all things . . . but in all other respects (it is) not good, for it is subject to disturbance and movement. Thus it is impossible for things down here to be altogether free from evil, for down here the Good is defiled, and " the good " down here is that in which there is the smallest share of evil ; being defiled, it no longer remains good . . . , it becomes bad. (CH 6 : 2-3)

4. So, then, good is in God alone, or God alone is the Good ; . . . only the name of

---
* *Or*: perfect.

"good" is in men, the thing itself nowhere.[13] For the material body leaves no room for it— a thing which is hemmed in by evil on every side, by labours and pains, by desires and angry passions, by deceits and foolish fancies. And ... each one of these aforesaid is believed to be the greatest good, but is rather the utmost evil; (CH 6:3) while the hardest thing of all is that we have need of them and cannot live without them. (CH 6:6)

5. As for myself, I am grateful to God who has thrown into my mind about the gnōsis of the Good that it cannot possibly be in the world; for the world is a fullness of evil,[14] but God of good[15] ... Nothing of the Good is to be obtained from things in the world; for all that falls under the eye are phantoms[16] and as it were silhouettes, while what does not fall under (the eye) is (real), and especially the essence of the Beautiful and the Good. (CH 6:4)

The theme continues. The "good" is he who gives everything, and only God can ever do that. He alone. He has no partner as the Valentinians declared, for there is nothing besides, outside, Himself. He lacks nothing; He can neither gain nor lose, for all are in Him. Nor can He feel the passions of joy and sorrow that shake our souls; He is ever serene, at peace.

There is no rebel, man or angel, to defy His word; His will is at once fulfilled. So He knows nothing of fear, or jealousy, or anger, or desire. It is such passions as these bring woe and evil to our lives; He, the pure and passionless, unchanging, unshaken, can feel no evil in Himself. The evil we see around us everywhere is, as the Areopagite and Mother Julian also taught, no real thing, but only an absence, a defect, of good.

" Certain is death for the born ", as the Gita has it, and all that comes into being is bound to cease to be. So creatures are never free from change, secure from loss or from desire for gain or progress. Everything in the universe is subject to growth and to decay; nothing here is absolutely free from blemish or wholly perfect. God alone, who was and is and is to be, unmoved and changeless, is Perfection Infinite; he who would share in that Perfection must put aside all earthly things and step out into the untrodden realms of Spirit. All things down here are overladen with tendencies to evil and to pain; even when they seem to us most attractive there is a hidden reptile lurking amid their fragrant petals.

It is indeed a great cause for joy and thankfulness to learn that nothing really good exists in this world; for then the soul goes straight to God, in whom alone its joy can be found. This world and all its delights, which we think we cannot do without, are fleeting and unreal, illusory; it is only the unseen unchanging Reality behind, which casts them as its unsubstantial shadows, that gives us true and lasting satisfaction. For He is our home, and only He can fill the great emptiness in our hearts that were made for Him.

12. God the Beautiful

11. Just as eye cannot see God, so it cannot see either the Beautiful or the Good;

for these are parts of God, properties of Him alone, inseparable intimates, perfect and most beloved, with whom even God Himself is in love.[17] . . . One may dare to say . . . that God's very Being, if indeed He has "being", is the Beautiful and Good. (CH 6 : 4)

2. If you can understand God, then you can understand the Beautiful and (the) Good, which are the radiance emanated (?) by God, for that Beauty is beyond compare, and that Goodness is as inimitable as God Himself. . . . If you seek after God,[18] you are also seeking the Beautiful. (CH 6 : 5)

3. For the path which leads to It is one, Devotion by means of Gnōsis . . .,[19] whence those who do not know (Him) and have not trodden the road of Devotion dare to call a man "beautiful and good", and that, though he has never even in a dream seen anything good, but is wrapped up in every kind of evil and has believed the evil to be good and so makes insatiable use of it and fears to be deprived of it, striving with all his might not only to retain but even to increase it. (CH 6 : 5-6)

God is not only perfect Goodness, but the perfect Source of all the beauty our eyes and hearts can see; nay, He is Himself the only real Beauty. "Hermes" here gives a Platonic list of epithets of the Divine, which were probably those used in the Eleusinian Mysteries. God loves, takes delight in, His own perfections, for there is no object of His love which can exist outside, apart from, Himself.

God is not other than these perfections of His; He is all that is beautiful and good, being, as Plato says, the Sun of the Spiritual World that rays them down. Creatures can know the beautiful and good only so far as they know God Himself; finding Him, they see His beauty, His goodness, everywhere. Those ignorant of, divorced from, God can never know what is beauty or goodness but, deceived by the world's illusions, mistake good for evil and ugly for beautiful, so that they fall into endless desire for worthless things. To seek the truly beautiful is really to seek for God, for there is no beauty that is not His; the search for happiness is fulfilled only on finding God. And He can be found only on the path of knowledge (*gnōsis*) and devotion (*eusebeia*), a balanced harmony of *jnāna* and *bhakti*, for to know God is to love Him, and it is the ignorance of His infinite love that plunges us in every kind of misery.

13. Has God Form?

1. All things are in God, but not as if lying in a place. . . ., and if you boldly grasp the idea you will more correctly understand Him who contains all things . . . There is nothing which can enclose the Bodiless, but

itself it encloses all, being the swiftest and mightiest (of all). Now think this out for yourself. (CH 11 : 18-19) The Bodiless is either divine, or else it is God (Himself) (CH 2 : 4), and by the act of (willing) God (makes) all things to be. (CH 10 : 3)

2. Now the universe is all-formed,[20] not holding the forms latent in itself, but itself changing (them), (CH 11 : 16) for without destruction there could be no birth. (St. 2 : 16) Reality (is) only (that which ever is) ; ... every changeable thing is unreal. (St. 2 a : 12-13). What, (then), is to be said of the Maker ? For surely He cannot be formless ;[21] and yet also if He is all-formed He will be like the universe, while if He has (only) one form,[22] in that respect He will be less than the universe. What shall we say He is then ? . . . Well, He has one Aspect, which will not come under the eyes, (for) bodiless He reveals all things through bodies. (CH 11 : 16)

When we say that God contains all things, we must not think of Him as a sort of box, or as a definite place wherein they lie. God is eternal, omnipresent, and cannot be confined like bodies in time or space. He is here, and at the same time He is there, He is everywhere—" out beyond the shining of the farthest star ", and yet at the same time dwelling in the simple hearts of children. This divine quality is shared by all that is spiritual.

The universe is always changing its forms, destroying some that others may be built. But the Real never changes its form—if it have a form—it is one, and ever-constant. The universe is one amid all its changing forms, and so is God *one* in every form of the universe that He has made in His own image, to be the " body " of His manifestation. Thus God has one form, though it is not such as eye can see; it is a formless form, the ideal Archetype of forms which reflect His beauty in all the forms of this the lovely universe that He has made.

14. God Reveals Himself

1. Now God has (always) stood unmoved, and in the same way Eternity has always stood beside Him, enclosing within itself the unborn universe which we rightly term " perceptible " ;[23] and this universe has been made as image of this God, imitating Eternity.... It can be admitted that God is also thus moved within Himself by the same motionlessness, because on account of His vastness stability is a motionless movement, for immobility is the law of His vastness.[24] (PS 31 : 1-2)

2. For His where and whither and whence and how and nature are unknown[25], and He moves in utmost stillness, and His stillness

(moves) in Himself. On this account eternity is without any time-limitation; but time, which can be defined, is eternal through cyclic recurrence in number and alternation; therefore both seem to be infinite, both eternal, ... God and Eternity are therefore sources of all existing things. (PS 31 : 3-32 : 1)

3. For one thing alone is His glory, the making of all things; (CH 14 : 7) neither can the Maker exist without that which comes into existence, (nor can the thing made exist without the Maker). (CH 14 : 5) God, Maker ... of the all, ... is both One and the All, the One not being doubled but both being one. ... For if anyone tried to separate the All from the One, taking the term " all " as a plurality and not as a plērōma,[26] he would by breaking off the All from the One destroy the All; but that is impossible. (CH 16 : 3)

4. Now Will is the energy of **God**, and His very Being is the willing that all things should exist.[27] For what is " God " and " Father " but the existence of all things which do not yet exist?[28] ... For He wills these things to exist, and in that way they also do indeed exist; ... (and) it is on

account of **the Good** that all other things exist, . . . for it is a property of the Good to become known to the one who is able to see. (CH 10 : 2-4) And inasmuch as the things which come into existence are visible, so He too is seen ; and this is why He makes (them), that He may be seen. Always making,[29] He is thus always seen. (CH 14 : 3)

God has always been, through all eternity holding within Himself this visible universe latent in, and modelled on, the spiritual ideal universe that existed always in His thought, fore-planned before all ages. Now a wheel may spin so fast that it seems to be at rest ; the swift whirling in all the atoms and worlds of our universe copies that of the ideal universe in His Mind ; so swift is His thought that it seems to be at rest. A star revolves and travels thousands and thousands of miles an hour, yet so far away it is that it seems to be at rest ; God's vastness, enclosing all, initiates all movement, yet because there is nothing outside Him to move Him He is Himself unmoved. (In this passage what is said of God is equally true of the universe, which is an image of God.) The whole universe moves within God, but God moves only in Himself and so, with relation to any " outside " point (nothing is really outside Him), He never moves in all eternity.

The unfolding of eternity is called " time ", which is itself unending, eternal, through constantly recurring changes which bring into manifestation all things as God has willed. It is this ceaseless, yet motionless, activity of God by means of " time " which is His supreme glory. As the film unrolls from latency on its round spool, so the unmoving cinema machine reflects so many movements on the screen.

Ever making, God and His creation are one, for it exists only in Him. He is Himself, and He is also what He has made, for He and that can never be separated from one another. There can be no poem without a poet, nor poet without a poem. To imagine the universe without a God is impossible to the clear thinker, nor can he be led by the seeming plurality of things to forget that they are all one unity in Him. The One and the All are not distinct but in a very real sense identical, though it is yet true that He is beyond all that He has made, as the poet is greater than his poem.

By His divine Will, which is always towards the Good, that is, towards *giving*, God brings into existence all things which are latent in His fore-knowledge. It is not that He makes them once for all, but He is ever willing them to exist; their existence is in His Will, and it is maintained so long as He so wills. In seeing them, we see God's Will, we look upon the manifested thought and Mind of God. This is why He made them, that we might see Him through them all, and find His Beauty even in ourselves and in those who injure us.

Look at the tender floweret opening to the sun's first rays; you see God's joy at working His eternal Beauty into the shapelessness of garden clay. Look up into the black velvet sky of moonless midnight, and see its vast spaces, its sparkling stars, every one of them a vastness of vivifying fire; you see His omnipotence and wisdom. Through all His creatures God reveals Himself to any soul who cares to see the wonders of His work; and yet what He really is in Himself must ever be a mystery, unknown to us who are but His finite creatures.

15. God and His Universe

1. God therefore is Father of the universe, and the universe of those in the universe. Now

then the universe is God's son,[30] and those in the universe (sons) of the universe. (CH 9 : 8) God makes eternity,* eternity the universe, the universe time,[31] and time becoming. God's essence is the Good, eternity's is sameness, the universe's is order, time's is change, and (the essence) of becoming is life. (CH 11 : 2) And just as God has no end, so also has His creation no end; (CH 16 : 18) (for) the universe has become immortal through the Father who is eternal. (CH 8 : 2)

2. God then is the Source of all things,[32] while eternity is the power of God, and the universe is the work of eternity, which has never come into being[33] and is ever coming into being through eternity, for which reason it will never be destroyed because eternity is indestructible. Nor will anything in the universe perish because the universe is surrounded by eternity. Eternity organises (Matter), putting immortality and durability into Matter. (CH 11 : 3)

3. Now the whole of this Body, wherein are all bodies, † (is full of Soul, and) Soul is full

---

* *Or*: Aeon.
† *Or*: all are bodies.

of Mind, and (the Mind) of God. God is in Mind, Mind in Soul, and Soul in Matter.[34] (Soul) fills (the Body) within and surrounds it outside,[35] giving life to the whole. (CH 11 : 4)

God produced this universe out of Himself, out of His own thought, and the universe continually produces things within itself throughout eternity unrolling itself as time. God is always good, that is, giving; eternity is always changeless; the universe is always under perfect laws whereby things grow and decay harmoniously by the action of time; and this growth and decay is what we call " life ". Because creation is not apart from God, nor could it exist a moment without His Will, it shares in some degree His eternal Being, and so it too is immortal and divine. It never had a beginning, for it always, with all its children, existed latent in God.

Manifested through God's eternal activity, the universe continually unfolds itself through internal changes which do not affect the immortal continuity of the whole. Cells in a human body grow and die, while the common life of the organism Man goes on; and because their life is common, in a sense the life of each cell goes on—in another cell, another form. It is God's power which pervades lifeless matter and makes it alive and indestructible.

The universe as a whole, like every form within it, is the vehicle of Soul—that is, in the event, of God. Thus God pervades the universe and every atom in it with His Being. He is Himself their life. All are filled with Him; without Him to sustain its existence nothing could exist. He is in all, and all are in Him; nay, rather He is they and all that are in them. As water in the drop and the drop in the sea of water, so are God and His universe in each other, the One in All, and the All in the One.

16. The Making of the Universe

1. Now God is everlasting, God is eternal;
. . . He is, was, and ever will be; such is God's (very) nature, which is wholly self-born. (PS 14 : 3) God is the source of all that is, of Mind and Nature and Matter, (having made all) in order to show forth (His) wisdom. .·. . And the force by which He works is Nature, (acting) by means of Necessity to bring about both end and renewal. (CH 3 : 1) The Oneness, being source and root of all, is in all; . . . without a source nothing exists, but a source (arises) from nothing but itself, while it is the source of other things. (CH 4 : 10)

2. God was, and Matter; that of which the universe was made was not, because it had not yet come into being; yet it was already (latent) in that from which it was to come into being. (PS 14 : 2) For there was Darkness in (the) Deep,[36] and boundless Water, and a subtle intelligent Breath pervading with divine power what was in Space. Then when all was (yet) indeterminate and unworked, a holy Light was sent forth, (CH 3 : 1)—the Word of the Creator, ... everlasting, self-moved,

subject to neither gain nor loss, changeless, indestructible, constant, ever like Himself, steady, well-ordered, being One after the God already known (about). (F 30) For the Word came forth all-perfect, fruitful and creative, fell upon the fecund nature of Water, and made the Water pregnant.³⁷ (F 27)

3. (Then came into being) the elements; all of them being separated out,³⁸ the lighter were **removed** on high, the (fire) being suspended aloft to ride upon the breath, while the heavier (sank down and) sand was deposited under the moistness; thus out of the slime (dry land) solidified. ... Then the sky appeared in seven circles, and gods visible in starry forms with all their signs; and the **vault of heaven revolved** in a circular course, upheld by divine breath. (CH 3 : 2-3)

4. Whence appeared this great Sun?³⁹ ... It appeared from the forethought of the Master of all; (F 31) the Lord of all ... spoke with His own holy and creative word: " Let a sun exist! " and even while He (spoke) it appeared. (For) the fire which tended upwards and was most bright and active raised (itself) on high from (the) water. (F 33) Now

he is set in the midst, garlanded with the universe,[40] and he lets (it) rush along not far from himself but, if one must tell the truth, joined with himself. Like a good charioteer, he has secured and fastened the chariot of the universe to himself, lest it should somehow fly off in disorder; now the reins are Life... and Immortality and Birth.... And in this way he works everything. (CH 16 : 7-8)

5. The Creator and Lord of all spoke thus: " Let there be earth! " and immediately earth came into being, fount of creation. (F 32) How did the whole earth appear? By gradual drying up in order..., (for) most of the waters having been bidden by the (Lord of all) to withdraw into themselves the earth appeared, (at first indeed) muddy and quivering, but later, when the sun shone out and continually scorched and dried it, the land was fixed firmly among the waters, being surrounded by the Water. (F 31)

6. But during a long while the nature of (the things lying down below) was inert... and remained barren, until the gods who had already been bidden to patrol the sky came near to the King of all[41] and told Him of the

stillness of things (below) and (said) that (these also) ought to be arranged. And they said, "We pray Thee to look into things which now exist, and find out (what those which will exist) in the future may need, (for) this is the work of no one else but (Thy) self." (KK 9)

7. When they had said this, God smiled [42] and said that Nature should be, and out of His cry [43] came forth an all-beautiful wonder-maid, [44] on seeing whom the gods were utterly amazed; and God the Forefather honoured her with the name of "Nature" ... and He commanded her to be prolific. ... God said, and she was, (KK 10) for God's Will is itself the full accomplishment, inasmuch as when He has willed (anything) the doing is completed at one and the same point of time. (PS 8 : 2).

8. (God said:) "How long shall the things which have already been made remain unpraised?" ... And He commanded the race of men to come into being. (KK 27, 29) Then when He decided to reveal who He is, He breathed into divine (men) a deep longing (for Himself), and freely bestowed on their

THE GOOD FATHER

minds a radiance greater than they had had in their breasts, so that they might first will to seek the yet unknown God, then desire eagerly to find Him, and lastly be able to succeed (therein). (KK 4)

We shall do well to study this important section along with §§ 1-4, which it supplements, and also to compare it with the Creation stories of Ancient Egypt and Irāq, the strange *Stanzas of Dzyān*, the Vedic Creation hymn, the Purānic account, the Hebrew legend in *Genesis*, the various Gnōstic systems, and the systems of the various philosophers of Greece. We shall be struck not by the differences so much as by the many points of similarity, which testify to a tradition of vast antiquity.

First, we must always remember that it is God's manifestation, the universe, which comes into being and evolves; He Himself is ever the same, eternally unchanged. Yet all come forth from Him, like the web from the spider, in order to reveal His wisdom, power, beauty and love. Nature is the instrument with which He works, and she is governed by His perfect and unswerving laws. There is a kind of triad here: Mind and Wisdom, Nature and Force, Matter and Necessity. God Himself is the Source and Base of all, the One First Cause, Himself uncaused.

In the beginning of His manifesting there was only He, together with that Power in Himself on which He was to act, the primal "root of Matter". All was still in latency, sleeping until the hour should strike for God to unveil His glory. Matter itself did not yet exist, for the "moistness" of § 2 had not yet differentiated from its parent darkness.

Then the darkness became a boundless Chaos-ocean, and the Creative Word, a Ray of divine Light, flashed down to brood upon, to fecundate, to act on it as fire will act on water. The "boiling" ocean formed "bubbles in space", and thus was born the energy within the atom; the "roots of elements" were formed, and each moved off to its appointed place. Out of the mingled "earth" and "water" dry land appeared, while on high the clouds of heavy water-vapour were discharged and unveiled the clear night sky, with its constellations and zodiacal signs ruled by the seven Planetary Lords. All these rotate incessantly around the universe.

The sun, lord of life and for us a fitting emblem of the Supreme, came forth obedient to God's call, formed from the purest "fire" in our solar system. He reigns now in the centre of our chain of worlds (note the heliocentrism of this Egyptian philosopher: S tries to evade it by a most fanciful interpretation) and rules his family much as a skilled driver controls his team of horses. He binds the planets to himself with the centripetal laws of gravitation, and guides them along the uncharted ways of space by the laws of generation. For it is the sunlight which is the cause of life—of coming into being, being and continuing to be—generating and maintaining it in all beings as the seasons follow in due order.

At God's command again dry land appeared out of the slimy blend of earth and water, slowly growing hard and firm under the sun's warm rays. Surrounded by the ocean waters, the land of our earth swims on its tireless journey through the unbounded seas of space.

The long Archaean Ages passed away while earth lay lifeless and inert until its conditions changed and made it suitable as a home for life. Then the Seven Rulers, eager to establish the control of Destiny over this new world, went before God, the Sovereign Lord, and urged Him to make it fruitful as the skies had already become, for He alone has power to work the miracle of bringing life upon the earth.

THE GOOD FATHER 51

God answered them with an approving smile, for all creation is a joy, a play, to the creative Artist, as the Montessori child knows well; and an old Egyptian tradition said creation was a sevenfold peal of laughter. This divine smile awoke the sleeping *Virgin of the World*, Nature, Mother of all the Living, whose wondrous beauty amazed the Seven Rulers. The "lover's kiss" stirred her to activity; immediately obedient to God's word, her maiden womb became prolific, and all the tribes of unthinking creatures were born, plants and animals of every kind.

More geologic ages passed until God willed a being who should be endowed with mind and reason to contemplate and admire the beauty He had made. He called the human race into existence to tend the world and to know their Creator. In some of the more godlike of men He set a brighter inner light than others knew, the Spiritual Mind or Intuition; and He put in their hearts a love for Him, an eagerness to seek Him, a desire to know Him, and the power to attain to Him. These are the true philosophers, the theologians, prophets, saints and yogis, who are the natural guides and teachers of their brothers who still lie in ignorance of God. (cf. §§ 7 : 2 and 37 : 2-3)

CHAPTER THREE

GOD'S COSMIC IMAGE

We continue to study God's relationship with His creation that culminates in Man, for the universe is in very truth God's "form", His deathless "Body". God is to man no remote stranger who must be sought laboriously as in a foreign world, but Heart of his heart and Soul of his soul. Man is a reflection of God, made in His image, sharing potentially His nature, and filled with Him. Man is immortal, not by gift of grace but as the child of the eternal God; he has only to realize himself to know the Divinity within him as in all the universe beside. All things reveal His glory as He incessantly produces and provides in sublime perfection. The very universe itself is a direct path for us to see, to love, to attain the Divine Artist who, out of His own Beauty has woven its marvels of adaptation and of harmony.

No haters of their kind, fleeing to the seclusion of a desert cave, were our Hermetists. Their books overflow with a lively poetic appreciation of the world's beauty, wherein they found their God. If they withdrew into tiny groups from the noise and confusion of worldliness, if they set aside the lures and callings of the flesh, it was only the better to contemplate and love the beauty of God's creation, through the clear lens of a pure and calm mind. In their love of Him who is the source of every good, their very presence and their prayers must have called down blessings on their fellow men, as do the Contemplatives in their convents and hermitages even in our day.

17. Man and the Universe

1. Now the universe is first of all living beings, while man, as a living creature, is next after the universe but first of mortals. Being mortal, he is not only " not good " but also " evil " ; while the universe is " not good " as being movable but not " evil " in that it is deathless. But man is " evil ", both as movable and as mortal. . . . Thus there are these three—God, the universe, and man ; God holds the universe, and the universe man. (CH 10 : 12, 14)

2. Those that come into being have no independent power but depend upon Him, (CH 11 : 6) and nothing evil or mean is to be ascribed to the Maker Himself, (CH 14 : 7) for even those things which to mortals seem worthless are fair in God's sight because they have been made to obey the laws of ,God.[1] (KK 51) (Now God sent man down here) to examine heaven,[2] and to know divine power,

and to witness the forces * of Nature, and to infer what is good and bad, and to find out every kind of cunning workmanship. (CH 3 : 3) Having **mind** according to the Father's will, man is beyond all other living creatures on earth, (CH 8 : 5) so that he may be able to tend the earth and delight in the Divinity, . . . giving God the utmost praise and thanks, while revering His image—not unaware that he is himself a second image[3] of God, of whom there are two images, the universe and man.[4] (PS 9 : 4—10 : 3)

God is Life, and the universe is God's Body. Life cannot remain in a dead body; the universe is alive, every part of it, and it will never die. Yet like all other bodies, the universe is liable to change and so it lacks perfection. Man, as a body, is also subject to change, and he is mortal—when he divorces himself from God, his inner Life, and tries to stand alone.

Nothing created, nothing born, can stand alone. All depend upon their Source, their eternal Base, the Divine, in whom is omnipotence, perfection. Looking casually at our world, we see floods, diseases, wars, famines, insect pests—and complain of God's arrangements: " Why did He make mosquitoes ? " we cry during a sleepless night. It is our lack of faith, our lack of thought. All these things obey God's laws; and that is reason enough for their creation, even though we may not as yet understand. That is why we are here—to learn God's wisdom as revealed in His works, and so to

* *Or* : workings.

gain knowledge and wisdom for ourselves. It is our God-given duty to co-operate with Him in tending the soil and in serving His world as best we can, but above all in offering Him our loving adoration. And we can do that best by revering all that He has made, treating our fellows with courteous consideration, preserving and adding to the beauty of our surroundings, and never tearing to pieces or carelessly trampling on even a forest weed. For all are parts of His glorious Body, because of Him worthy of our deepest awe and reverence.

18. Thought and Feeling

1. Now mind is not cut off from God's essential Being, but has as it were been unfolded. (from It) just like the light of the sun. (CH 12 : 1) for mind differs from thought to the same extent as God differs from divine influence;[5] divine influence arises from God and thought from the mind, being sister of speech. . . . Neither can speech (be understood) without thought, nor can thought be expressed without speech. . . . So feeling and thought are both infused together into a man as if they were twined together: for neither is thought possible without feeling, nor feeling without thought. . . . Now the mind gives birth to all thoughts—good when it receives the seed from God,[6] and the contrary when from one of the

spirits. (CH. 9:1-3) The feeling and thought, then, of all living beings enter from without, being breathed in through the surroundings. (CH 9:9)

2. Now the universe also has a feeling and a thought of its own, not like the human, nor so elaborate, but greater and more simple,[7] for the feeling and thought of the universe is one—to make all things, and to re-make (them) into itself, being an instrument of God's Will.[8] ... Rushing along, it gives life to all and, putting an end to all, it renews what has been broken up, just as a good gardener[9] supplies renewal to them by putting down (new seed). (CH 9:6)

3. God ... is not without feeling and thinking;[10] ... and this is the feeling and thought of God—to move all things; for all these things, as many as there are, ... are in God, and arise from God and depend on Him ..., or rather I should say that He does not contain them but, I declare the truth, He *is* all of them. (CH 9:9) And that is how all things and all persons depend on God;[11] (CH 16:17) He is unwearying and there is no variation in (His) skill, but He possesses

the same kindnesses through all. (CH 18:3) There will never come a time when one existent thing shall be forsaken. (CH 9:9)

4. Truly so lofty is the doctrine of divine things that it is beyond the efforts of human minds, (PS 19:1) but to some it seems incredible, to others a mere fable, to others again perhaps something to be laughed to scorn.[12] (PS 12:2) For thinking is believing, and to disbelieve is to be unthinking. Now speech does not at first attain to the truth, but the mind is mighty and when it has been led by speech some distance on its way[13] it attains to the truth. (CH 9:10) And thus it happens that we men see as if through a fog the things which are in Heaven, so far as it is possible in the condition of the human mind. (PS 32:5)

All mind is derived from God and is as much a part of God as sunlight is of the sun. Following the sunbeam to its source, we find the sun; following the mind, we can likewise find the Divine from whom it came. As God rays out His inspirations to goodness, wisdom, truth, so the mind rays out its thoughts and plans, which become intelligible when expressed in words. Now when our thoughts come from pure mind they reflect God, the Source of mind; but when they come from feelings, emotions or desires they reflect only the influence of some obsessing spirit. For we are not separate or isolated beings, each living a private life in some enclosure, but we are a unity; the thoughts and feelings of others, living or "dead", pass through us as water through a fish's gills.

We are not distinct, apart, from the universe, but parts of its conscious life. This world—the whole universe—has a life, a consciousness of its own, as Fechner taught—unlike ours, vast and good and simple, with but one desire and aim—to fulfil God's Will by bringing countless things into being throughout all time, replacing with new beings those that are reabsorbed.

God too, for we are His image, feels and thinks; His thought is to make and to sustain, and His feeling is to love wisely all that He has made. Because He is eternal, and we are enfolded in His love, we know that He will never fail us or forsake even the least of His humblest creatures. Because He is Himself in the universe, we know that we can find Him therein, and that He does not altogether transcend the reach of our thought and feeling, which are akin to Him; we can find Him through the mind and through the love of our own heart.

Yet it is not easy to understand God and His works. Indeed, the frivolous dismiss the effort with a sneer, saying, "Myths, grandmothers' tales! What is the use of Religion in our days? Science and Economics are worth while!" But it is when we think of God we come to believe and to trust in Him; unbelief and want of faith spring from the lack of real thought, the mind being swept away by prejudice and ignorance into hasty assumptions; faith is the child of study, not of lazy credulity or indifference. True, we cannot find God through words or reason alone, but they are a signpost to indicate the way. If the mind in silent prayer and contemplation goes along that road, it will find Him, the common Source and Goal. So our ability to know

—and that is, to love—God and His ways, is limited only by the clarity of our mind and its steadiness in pursuit of truth.

19. The Content of Space

1. Nothing that exists is void; it is only what does not exist that is void; (CH 2 : 10) for all parts of the universe are wholly filled with bodies[14] of various kinds and shapes, each having its own form and size, so that the universe itself is full and complete. . . . Nor do I consider even that which is said to be outside the universe as (void) . . ., seeing that it is filled with things which can be conceived by thought, that is, similar to its own divinity. (PS 33 : 1-2)

2. And so . . . you must call nothing void without saying what it is void of, . . . for . . . it cannot possibly be empty of at least breath and air. (PS 33 : 3) Is not air a body ? . . . And does not that body pervade all that exists and (so) fill it ? And is not a body made up of the four (elements) mingled ?[15] Therefore, all that you call void are full of air, and if of air then of the "four". . . . So these things . . . ought to be termed

empty, not void, for they are full of something. (CH 2 : 11)

3. Now that Space[16] wherein the All is moved is ... bodiless, ... Mind wholly entire, self-embracing, free from every body, inerrant, impassive, intangible, itself stayed in self, containing all,[17] and preserving the things that are, whose rays[18] are as it were the Good (and) the Truth, the archetypal light ... of Soul. (CH 2 : 12)

We often loosely say that such and such a thing is empty, but this whole universe and everything in it is a fullness. The "empty" jar is full—of air, wherein are floating tiny drops of moisture, specks of dust, and "molecules" of heat; so that in the "emptiness" of that jar all the "four elements" of ancient science can be found. Nothing is empty, really, save what is not a thing, the non-existent. There is not even an ".empty word" that is not full at least of silliness or idle mischief, if it be not full of evil meaning and purpose.

All things are filled by "Space" ($ākāsʻa$), and all things float, are buoyed up, in "Space". That all-sustaining, all-pervading Something is the Real, whose epithets are negative while most active, whose radiance illumines Soul with the divine light of Truth—which is God in us, the Ray of Mind.

20. The Immortal God is in All

1. There is nothing of what comes into being, or has come into being, where God is

not, (CH 12 : 21) for God is all things,[19] and all are from Him,[20] and all are of His Will[21] and inimitable Wisdom. For the All is good and beautiful, but it can be felt and understood by Him alone. Without Him neither has anything been, nor is, nor shall be, for all are from Him, and in Him, and through Him. (PS 34 : 3)

2. Whether you speak of matter, or body, or essential being, know that these also are forces of God ; . . . and this is God—the All, and there is nothing which is not (included) in the All. Hence beside God there is neither size, nor place, nor quality, nor form, nor time, for He is all, and the All pervades and surrounds all.[22] (CH 12 : 22-23) If you learn to understand this, . . . you will give thanks to God. (PS 34 : 4)

3. The entire universe . . . is a fullness of life, and through all eternity there is nothing in it . . . which is not alive, for there has never been one dead thing in the universe,[23] nor is there (now), nor will there ever be. For the Father willed that the universe should be a living creature[24] as long as it exists, so it also must be a " god ". How then could . . . there

be dead things in the "god", in the image of the **Father**, in the fullness of life? Deadness is corruption, and corruption (is) destruction; how then could any part of the Incorruptible be corrupted, or any whit of the "god" be destroyed? (CH 12 : 15-16)

4. Nay, death has nothing to do with these, . . . for death is destruction, and nothing in the universe is destroyed. For since the universe is a "second god" and a deathless being—and an image of the Greater and united to Him—it is impossible for any part of the deathless being to die, and all in the universe are parts of the universe. The term "death" is a name void of fact. (CH 8 : 1)

God, the Real, is in everything that *is*, for all derive from Him and are sustained by His eternal Will. So in a sense all things are divine, though their divinity be known only to God and to him who becomes like God. It is He who acts in all the laws and forces of this material universe; Nature is His obedient servant, and nothing can happen outside His Will. Even the midget or the ant dies because it is His Will, for all are in Him and live by Him; He is the life, the very being, of all that is. Knowing this, a man will lose all fear, be freed from every passion and filled with peace and joy, seeing in all events the plan of his all-loving God, in friends and foes alike the agents of His Will sent to him by His love.

Nothing in God's universe could ever die, for all is in Him and He is Life; they exist only in Eternal Life. Never could death enter into the Body of this God of Life; and our universe is His Body, closely linked with Him, so that all the universe is full of life. There is no death; what seems so is but change of form within the living Body of the Immortal God, "Living" or "dead", all things in this universe are alive, because He is Life and they abide in Him. To know this is the way to bliss.

21. One God Made the Universe

1. Now gaze through me,[25] (Mind), upon the universe which lies under your eye, and carefully observe its beauty, a body fresh though none is more ancient, in the prime of life and ever new, nay rather, in ever greater bloom. . . . All is full of light, . . . for by the attraction of opposites and the blending of dissimilars (the fire) has become a light shining down through God's working.[26] (CH 11 : 6-7)

2. See the moon, outstripping all (the planets) in the race, an instrument of Nature that changes matter here below.[27] Then the earth, set firmly in the centre of them all, foundation[28] of the fair universe, feeder and nurse of terrestrials. Now gaze upon the

host of deathless living beings, how great it is, and (upon) that of the mortals, . . . and all are full of soul, and all are in movement, some of them around * heaven and others around † the earth. (CH 11 : 7-8)

3. And that all these have come into existence . . . you have no need any longer to learn from me, for they are bodies, and have a soul, and are moved; and these cannot come together into one without someone to bring them together. So there must be some (such) a one, and He must certainly be *one*.[29] . . . One speed having been decreed for the whole **motion of them all**, it is impossible for there to be two Makers or more; one system is not maintained by many, but there will be a rivalry among the many. And if there were another Maker for the changeable and mortal creatures, he would desire to make the immortals as well. How then (can the life of the immortals be) other than (that of) the mortals? . . .[30] Thus the Cause of all life [31] is (the Cause) of (that of) the immortals. (CH 11 : 8-9)

* *Or* : in.
† *Or* : upon.

4. So it is both clear that there is someone who makes these things, and also obvious that He is one, for there is also one soul, and one matter, and one life. Who then is He? Who else could He be but the One God? For to whom else does it belong of right to make ensouled living things? So God is One; if many, absurd! ... And how is it a great thing for God to make both immortal life and change, when you yourself do so many (different) things? For you see, and speak, and hear, and smell, and touch, and walk about, and think, and breathe, ... but the (doer) of all these things is **one**. ... For (no man) can exist if he does not show forth any of these things; how much more, then, God? ... God—but it is not right to say this—would no longer be God ... (God), then, makes all things;[32] (CH 11 : 11-13) worship and adore Him with reverence; and the worship of God is one—not to be bad. (CH 12 : 23)

"Hermes" tells his disciples to look round them thoughtfully at the beauty of this universe when it is now millions of years old, and see how it is still full of life and its energies show no signs of running down. The sun's fiery heat has been tempered for us by distance and the atmosphere into a mild life-giving light which spreads beneficence on every side.

They should also look at the moon, which runs so swiftly eastwards round the earth, governing the tides and influencing the growth of plants; and at the earth, which seems the very centre of heaven's cycling bodies, and which bears and feeds such swarms of living creatures. The sun gives life, the moon forms bodies, and the earth gives food to them. All these, animals and plants and stars, are full of soul and constantly in movement under a single law.

How could all this vast and wonderfully organised universe have just made itself? A statue does not carve itself out of the marble block, but awaits the sculptor's chisel. So there must have been a Creator of the universe, who made the laws which everything obeys. Now had there been two Gods or more, there could not have been a single system running through them all, for each God would have had his own laws to impose, and they would have divided the universe into separate spheres of influence. And that would have been a chaos, not a cosmos; all would have fallen into anarchy. No, there could be only one God, and He who made the tiny ant made also the mighty sun and all the stars.

The whole universe is clearly a wondrous unity, so it could have only a single God to bring the all-pervading Soul and the multiform Matter together. All the "gods" or angels work under Him, Nature and the Seven Lords obey His Will, so He is really the only Worker. We need not, like many Gnōstics, imagine a separate Demiurge to make material forms. Even man is one though he has so many kinds of activity simultaneously at work, so also God is God by reason of His manifold activities in creation. This is the God who alone deserves our worship, and that worship is to be as much like Him as we imperfect human creatures can.

22. God the Universal Worker

1. If you give yourself up to me [33] for a little while, you will easily understand that God's work is one—so that all things may come into being.... And this is goodness;... for just as a man cannot live without **breathing**, so also God cannot (be) without doing good—and that... is life. And that is, as it were, God's (very Being), to move and give life to all. (CH 11 : 13, 17)

2. Yet... He has no other as fellow-worker;[34] being therefore a solitary Worker, He is always at the work, Himself being what He makes.[35] For if He were separate from it, all would collapse and all would of necessity die,[36] because they have no life (in themselves). But seeing that all living creatures exist,... and one life is in all, (and life) comes from God, it follows that all things arise from God. (CH 11 : 14)

3. Now God, being the Creator of all, makes all things like Himself; but these, coming into being good, **begin to vary**[37] by the contact of forces. (CH 9 : 5) God has not made *

---
* *Or*: Caused to be.

evil,[38] but the continuance of generation makes it erupt on them, and for this reason God has made Change, as it were the purifying agent of things which have come into being. (CH 14 : 7) God's working is a power which cannot be excelled, and nothing either human or divine can be compared to it. . . . Now God is not idle, or all things would be idle, for all are full of God. . . . The Maker is in all, being active (everywhere). . . . So never imagine that anything below or above is like God, or you will fall away from the truth, for nothing is like the Only and One.[39] (CH 11 : 5)

4. Mind is seen in thinking, God in making. For this very reason has He made all, so that you may see Him through all.[40] (CH 11 : 22) He is not any one of these things, but is the Cause for their existence,[41] both for all and for each single one of all the things that are, omitting nothing at all save the non-existent. . . . Thus God is not mind,[42] but Cause of the mind's existence . . . , nor light, but Cause that light exists. (CH 2 : 12-14)

There is but one God to create all; and because God's very nature is to create, to *give*, His whole Being is absorbed in that activity. It is His only work, to do good by putting His life into forms. He works alone and ceaselessly. Nor is what He makes in any way other than Himself; separate, it could not exist for a moment—He being its very life, the basis and support of its being. Everything lives only through His life within it.

The painter's picture is full of his own character, the author is revealed by his novel; so everything that God creates resembles Him, carries His "signature", as it were. But after it comes from His hand, beautiful and pure, time passes over it, and it is moulded by the circumstances wherein it is placed. Each being reacts to stimuli in different ways, and so some grow more godlike while others are stained with the slime of earth. God is not the cause of this "evil"; it is a natural result of material existence in a universe of change. It comes from and increases with the passing of time, like rust forming on a steel knife, so it can be checked only by lessening the time. This is why God ordained the purifying change that men call "death", "lest one good custom should corrupt the world" by surviving its usefulness. God's wisdom is supreme, inimitable; it is for us to admire and not to criticise in our ignoance. His activity is unending, for if He abstained from action the universe could not run for a single day.

Through man's thoughts we see into his mind; through God's creation we can see into His Nature. This indeed is why He makes everything. He is no more identical with His creation, however, than the sculptor is with his statue, but He is the Cause for everything. "Hermes" does not teach a Pantheism adapted to a lazy mind. God is both *in* and beyond His universe.

23. God Unmanifest made Manifest

1. The Unmanifest always *is*, for He has no need to manifest, . . . because He always

is, and makes all things else manifest, Himself being (still) unmanifest.[43] . . . He is not Himself brought into being in (our) imagination, but (presents) all things (through) thought-images.[44] . . . So it is clear that not (being) one brought into being He is unimaginable, then also invisible; but He presents all things through the imagination and so manifests (Himself) through all,[45] and especially to those to whom He wills to manifest.[46] (CH 5 : 1-2)

2. Pray then first to the Lord and Father, (the) only and one (Good), to receive His grace, and that a ray of Him[47], even if only one, may shine upon your mind, so that you may in thought be able to grasp so great a God. For thought alone can see the Invisible, because it is also itself invisible. (CH 5 : 2)

3. If then you are able to see with the mind's eyes,[48] He will manifest (to you), . . . for the Lord willingly appears[49] through the whole universe, and you can behold the image of God and take it in hands. (But can you anywhere) see (your own) thought? So if even what is in you is invisible to you, how can He

(who is) in Himself appear to you through the eyes ? (CH 5 : 2)

4. But if you desire to see Him, think of the sun, think of the moon's course, think of the order of the stars,—who is it who watches over the order ? . . . Who is it who has settled for each one the place and the extent of its course ? . . . Who is it who has set the boundaries around the sea ? Who is it who has established the earth ? For there is some One who is the Maker and Master of all these ; . . . because every order (is made). (CH 5 : 3)

5. Would that it were possible for you to grow wings and soar into the air ! Poised between earth and heaven, you might see the solidity of the earth, the fluid mass of the sea, the streaming rivers, the free air, the swiftness of fire, the course of the stars, and the speed of heaven's revolving round them all ! O most blessed would be . . . that vision,[50] (to see) all these (swept along) under one impulse, and to perceive the Unmoving in movement and the Unmanifest revealed through the things which He makes ! (CH 5 : 5)

6. Such is the order of the universe. But if you wish to see (Him) through mortals also,

those on earth and those in the deep, . . . think how man is created in the womb, and carefully observe the Creator's skill in work, and learn who it is who fashions this beautiful and divine image of the (Heavenly) Man.[51]
. . . See how many crafts on one material, and how many labours (in) one sketch—and all most beautiful, and all proportionate, yet all different! Who has made all these things? What sort of mother, what kind of father, save the Invisible God (who) has created all things by His own Will? (CH 5 : 6-7)

7. Now no one says that a statue or picture has ever come into being without a sculptor or a painter, and has this work come into being without a workman? O what depth of blindness, what great impiety, what colossal ignorance! Never rob things created of the creator! (Now who) is the father of all? Surely it is He alone! And this is the work for Him—to be Father, to give birth to and make all things. (CH 5 : 8-9)

8. Just as it is impossible for anything to come into being without the maker, so also He could not exist unless He were ever making [52] all things, in heaven, in the air, on earth, in

the deep, in every (part) of the universe, in all that is and that is not. For there is nothing in all this which is not He; He is both the existent and the non-existent,[53] for He has made manifest the things which are, while He keeps in Himself [54] the things which are not. (CH 5 : 9)

9. Such is He who is greater than the name of God, He the Unmanifest, He the most Manifest.[55] He is perceived by the mind, He is seen by the eyes.[56] Such is the Bodiless, He of many bodies, or rather of every body. There is nothing which is not He,[57] for He is indeed all (that) exists. And this is why He has all names, in that (all things) are (of Him the) One Father; and that is (also) why He has no name,[58] in that He is Father of all. (CH 5 : 10)

God is self-sufficient in Himself. He lacks nothing, for He has, is, all; there is no need for Him to create, save in His own inherent goodness, which must give out Himself; He manifests Himself through His creation solely because it is His will. He shows Himself to us by images in our minds, which are reflections of His all-inclusive Mind. The things we think we see and hear and feel have no real existence in themselves; only God really exists. He it is whom we see in everything, and not the "objects" of this phantasmal world. Those whom He endows with Spiritual Mind see Him most clearly, by the light of Mind, the gift of His grace—without His grace, He, the "Dark Father", must ever remain hidden and unknown to us His children.

So we must ask His grace to illumine our minds with light from Him, the Source of Light, the Sun of the ideal world—so that we may understand our God and rejoice in His Light, which is invisible to our poor mortal eyes and can be seen only by the thought of a God-illumined mind.

God is always ready, eager, to give Himself to us, and we can even take Him in our hands by faith when we touch a tiny flower or a scintillating dewdrop, for they are His "image", intimately united with Him. Yet we cannot see His own, His real "Form". Can we see the flying thoughts in our own mind? Then how can we with fleshly eyes look on the God who dwells in the "darkness" of His own abyss-like Self? If we would see God, we should gaze on His works, which reflect His power, His beauty, and His wisdom—and then go beyond them to their Source.

If we could soar up above the ground into the pure layers of the upper air, and then look down upon the wonders of our world and all the marvels of the universe around, all obeying the laws of *one* Divine Creator—what joy it would be to see how the Invisible shows Himself to us in His creation! Then if we watch how the baby's body forms in its mother's womb, its little limbs and vital organs all perfectly shaped and adapted for their future work—what reverence should we not feel for the sublime Maker here revealed! It is His power alone that does all this; the human parents have no share in this amazing artistry. And yet He lavishes upon the tiniest creature, born for an hour of drifting in the unseen deeps of ocean or to dance in crazy delight a single tropic night in some far desert, the same skill and care as upon the human brain. Into a seed so small we hardly see it He packs the mighty forest tree with its potentialities of leaf and flower and fruit and seed.

None in his senses could think such works of perfect art could make themselves without an Artist. Such talk would be both foolishness and blasphemy as well. And that sublime Artist could be none but God, the one and only Good, the Father and Maker of all. But if God once ceased to make, to give, He would cease to be, for His Being is to give. What He makes is but Himself made manifest, and what is not yet created is held in Himself, latent and unmanifest.

Such, then, is the God of whom we have tried to speak, the God who cannot be named by any name, He is so great. Only by the enlightened mind can He be seen, and yet He can also be "seen" by the eyes that look understandingly upon His works. He is Himself beyond all forms, yet every form is a form of Him, for He is all in all.

24. A Hymn to the Supreme God

1. Who then can speak well of Thee or unto Thee? And whither also looking shall I bless Thee—up, down, in, out? For *Thou* art (the) direction [59] of all beings; there is no space [60] around Thee, but all is in Thee. (And what gift shall I bring to Thee?) All are from Thee [61] who givest all and takest nothing, [62] for Thou hast all, and there is nothing that Thou hast not. (CH 5 : 10)

2. And when shall I sing hymns to Thee, for it is impossible to fix an hour or time (that is without) Thee? For what again shall I sing hymns to Thee? For what Thou hast made, or for what Thou hast not made? For what Thou hast revealed, or for what Thou hast concealed? (CH 5 : 11)

3. And further, how shall I sing hymns to Thee? As being of my own?[63] As having anything of my own? As being other (than Thou)? For Thou art whatever I may be, Thou art whatever I may do, Thou art whatever I may say.[64] (CH 5 : 11)

4. For Thou art all, and there is nothing else which (Thou) art not.[65] That art all that has come to be, Thou art what has not come to be—(Thou art) Mind when thinking, Father when creating, God when active, and Good when doing all! (CH 5 : 11)

Swept on by the grandeur of his thoughts, "Hermes", or the Hermetist, breaks out into a paean of jubilation, which ranks among the loveliest poems of praise in human language. With it we close our poor account of God, and turn to a closer view of Man in His creation—his responsibilities, dangers and glorious opportunities.

God is ineffable, cries "Hermes", and all our sweetest praises cannot but fall short of His infinity.

(cf. § 38 : 6) He is not to be found in any one direction, nor is any place His special shrine, nor church nor mosque, nor temple, nor holy hill; for every place is His, and He is everywhere alike; wherever we turn we may see His glory, for He is in all that can meet the eye. There is nothing we can give to Him who is the owner, the very being, of all that is. Nor is there any special time or day for His worship, for all days, all hours, are His equally, and in the real world "there dawns no Sabbath, no Sabbath is o'er; those Sabbath-lovers have one evermore." Nor can we say which is the greater blessing we receive from Him—the gift of things created or the withholding of things He has not made but has withheld as mysteries in His own eternal Self.

Nor have we anything of our own to say, nor are we ourselves our own or apart from God, that we might come before Him as separate beings to adore His glory. He is everything in all of us—our life, our words, our deeds; and we of ourselves are *nothing*, nothing but the echoes of His creative "Word" uttered in the night of ages upon the silence of God's eternity.

CHAPTER FOUR

MAN IN THE UNIVERSE

Our fourth chapter tells us how man gets his body, and what happens to him when he has to give it up again. We learn how the "evil" man, who has identified himself with the flesh and its desires, fares when he can no longer gratify them, and how the "good" man, whose life aimed at serving others and knowing God, is rewarded by a glorious assimilation to the Divine. We learn also about the inner world and its inhabitants, and how reincarnation helps the soul to evolve, and the old old question about Fate and Free Will is solved by throwing the responsibility for his choice on a man's own shoulders; he can choose the upward or the downward path as he will, but having chosen he must reap the consequences of his choice. Oppressed by the number of those who reject the spiritual life, "Hermes" gives way to a gloomy forecast of the future of his beloved fatherland, but then outlines God's plan for the salvation of individuals who try to choose aright.

25. Man Comes into the World

1. (God ordained) the births of men ... and He puts each soul in flesh by means of the coursing of revolving "gods". (CH 3 : 3)

These (four elements) combine according to the plan of the "harmony", and (the composite bodies) arise from their co-operation. (Now in the seed there is) a life-breath adapted to the life-breath around it. This, entering into the womb, is not inactive but changes (the ovum), and during the changes (this) increases in strength and size. Then over the whole extent (of the embryo) it knows how to (take up) a copy of the model, and is moulded (in that form); after the model it **assumes** the species-form, through which that (which is being born) is fashioned into a copy of the species-form. (St. 15 : 3-4) For every living being . . . of whatever (species) . . . bears its likeness, though . . . the individuals yet differ (slightly) from it.[1] (PS 35 : 1)

2. Now Nature[2] adjusts the composition of the body to the "harmony"; (the) soul, taking over (the body) just as she has prepared it, thereupon confers life upon Nature's work, . . . and Nature harmonizes (it) according to the ruler of the star-blend. . . . For the purpose of the "harmony" of the stars is to bring about a "sympathy" according to Destiny. (St. 20 : 5-7)

3. It is the soul which is nearest that is assigned (to the new body), not because of (any) congenital likeness (thereto), but according to Destiny; for it has no longing³ to be with a body, (St. 15 : 6) whence also its association with the body must have taken place under compulsion. (St. 25 : 4) Their lot is to live, and acquire skill in proportion to the fate decreed by the circling "gods", and to be dissolved into (the elements). (And some of them) will be (famous), leaving behind them great memorials of their handiwork, (but the) names (of the majority) time will make dim.⁴ (CH 3 : 4)

From corrupt and incomplete passages mainly preserved to us by Stobaeus, we learn how the body of each man is prepared for him, as destiny has decreed before his birth.

The body is built up out of the four "elements", or (to use the astrological term) "triplicities", in the proportions laid down in the natal horoscope; the positions of the planets in "signs" and "houses" and "aspects" exactly correspond with those required to work out the destiny of the life that lies ahead. When the sperm, vitalized by the heated air of coition, enters the ovum, it brings about changes until the embryo attains a certain size, while it is slowly moulded by the planetary influences set to work at the moment of conception into the "shape" of an inner body already formed by the experiences of the individual soul's former births, as shown in the ante-natal horoscope. The human form is gradually achieved (and plants and animals grow in an analogous way), and then when the new body is ready the human soul enters and takes up her abode in it, for it is now perfectly adapted to her real nature and her needs.

The soul is drawn into the new body, not by the desire to be incarnate but by the simple law of attraction between similars. A soul with no kinship with body (that is, with no desire for those experiences which can come only through a physical body), can therefore never fall into incarnation at all, but will live always on the inner, higher planes. The tendencies of her past (*Skt.* vāsana) draw her into that body which is most nearly consonant with them, so that her destiny may be fulfilled and her desires exhausted. The purpose of her incarnation is that she may thus, by experience, evolve and grow in wisdom, but it is her own destiny or karma which decides whether success and fame, or failure and oblivion, reward her efforts down here in this land of exile. Of course, S is in error when he thinks the last sentence teaches the non-survival of the soul; " Hermes " speaks of what is left behind on earth.

The Arabic Hermeticum, *de Castigatione Animarum*, gives a most valuable explanation of the Hermetic doctrine of Reincarnation.

26. Human Love

1. Now each sex is filled with procreative force, and there is a combining of the two (forces), or rather what is more true, an incomprehensible oneness which you might correctly style " love " or " passion ", or both.

This, then, is to be accepted by the mind (as) truer than all truth and clearer, that from that (Lord), the God of all Nature, has been devised and bestowed upon all for all time this mystery of procreation, wherein are inherent the highest affection and joy, gladness, yearning and divine love. And there would have been some need to say how great is the compelling force of this mystery, had not each one been able to know it out of (his) inmost feeling by observing himself. (PS 21 : 1-2)

> Though they chose celibacy for themselves, our philosopher-devotees knew well how the power of sex sways the overwhelming majority of mankind. They freely admit that it is God who in this creative act which Nature's children can perform has sown the delights, the intoxication, which have made it such a lure to almost all that live. Nor do they forget how the love and longing for a purely human union serve to initiate the soul into that higher love which at last blends man and God in undying unity. The mystics of every creed and age have found the lower love provide an effective vocabulary when they have tried to describe the ineffable experience of the higher. I may just cite the *Gita Govinda*, the *Song of Songs*, and the writings of the Sūfīs and the Sikh Guru Arjan.

27. Death and After

1. Now, through ignorance of the truth, death frightens the majority as the greatest

evil. Death comes to pass by the breaking-up of a worn-out body,⁵ and on the completion of the number (of years for which) the body's (power of) adjustment (lasts); the body dies whenever it can no longer bear the vital forces of the man. So this is death—breaking-up of the body, and disappearance of bodily feeling. (PS 27 : 4) The dissolution is not (really) death, but the **separation** of a mixture; it is dissolved not to be destroyed but to become new.⁶ (CH 12 : 16) For change is the (condition for) survival of every body—that of the immortal without dissolution, and that of the mortal through dissolution. (CH 16 : 9)

2. Life is the union of **matter** * and soul;⁷ death is not the destruction of what had been combined, but the breaking-up of the union. (For nothing dies, but all things on earth are changed), and they say that the change is "death", because the body is broken up while the life passes into the unseen. . . . I say that even the universe is changed (eternally), because every day (some) part (of) its (life) becomes invisible, (but) it is never dissolved. (CH 11 : 14-15)

* *Or:* body, or mind.

3. Now beyond all (beings) man (is immortal) who can even receive God and be of one substance with God, for with him alone of living beings God mixes as a friend. (CH 12 : 19) A human soul—not all, indeed, but the pious—is something spiritual and divine; and when such a soul has fought the good fight of devotion—now the struggle of devotion is to know God and to do wrong to no man—she becomes wholly mind; (CH 10 : 19) it is possible, therefore, for the Mind, being the ruler of all things and (a **power**) * of God, to make the soul whatever it likes. (CH 12 : 8)

4. As soon, then, as the mind puts away the earthy body, it immediately puts on its own tunic,[8] that of fire—for mind, which is keenest of all intelligibles, has as a body fire, the keenest of all the elements. (CH 10-18) Having put away the (earthy) body, it has put away also the capacity for passion. (CH 12 : 11) Thus the mind, which is divine in nature, having been purged of the wrappings, ., . . moves about in every plane, leaving the soul to be judged and dealt with as it deserves.[9] (CH 10 : 16)

* *Or* : a working.

5. Now it is quite needless to worry[10] about this (death), but there is another which is unavoidable, which either human ignorance or incredulity thinks little of. (PS 27 : 4) (Thus) in the life on earth souls imperil the hope of a future eternal life ; (PS 12 : 1) for **man** is brought up along with **evil**, and therefore he delights in it. (St. 11 : 5)

Most of us fear death because it plunges us into the unknown. But really it affects us very little, for it is merely the breaking-up of a body which can no longer bear the strain of life. This must at all events happen when the lifetime fixed by destiny expires, and it leaves the soul free, unhurt, to proceed elsewhere, while other individuals take her place on earth.

Death really destroys nothing but the link between the soul and body, to which the soul had so reluctantly to submit at birth. It is her release from exile and confinement, her " going home for the long holidays ", while the walls of the deserted prison crumble into ruin. Should she weep for that ? Yet even the empty body is not actually destroyed, for its dust is used by the economical Mother, Nature, in building bodies for new plants and animals.

Man is the highest of living creatures, the least subject to mortality, for by his inmost nature—which is, immortal, heaven-born, divine—he is able to commune with God, to move with the Eternal on terms of loving intimacy, and even to receive God into his very self and so to be consubstantial with Him (*sunousiastikos*). Those who set their faces to the Truth, who try sincerely to serve God, by seeking Him and doing good to all His children, when freed from the body's harsh captivity become like Him, pure Mind, and through His power attain the degree of godhood to which they have aspired.

Set free from this body of the gross lower elements, the spirit steps out in its subtle fiery "astral" body, and is swiftly purified by its flames from all the passions which have defiled its "Spiritual Robe". Having passed through this purgatory, she moves on into the spirit-world, where she is free of every plane. We need not fear this kind of death, which sets us free from bondage, but there is excellent cause for us to dread lest our misuse of life endanger our eternal future by plunging our souls into agelong misery. For owing to the many evils inherent in our environment here on earth it is fatally easy for us to be lured away into the choice of evil instead of good. Then the seared conscience will be our judge, burning us in remorse at the sight of the results of all our evil deeds and thoughts which we can no longer undo.

28. The Judgment of Souls

1. When the soul has departed from the body (PS 28 : 1) she remains separate so that she may render to the Father an account of what she has done in the body; (F 1) then (comes) an examination and a weighing of her merit, and she will pass into the power of the Chief Spirit.[11] And when he sees [12] that she is pious and righteous, he lets her remain in the places which are suited for her; but if he sees that she is marked with the stains of sin and defiled by (incurable) vices, he drives her down

from above into the depths; he hands her over
to the warring storms and whirlwinds of air,
fire and water, so that between sky and earth
she may ever be tossed to and fro [13] by the
waves of matter, and torn by agelong
penalties; so that in this (respect) the eternity
of the soul is a handicap, because she is
brought under an agelong punishment by undying feeling. (PS 28 : 1-2)

2. Know then that we should dread and
fear, and take care lest we be involved in
these things; for those who disbelieve (now)
will after their misdeeds be forced to believe,
not by words but by experience, nor by threats
but by the actual suffering of the penalties.
... After death they are crushed by more
severe [14] things if by chance while they lived
their (offences) were hidden, for Deity fore-
knows all things, and penalties will be inflict-
ed that exactly fit the nature of the sins.
(PS 28 : 2-3)

3. The only safeguard is the highest
devotion, for no evil spirit or destiny has
power over the devoted man; God defends the
devotee from every ill,[15] (so) the one and only
good thing in men is devotion. (PS 29 : 1)

4. God the Father or Lord of all, who alone is all, willingly shows Himself to all—not where he may be in a place, nor of what kind he may be in quality, nor how great in size, but in the understanding alone of the mind He shines upon the man who dispels the darkness of error from the intellect, accepts the radiance of truth, and so merges himself with the entire consciousness in Divine Mind; freed by the love of Him from that part of his being which is mortal, he (then) becomes assured of the future immortality. (PS 29 : 1-2)

5. This then is the difference between the good and the bad; for (in so far as) one shines brightly in devotion, reverence, intelligence, worship and adoration of God, he perceives true Reason as if with (these very) eyes, and in the certainty of his faith[16] he surpasses other men as much as the sun (excels) the other stars in light.[17] (PS 29 : 3) This is the reward for those who live devoted to God and serving the world; (PS 12 : 1) (never) then should you say anything about Him, the One and Only Good, thinking that it is impossible, for He is all Power. (F 26)

MAN IN THE UNIVERSE

And after death, the judgment. We find here a clear memory of the familiar scene in the *Book of the Dead*, where the heart of the deceased is weighed in the balances against the feather of truth and righteousness by Thóut (Hermes), with the "Chief Spirit", Osiris, whom Porphyry calls Serapis or Pluto, looking on as "Judge". The pure pass on to places suitable for them, to revolve for ages with the "Undying Stars" in the "Boat of Rē"; those who are foul with sin are driven down into the hurricanes of chaos, where all the elements are at war with each other and life is a nightmare of unending strife. Here as long as time shall last these wretched souls are held imprisoned, vainly longing for death to end their torments. Dying, they cannot die, and their emotions are a ceaseless torture to their spiritual senses. All religions speak of hell in these ghastly terms.

This indeed is a hell to fear. It is easy for us who do not yet see its agonies to scoff and turn away to fresh defiances of God's eternal laws—but after death comes the reckoning we cannot evade. God cannot be deceived; our sins will find us out and exact their penalties to the last farthing. It is probable, indeed, that the punishment so exactly fits the crime that it is a ghastly compulsion to repeat the sin in memory, again and again, in a growing horror and remorse, as ghosts are said to repeat night after night their tragedies. Hypocrisy, unearned good name on earth, must now be doubly paid for; the penalty falls with greater weight when long postponed, and those who in life have partly expiated evil deeds have less to pay in the hereafter. It is good to remember that the dreadful Judge in this trial is really our own conscience, which chastises us with stinging whips of regret, through the laws which God has made (cf. §§ 27 : 4 and 29 : 5) and so purifies us of the stains of evil.

Nothing can save poor erring man from such a fate as this but the most sincere devotion, in deeds and not only in words, to God. For God protects His lovers from every kind of harm; He frees them from bodily desires which enslave them to Fate, and at the hour of death stands by to claim His own. So the only really wise course for man is the uttermost devotion to God.

Gladly his God illumines the mind of the seeker after Him with a clear vision of the Real revealed in His divine attributes, and thus He expels all ignorance of Him and draws the devotee into union with Him. Love for God flames up, and in its purging fires "all the dross of earthly things is burned and burned away". The devotee is assured of a liberated life through all eternity, free from the fear of falling away from the God on whom his heart is set.

It is man's growth in the Godward qualities which makes him "shine as the stars of heaven" while he gazes on his Father's face as if he saw the beatific vision through eyes of flesh. This is the reward a good and pious life has earned. Feeble as man is alone, we must never doubt God's sanctifying power to work this miracle, for to Him "nothing is impossible", and it is His nature and His joy to give Himself in love to those who seek for Him, whether they be men of importance or unknown to the world.

29. The Path of Souls

1. Moreover, Soul is a bodiless substance (St. 16 : 1) and it confers intelligent life (upon man); (St. 20 : 1) and even while in a body it does not step out of its own substantiality, for it chances to be self-moving. (St. 16 : 1)

2. Souls . . . are of one nature with each other in that they are (all) from the one place where the Creator modelled them, and they are neither male nor female,[18] for such a difference arises in bodies and not in the bodiless. (St. 24 : 8) But He ordained as a law that all should be everlasting, inasmuch as (they arose) from one substance, . . . and He assigned to them divisions in upper space. (KK 16) 'All the souls (which) are rolled along[19] in the whole universe are, as it were, parted off from one Soul, that of the universe, . . . the human (souls) when they have attained the beginning of immortality, change into spirits, and thereafter pass on into the choral dance[20] of the " gods " ; and that is the soul's most perfect glory.[21] (CH 10 : 7)

3. The dignity of a soul is Gnōsis, for the Gnōstic is also good and pious and already divine. . . . He does not speak much[22] or listen to much, for he who spends time in conversation and gossip * is beating the air.[23] For God the Father is not taught by speech and hearing, (CH 10 : 9) and the proper thing for man is to become one with Him. (F 17)

* *Or*: discussion and argument.

Now Gnosis is wholly different from feeling, for feeling occurs when the (material) is dominant, (and it uses the body as an instrument) because it cannot exist without it, whereas Gnosis is bodiless, and it uses the mind itself as its instrument; and the mind is (opposed) to the body. (CH 10 : 9-10)

4. Mind pains (the) soul,[24] stealthily taking away its pleasure, from which comes a soul's every disease.[25] Now a soul's greatest disease is godlessness;[26] closely after that follows a fancy for all bad things and nothing good. So Mind, by counteracting this, clearly wins good for the soul, just as the doctor also wins health for the body. But any human souls who do not take Mind as pilot suffer the same fate as irrational animals, they cease not from senseless raging and lusting, nor do they (ever) have surfeit of evils. (CH 12 : 3-4) In irrational creatures the mind works a law of nature, co-operating with their impulses.* (CH 12 : 10)

5. From the moon down to us is the home of souls, (St. 25 : 9) and this space is made up of ... **sixty** sub-planes; (St. 25 : 11) in these

---

* *Or*: passions.

planes ... dwell the souls, each (in that) for which it has affinity. (St. 25 : 13) Though in these the air has its own way, ... while it is in movement the souls have the power to dart up or down ... unchecked, for they flow through it without mixing or adhering, like water through oil. (St. 25 : 10) Now they are of one and the same composition but no longer of rank; for by so much as each of the planes is higher from earth than others, by so much also the souls in it surpass in eminence those in another. (St. 25 : 13)

6. Now in these same planes ... wander about (both) the souls which have been released from bodies, (and) those which have never been embodied. Each of these has a place according to her merits, so that the godlike and kingly dwell in the highest of all, while the lowest in rank and as many as are grovellers on the ground (dwell) in the lowest of all, and the middling (souls dwell in) the midst. (St. 26 : 1)

7. Nor do (all) go indiscriminately to one and the same place, but (each) is sent to her own plane, and (this will be) clear from what she suffers while she is still in the body, made

dense against her own nature[27] ... For suppose men and **other living creatures of all kinds*** have been shut up in one and the same cage, and ... then that (all) these are set free from the cage at one moment. Does not each turn by the inner instinct to the place natural (for it)?[28] So does each soul, whether incarnate as a human being or living on the earth in another form, know where she has to go. (St. 25 : 5-8)

8. Those who have been set free return to the same or even loftier (planes), unless it be that some of them have acted (against) the dignity of their own nature and have transgressed the commandment of the Divine Law. (For) the providence above banishes (these) to the lower planes according to the measure of their sins,[29] just as it also leads up from the lower to higher (planes) those who are inferior in power and merit, (if they have obeyed the commandment of the Divine Law). (St. 26 : 2)

9. Now in (those) on high there is no disagreement, but all have one purpose; there is one mind for them, (and) one feeling, (for) the love-charm for one another is the common

---

* A long list is given in the text.

love (for God) producing one harmony of them all.³⁰ (CH 18 : 14) There is a communion of souls;³¹ (CH 10 : 22) man being joined in kinship to the angels reveres them with reverence and a holy mind, while the angels on their side look after and guard all human affairs with sincere affection. (PS 22 : 4) The (souls) of the angels commune with those of men; the greater are in charge of the less—angels take care of men, and men of irrational (creatures), and God of all, for He is greater than all. ... Blessed is the soul that is filled with Him, and miserable the one devoid of Him! (CH 10 : 22-23)

10. (It is) not that God ignores man;³² indeed He is very well acquainted with him³³ and wills to be known (by him).³⁴ This is the only salvation for a man—the Gnosis of God; this is the way up Olympus, (and) by this alone does a soul become good ... of necessity.³⁵ (CH 10 : 15)

11. Behold an infant's soul, ... one that has not yet accepted its separation because its body is still tiny³⁶ and has not yet³⁷ grown to full size. How altogether, beautiful it is to see not yet made muddy by the body's passions, all but hanging from the Universal

Soul! But when the body has increased in bulk and has drawn the soul down into its mass,[38] it produces forgetfulness; and having broken itself off from the Beautiful and Good it no (longer) shares in that, and through forgetfulness it becomes evil.[39] (CH 10:15)

12. Now if ... a soul remains evil she does not taste of immortality, but rushing back headlong she returns along the road that leads to creeping things; and the unhappy one, having failed to know herself, serves strange and laborious bodies.[40] And this is the doom of a wicked soul. Now ignorance (of God) is a soul's evil, for a soul which has not learned anything of the things that are ... nor the Good, is blinded and tossed about[41] by the bodily passions, ... not ruling but being ruled. This is the soul's evil.[42] (CH 10:8)

13. For this is the greatest evil for men.[43] All things else that are rashly done by men are ventured on from either error or need or ignorance, (and) all these are guiltless before the "gods"; only impiety comes under punishment. (CH 16:11) Justice on high knows how to assign his due to each,[44] even if they are (all) exiled from the happy plane;

(St. 24 : 5) to each man will follow a suitable reward.[45] (KK 62)

Soul is a real thing, no unsubstantial fancy, even though it may have no body our senses can perceive. Whether it be in a physical body or no, its nature is the same; it has the power to initiate activities which need a body of some kind for their expression.

All individual souls are essentially alike, for they all come from one common Source—the Universal Soul which God created—and in them there is no distinction of sex as in the body. The Corelli fantasy of "twin souls" finds no corroboration in Hermes. The individual souls, broken off from their source, wander from plane to plane as pilgrims until they come to know God; then they attain the immortality to which He destined them, and as spirits they join the divine beings, angels who are ceaselessly engaged in adoration of His glory.

So the aim of souls is to know God through the mystical experience of union with Him in love, for that brings all the virtues in its train. Such a one is reticent and avoids unnecessary speech, for he knows that God is not found by noisy propaganda or by listening to many lectures, or in arguments upon Theology, but in the silent experience of the heart; relying no more on outward things but on the inward spiritual realities, he is liberated even while his physical body is still alive. He remembers that the knower and lover of God, the true Gnōstic, may not always be seeped in ecstasies and thrilling feelings of devotion; his constant aim is to be united with God, and not merely to enjoy the rapture of feeling His presence in the heart. It is a poor lover who loves God only for the reward of such delightful feelings. Union with God is performed in the will, and it may not always percolate through into the consciousness; nor need it.

Now vice grows in the soul through the wrongful avoidance of pain or the selfish thirst for pleasure, so it can be destroyed by the brave endurance of suffering. The gift of the higher Mind, by which God can be known, does not fill the soul with easy bliss—rather, it often drives her to asceticism, so that she may overcome the obstacles to her realising the Divine. Experience teaches her—and our modern world in its disastrous neglect of God will soon learn this to its full satisfaction —that all evils arise from the lack of true religion ; so their cure must lie in true sincere devotion, spurring man on to overcome his passions. No other motive for self-conquest can be so strong as the love of an infinitely lovable God. Those who disobey their conscience soon become the prey of every kind of passion, and like the beasts they are swept along by every wind of impulse.

Where do souls dwell when free from the physical body which entombed them down here ? They dwell in the quarter-million miles of upper space around our earth, on many planes according to their own evolvement. Even the subtlest matter cannot impede their movements ; they can pass freely up or down from plane to plane upon their business, but each has her home in that plane for which she is best adapted. Some are far nobler, wiser, stronger, more loving than others ; these live upon the higher planes, while the less developed are on the lower. Those who have "died" live on these planes together with those awaiting birth.

At "death" each soul goes straight to the habitat for which her powers and virtues make her fit, for she is eager to be free and overjoyed at escaping from the body. If she has spent the recent life on earth nobly and well, she is guided to a higher plane than that from which she descended, but if she has wasted her opportunities or delighted in evil, she has to fall to lower planes, or even, in extreme cases of depravity, she is cast down to hell.

Among those on the higher planes there is a perfect harmony, for they are all united by their common love for God which is the basis of their love for one another. Indeed, this chain of lovingkindness runs through the whole universe, angels protecting and helping men, while men respond with grateful reverence and in their turn look after the lower animals. At each level the stronger and wiser help the weaker and more ignorant, bound together by loving ties of service. And over all is God, the Source of all true joy and blessing. For man becomes God's co-worker and His friend by serving His lowly creatures on the earth.

God does not despise or forget His human creature, but knows him intimately and acknowledges him as His own dear son. It is His Will—and God is almighty, so His Will is always fulfilled—that man should know Him too, and so be saved from the darkness of ignorance and sin. For nothing can lift man up to God's highest heaven save this knowledge of Him, which is itself the unitive love of His Divinity.

How pure, how beautiful is a child's innocent soul, still free from egoism, not yet trying to stand apart as a self separate from the All, unstained by evil, so that she almost seems divine! But as her body grows " shades of the prison-house begin to close " around her, until she forgets the beauty of the spirit-home that is her real native land, and then, as she sinks deeper into the clinging flesh, she no longer trails her " clouds of glory ". Darkness comes over her, and her sweet beauty slowly fades away like " the roseate hues of early dawn."

The soul choosing to remain bound to fleshly delights cannot but return again and again to those false joys in which she put her faith. Bodies adapted to such a fallen soul gather round her, and the seeing eye beholds her bestial ugliness as if it were indeed the body of a beast. But such an evil choice is impossible for one who has once known God; knowing Him, one can never again feel the slightest real attraction for any other thing.

The slips and errors of God's lover arise from frailty or ignorance of the law, and signify but little; forgiveness and atonement are not hard for these. But the one unpardonable fault in men is a wilful ignorance of God; the man who turns away from Him finds no salvation; in ghastly isolation (avichi) he is left to reign in the hell his evil choice has justly earned for him and built around him.

30. Providence and Destiny

1. Now the race of men is **apt to err** because it is mortal and made up of evil matter, and it is subject to Destiny on account of the forces at birth, and to Justice on account of its errors in life. The sudden slip especially happens to those who have no power to see God,[46] and on these especially Justice lays hold. (St. 7 : 3) Now then, once the intelligible substance has drawn near to God it has control over itself, and in saving itself it saves the other also. As long as it is (by itself), it is not under Necessity, and its choice is made in accordance with forethought, but if it falls away from God it chooses the bodily nature,[47] and thus (falls under the Necessity) of the world. (St. 8 : 5)

2. (The lord of the horoscope is the Sun); under this are ranged the band, or rather, bands, of spirits—for these are many and varied—lined up under the (command) of the stars; to each of them (are entrusted) an equal number ... both "good" and "bad" ... in their influences. These have been invested with authority over all doings upon earth ...; they remould and **pull away*** our souls to themselves ... when ... each of us is born and ensouled.[48] ... These then make their way through the body into the two (irrational) parts of the soul, and set it vibrating, each one towards its own activity. ... So they control the whole of this business on earth, through our bodies as instruments; and " Hermes " called this administration Destiny. (CH 16 : 13-16)

3. But the rational part of the soul remains free[49] from the tyranny of the spirits, fit to receive God. Therefore on the one upon whose rational (part) shines a ray (from God) the spirits have no effect, for none of the spirits or (planetary) "gods" can do anything against a single ray of

* *lit.* : wake up.

God; but such men are extremely few. (CH 16 : 15-16)

4. Forethought is the self-sufficient Reason of the heavenly God, (St. 12 : 1) and while Necessity is a firm and unalterable decision of Providence, (St. 13) Destiny is subordinate to Providence [50] in accordance with Necessity, and the stars are subordinate to Destiny. . . . For in accordance with her they bring all things to pass for Nature and men, nor can anyone escape from Destiny; (St. 12 : 1-2) without her nothing bodily, either "good" or "bad", happens to take place. (CH 12 : 5) He who has become aware of himself . . . should . . . let Necessity go its way . . . as it has nature. He (should) only seek himself and, becoming aware of God, rule the passions, and let Destiny do what she will with her clay —that is, the body.[51] (F 21)

5. Now Providence is what fully controls the entire universe, while what constrains and surrounds (the individual things) is Necessity; and, working along with Necessity, Destiny drives and pushes all things around, for her nature is to compel.[52] . . . But Providence foresees (all things at once); while (through)

the grouping of the stars Destiny is the cause (of birth and destruction to those on earth). This is an inevitable law according to which all things have been arranged. (St. 14 : 1-2)

6. But we have the choice; it is for us to choose the better and equally (we may choose) also the worse, **according to our will.**[53]* For having clung to evil things, (the soul) comes into intimacy with the bodily nature, (and) for this reason Destiny has power over the one who has chosen (the worse). . . . Now (only) the intelligent essence in us is absolutely free; it ever remains so, and in the same state, not sharing in the nature of things that come into being; and this is why Destiny does not touch it. (St. 18 : 3-4)

<blockquote>
Man is frail and easily makes mistakes, misled by the world's illusions and swept along by his body's tendencies. Even those who know God may slip at times, but especially liable to fall are those who are blind to the Divine, and these have to pay the price of ignorance. When, as in the devotee, the higher self draws near to God, she gains power over the lower tendencies and, acting freely in accordance with God's Will, she at once redeems even her body from the evil inherent in materiality. Such a soul is free to think and act unbound by Destiny; but if she lags behind in following God's Will she at once loses touch with Him,
</blockquote>

---

* Mead's reading (*hekousiōs*).

chooses the world instead of the Divine, and so falls under the sway of Fate that rules the lower world.

Now Fate or Destiny Works through the places the planets held at the moment of birth; their " good " and " bad " influences act in man through " spirits " which tempt him to act in the several ways suggested by their own natures. Thus Mars makes him brave or violent, and Saturn calm or selfish. These planetary influences play upon man's lower nature of passion and desire, stirring his emotions into their own kind of activity, and thus they " possess " and use his body as their tool. The astrology student will understand this clearly. " Hermes ", that is, the seer in our Chapter One, speaks of this in § 2 : 4.

But the soul's higher part, ruled by Mind, is free from all such influences, being open only to the pure light of God's ray shining down on her. Over these devotees who are guided by God's Will alone the horoscope of destiny loses all its power; only those who choose the flesh lie under its sway. This has also been observed by astrologers in following the careers of dedicated men, who are said to " rule their stars ".

It is really the Supreme God who has planned all things from the beginning, and He knows which way each soul will choose to go. In fact, as time is real only for us, and past, present and future are at once visible to the Eternal Mind, that choice has actually been made even at the moment of creation, and it is perpetually being reaffirmed as the ages roll on. It is God who made these laws of Destiny which no man can escape save by taking refuge with God Himself. As the deep stream of life sweeps on round the wheel of births and deaths, all events in the material universe take place under these inevitable laws. So the wise man does not complain of troubles that come his way, nor does he fight against them; seeking God in himself, he gives his attention to self-control and the practice of virtue, and yields his body a willing victim to the forces that rule the world of flesh.

Yes, it is God who plans the general scheme of things, while details are worked out and adjusted by the laws of destiny which He has made. So we are always in His hands. We cannot evade His laws, but we can overrule them if we take the Godward path; identifying ourselves with His ever-free Will, we enjoy free will in ourselves. But if we choose the downward way, we lose that freedom which is in God alone, and even against our will are swept along like blown leaves by the forces we have invoked. It is only the higher self, the God-given Mind, which is eternally free, because its origin is in the Divine above all laws. Until we have enslaved our will by choosing evil, we enjoy God's freedom inherent in our spirits, which are His " sons ".

31. The Vital Choice

1. God is not to blame,[54] but we are responsible for evils, preferring them to good. (CH 4:8) He is not to be heard or spoken of;[55] nor is He visible to eyes, but to mind and heart. But you must first tear off the shirt *[56] which you wear, the gloomy wrap, ... the conscious corpse, the tomb carried around, the domestic robber—an enemy that hates (you) through the things it loves, and grudges through what it hates. ... It crushes you down

* *Or*: cloak.

to itself, so that you may not look up and, seeing the beauty of the Truth and the (one and only) Good, hate the evil of this thing. (CH 7 : 2-3)

2. Unless you first hate the body,[57] ... you cannot love your self; but having come to love your self you will have Mind, and having Mind you will share also in experience...., For it is impossible to be attached to both—the mortal and the divine; ... the choice of one or the other is left[58] to the one willing to choose. Both are not such as can be taken; when one is slighted, the force of the other manifests. (CH 4 : 6)

3. So let us seize upon the beginning, and travel with all speed.[59] For it is very hard[60] to leave familiar and present things[61] and return home to the old and ancient things; the things that are seen delight (us), while the unseen things give rise to unbelief; and the evil things are more visible, while the Good is invisible to the manifested because it has neither form nor figure; it is impossible for the Bodiless to appear to a body, (CH 4 : 9) but we (must) conceive (Him) **by conjecture** while suffering violence. (CH 16 : 6)

4. For the Good cannot be transcended; It is infinite and endless,[62] and in Itself beginningless [63] though to us the Gnōsis seems to have a beginning; indeed Gnōsis does not begin to be when it is about to be known, but it only appears to us to begin. (CH 4:8-9)

5. Now then, the choice of the better [64] turns out best for the chooser, seeing that it not only deifies the man but also proves (his) devotion to God. But that of the worse destroys the man, while he has no (less) offended against God; to the extent that just as processions pass along in the midst (of the crowd) and they themselves can do no work* and impede others, so in the same way these only make a showy procession in the universe, led along * by things of the body. (CH 4:7)

Nothing is evil in itself, but it is our own fault if we choose the unreal instead of the Real and then have to suffer for our folly. The Real is not perceived by senses but in our thought and feeling, and to raise these to the required state of sensitiveness to the Divine we must firmly reject the desires of the flesh which make them more gross and so stand in the way of spiritual aspirants. If we would enjoy God's beauty we must bring the body sternly under control. Gnôsis awakens of itself in the heart of one who earnestly seeks for God, and this *mumukshatva* is the main qualification for

* *Or*: astray.

discipleship. But the true and universal Self can only be loved and served by him who refuses service to the narrow personal and selfish Self. There is nothing here more fanatically ascetic or "Manichean" than we find in every mystic—Christian or Asian—it is a commonplace of the Inner Life, and St. Paul speaks eloquently of the struggle in himself. Ascetic Theology is the preface to all sound Mystical Theology.

The phrase "to hate the body" here means only: to reject its authority. Jesus, and the Hindu sages, no less than the Platonists and Stoics, taught that we cannot compromise between God and Gold, between the spirit and the flesh, things mortal and things divine: either the one or the other may hold our loyalty, but not both at once. We have to choose our master, serve him faithfully, and accept the wages that he pays.

No religion worthy of the name has ever claimed to be easy to follow; long years of effort, dismal defeats alternating with rare successes at first, are needed in the treading of every path to God. To reject what we see and know, to trust ourselves in life's storm and darkness to the unseen and unknown, of whose very existence we can at first have no proof, calls for a brave venture of faith. But that faith is itself our "passage-money", and without it we can do nothing. While we live encased, veiled, in flesh, we cannot help seeing God but dimly as in a glass.

It is our joy to know that our enjoyment of Him, once found, will be infinite like Himself, an unfathomable abyss. We can never come to the end of the glory of that life in God; it goes on and on for ever, deeper and deeper into the eternal Abyss of bliss. When we first see Him, we have an illusory sense that Gnōsis itself is born; but our knowledge and love of God are really timeless and eternal. Never was there a time when it did not exist or when we, unknown to our little incarnate intelligence, were ignorant in our true selves of the Infinite

Being in whom we have eternally had our being. Is the fish ignorant of the sea, the bird of the air, the flower of the sunlight? Yet our link with Him is infinitely closer than all these.

To choose the homeward way to Him is indeed wise, for it makes the chooser divine and also is a powerful example to others. But if a man foolishly chooses the lower, and enthrones the world in his heart instead of God, it ruins him, and it may also hinder God's work, just as a procession through a crowded street blocks the road for others. Such souls are swept along by desire round and round the wheel of births and deaths unrestingly, the prey to passions, hell upon hell.

32. Reincarnation

1. The impious soul remains in its own substance, punished by itself [65] and seeking an earthy body into which it may enter—but (only) a human one,[66] for no other body can contain a human soul; it were not right for a human soul to fall into an animal's body, for God's law is such as to protect the human soul from such an outrage. (CH 10 : 19)

2. Now what punishment is greater than impiety? What kind of fire has so fierce a flame as impiety? What ravenous beast (can) so maul a body as impiety the very soul? ... For in this way is a soul chastised: the mind

enters into the impious soul and torments it with the lash of its sins, being scourged by these (it is punished). (CH 10 : 20-21)

3. Nature is tent-maker and modeller of (the) vessels into (which) the souls are thrown. Two forces work at her side, Memory and Skill. Now Memory has this role: to see that Nature adheres to the type set from the beginning as a model, and that the (image) be formed as a (copy) of the **pattern*** on high; ... and Skill (sees) that ... on the whole for each (there is a body such) as is **suitable**.[67] (St. 26 : 4)

> For some time after "death", the soul that has rejected God remains discarnate, a mere mindless mass of passion, while, tortured by flaming memories of sensuality, it longs for another human body in which it can be born, to taste once again "the fleshpots of Egypt", the delights of incarnation. The teaching of some that the human soul may actually fall into the body of a beast is here emphatically denied by our Hermetist—even though this passage be clearly an interpolation by another writer, as S points out, we cannot date it by this fact. Such crude ideas of transmigration are only a literal misunderstanding of such Puranic and Pythagorean metaphors as we find in our § 29 : 12. The human soul is characterised by the presence of reason, which is not in the animal; any creature totally deprived of reason would no longer be a human soul; from the point of view of humanity it would simply cease to exist.

* *Or*: paste.

Surely a Godless universe would indeed be a hell; its inconceivable vastness, man's tragic pettiness and loneliness in those boundless spaces, would indeed be a nightmare if he were once convinced that he is not a soul and kindred to the All. Atheism also undermines the control of man's moral conduct and, as we have seen in recent years, throws wide the gates of hell, releasing savage bestiality upon mankind. It is the conscience which flays the wicked soul with the memory of her sins and drives her at last to penitence. M also sees here the working out on earth of the "karmic laws", the soul being taught by having to suffer in herself the exact wrongs that she has done to others in the past.

The time for rebirth having come, the embryo is worked upon by two forces to make it into a suitable body—one ensures that it resembles the incoming soul, whose subtle body is taken as its model; and the other sees that it is such as can be used for the working out of her destiny in the dawning life. (Cf. also § 25)

33. The Ideal King of Men

1. Now the King is last of all the "gods", but first of men,[68] and as long as he is on the earth he has been deprived of the real godhood, but compared with (ordinary) men he has something special which is godlike. For the soul that has been sent down into him is (from) a place which lies above those whence they are sent down into other men... Those who have well and blamelessly run the course throughout their own lifetime and who are

about to be deified (become Kings), so that by reigning they may be trained in advance to use the authority of the "gods", (while) those who are already godlike but (in) some trifle have trespassed the Divine regulation (become Kings), so that they may undergo punishment through being incarnated, ... but (that) they might (still) enjoy that (pre-eminence) when bound which they enjoyed while free. (St. 24 : 3-4)

2. Let us then praise God, but then we shall pass down to those who have received from Him the sceptre, (CH 18 : 15) and hasten on to the rulers of public security and peace, the Kings, to whom especially the supreme power over the greatest has been raised to a peak, ... of whom also the foreign land is terrified even before (their) movement. (CH 18 : 10) A King's virtue (is shown in making peace), and the very name confers peace—a King is so called for this reason that with gentle step he sets foot upon the summits and prevails by reason *, so that even the name (is) a token of peace. ... Moreover also, ... even the mere image of a King appearing has

* *Or*: a word.

before now assured freedom from fear and injury. (CH 18 : 16)

The natural leaders of men stand between them and the gods or angels, and belong to a higher spiritual plane than ordinary folk. Some are those who draw near the goal and are about to merge in the Divine; through a royal life they learn to use the greater powers that will soon be theirs. Others have attained to God, but have still some slight imperfections to wear away by the sufferings of bodily life, though they have not merited humiliation in this their final birth. The encomist does not tell us here about the tyrant, the monster of lust and cruelty, who may disgrace a seat of power —the Nero, Caligula, Hitler or Ivan the Terrible.

It is right to praise those whom God has set as rulers over us, men whose very name inspires obedience and restores peace. The last part of this paragraph is an elaborate word-play upon the Greek word for *King*, giving an impossible derivation such as used to please the fancy of the ancients. It sets out a noble ideal for the ruler of any grade—to rely on justice and persuasion, so that he is the dread of the wicked and the comfort of the righteous. This late passage, to which we probably owe the survival of the whole Hermetic Corpus as harmless to Roman Government, may well, as S suggests, refer to the bloodless victory of Diocletian over the Persians in A.D. 297. Its literary style is highly ornate and artificial, a complete contrast with that of all other Hermetic books.

34. The Age of Darkness[69]

1. Egypt is the image of Heaven ... and, if one should speak more truly, our land is the

sanctuary [70] of the whole universe. And yet ... there will come a time when it will be clear that the Egyptians have in vain obeyed the Deity with devoted mind and careful reverence, and all the holy worship of the gods will ... be frustrated. For the Deity is about to hasten back from earth to Heaven, and Egypt will be forsaken; the land which has been the home of religion will be abandoned, widowed of the presence of divinities. (PS 24 : 2)

2. For when foreigners [71] are filling this land and region not only (will there be) a neglect of religious duties [72] but, what is harder, a prohibition by so-called laws against religion, devotion and divine worship, with a penalty prescribed. Then this most holy land, the home of shrines and temples, will be choked with funerals and corpses. (PS 24 : 2-3)

3. O Egypt, Egypt! [73] of your religion only stories will remain, and those incredible to your (own) posterity, and only words cut in stone will remain to tell of your pious deeds! And the Scythian or Indian, or someone else like him, that is, foreign neighbours, will inhabit Egypt. (PS 24 : 3)

4. Now I cry to you, most holy River, foretelling to you what is to be! You shall overflow torrents full of blood [74] even to the banks, and the divine waves shall be not only polluted with blood but wholly befouled. And the number of tombs shall be far greater than the living; even the survivor will be known as Egyptian only by the language, but in actions he will seem a foreigner. . . . Worse than this, and far more wretched, Egypt herself will be driven on and stained with far more hurtful evils; she, the holy and once most beloved of God, the only colony [75] of the gods on earth in reward of her reverence, the teacher of holiness and devotion, shall become the type of utmost cruelty. (PS 24 : 4-25 : 1)

5. And then in the weariness of men, the universe will no longer seem worthy of wonder or adoration.[76] The whole of this good thing— than which nothing that was, or is, or shall be, could be seen—will be put in danger, and will become a burden to men and on that account disdained. Nor will this whole universe— God's incomparable work, . . . a good thing made up of many-formed variety of images, the instrument of God's Will for His noblest

work, ungrudgingly supporting man, in a unity of all the things that can be revered, praised and loved in brief by those who see—be loved (any more). (PS 25 : 1-2)

6. For darkness will be preferred to light,[77] and death will be held more useful than life; no one will look up to Heaven; the pious will be deemed mad[78] and the impious a sage, the insane will be held brave and the most wicked good. For the soul and all things about it, whereby we assume that either it is born immortal or that it will attain to immortality, as I have explained to you, will be considered not only a jest[79] but even non-existent. Nothing holy, nothing pious, nothing worthy of Heaven or heavenly things, will be heard or believed in the mind. Nay, believe me, even capital punishment shall be decreed for the man who has given himself to the "Religion of the Mind". (PS 25 : 2-3)

7. The sorrowful departure of the gods from men takes place, and there remain only bad angels[80] who, mingled with humanity, drive the poor wretches by main force into all the evils of recklessness— into wars, lootings, deceits, and all things

that are opposed to the nature of souls.[81] (PS 25 : 4)

8. Then shall the earth be no longer firm, nor shall the sea be sailed upon, nor shall the sky **continue** with the courses of the stars, nor shall the orbit of the planets in heaven be consistent. Every divine voice shall be muted in a needful silence; the fruits of the earth shall decay, nor shall the soil be fertile; and the very air shall grow weak[82] in gloomy stagnation. Such an old age[83] as this shall come to the universe: irreligion, disorder,[84] unreason, the (loss) of all good things. (PS 25 : 4-26 : 1)

And now we come to the famous " Prophecy of Hermes ", on which S vainly tried to fix the date, not only of the Perfect Sermon in the midst of which it appears but thereby the whole Hermetic literature, to the century or so before the Palmyrene sack of Alexandria in A.D. 269. F, in his notes on the last volume of S's valuable and scholarly work, shows how utterly unreliable such a theory must be; it is really little better than guesswork, without data. He points out that the so-called " prophecy " is really cosmic eschatology, akin to that in St. Matthew's Gospel (c. 24) and the late Jewish apocalypses; the Palmyrene invasion did not at all affect Egypt's religion, but the Jewish revolt of A.D. 115, stirred up by fanatical Messianists into persecuting Egyptian " pagans ", definitely did; if any historical allusion is to be found at all, it may as well be to this, or even, as Petrie has it. to the early Persian invasion under Ochus in B.C. 342—to which period other passages in our texts also seem to refer, *e.g.* the strange objection of our writer to his work being translated into the barbarous Greek tongue in CH 16—as to the impossibly late 3rd century A.D.

Swept along by his bias that " Hermes " is a fusion of Stoics and Platonists, and must therefore be late, S totally ignores the weighty evidences adduced by M, chiefly in the close parallels with Philonic and proto-Gnostic texts. It would, in fact, be as just to call " Hermes " an Occidentalized Vedanta, and to trace its descent from Sankara. No, this is not science, but prejudice. Parallels to almost every sentence in our " Gospel of Hermes " could be quoted from almost every religious literature in the world. It is quite absurd to imagine patriotic Egyptians writing a philosophy based on the ideas of the despised foreigner when those same foreigners in one voice declare that their philosophy derives from the carefully hidden lore of Egypt's own temples. It is vain for us to look for Egyptian *originals* of our texts ; they would have perished in the Serapeum fire, and being esoteric there could have been only a very few copies of them any way. They were not translated, but interpreted, into Greek, explained, re-expressed, with the aid of the precise Greek terms of philosophy then in wide use over the whole Mediterranean area. Only the Egyptologist trained in the recognition of yogic word-symbols could hope to trace fully their ancestry in the fragmentary hieroglyphic texts still preserved to us. And where is such a man ? Yet Pythagoras and Plato, no mean intellects, nor biased toward the " barbarian " cultures, repeatedly declare their debt to Egypt ; our semi-scholars think they know better than the eye-witnesses themselves whence that wealth was drawn ! But we have no right to call these men liars, or fools ; our knowledge of religious origins is still infantile.

For the Egyptian, Egypt is the Holy Land *par excellence*; every village has its own deity truly seated in the shrine, and the story of her cults runs back through three unbroken millennia of history to the dim ages, where it is lost in the misty semi-myths of the primal dynasties of gods. As an example of Egypt's religious faithfulness, we may note that offerings to certain deified kings were continued for thousands of years. And now our sorrowful prophet truly tells us of the then future day when all this will cease, and none will worship Egypt's gods any more.

The land will be filled with foreigners, to whom her cults will seem a grotesque superstition soon to be proscribed by law. S takes this sentence to refer to the Christian suppression of pagan rites in A.D. 353-391, and to be an interpolation in our text. This may well be so. But we need no more look for exact history in such apocalyptic material than in the books of *Daniel* and the *Revelation*; it is well within the powers of a normal mind to forecast the eventual result of influences already set in train as far back as the first Greek colonies in Egypt, around B.C. 500. Egypt, highway from East to West, could not long remain with an isolated national religion in an age of international commingling and rivalry. Because her sand and climate so wonderfully preserve her memorials of the past, Egypt has always seemed to outsiders a land of the dead; her religion was really one of joy and of robust, almost Epicurean, at least in earlier days—commonsense.

It is impossible to read this emotional apostrophe and fancy that its writer is building his religion upon a foreign philosopher. No, the Platonism in our books is secondary, due to the use of Greek as the international tongue of culture in that day. This is the genuine heart-cry of a devotee of Egypt's national gods when he sees, in imagination, the full national apostasy which has twice swept over Egypt since his day—first to

Christianity, and then to Islām. The Scyths and Indians were types of the "barbarians" then on the frontiers of civilisation; the *Sibylline Oracles* tell us how they scourged the Egyptian religion early in the 2nd century.

The holy Nile, the life of Egypt, whence comes all the water that feeds her fields, will then be full of blood as at the word of Moses, while the people will be stripped by their apostasy from all that is Egyptian save the language alone, being filled with unequalled wickedness and barbarism. Does S suggest that this was fulfilled when they became Christians? History would not support him in that.

How can gods stay where they are no longer wanted? no longer believed in? They withdraw, and their place is taken by evil spirits (cf. § 5 : 3), who obsess poor mankind and drive it deeper into such miseries as lacerate our world today. It is natural that when worship ceases, the functions of the gods which depend on the rites also cease, and all falls into disorder. So the very laws of Nature are disturbed, its seasons confused so that the harvests fail, and the harmony that holds the universe in one is broken up; the temple oracles are silent and their shrines are empty caskets whence the soul has fled; even God's voice in the heart of His devotee falls silent.

It is interesting to compare this description of the "last days" in which "the love of many will grow cold", with those in the New Testament and in the Purānas, and then to compare these with the world's actual condition in our own generation. Is this coincidence, or is it real prophecy? Nothing like what we read here took place when the Palmyrenes took Alexandria in A.D. 209, and Zosimus, writing in about A.D. 295, seems to know nothing of persecution among the Hermetists up to his day. Yet our § 39 also speaks of it, though that is certainly earlier than Zosimus. The possibility of true prophecy, as an occasional phenomenon, is established by modern study of the mind in such experiences as cryptaesthesia, clairvoyance, and phantasms of the dying. The materialists have given a wholly unscientific value to time.

In fact, F, reviewing the work of S, decided that the whole of §§ 34-35 form no reliable evidence for dating our Hermetic works. It is unlike anything else that we find in them and, he says, " must have once been a separate document ". M also thinks it may be an interpolation of the 4th century, under the shadow of growing Christian power and ruthless intolerance. But I admit that I am not convinced.

35. The Restoration of All Things

1. Now when all this has taken place, . . . then the Lord and Father and God, . . . setting . . . His Will against disorder, and recalling the error, and purging away the evil,[85] . . . leads His Universe back to the ancient state, re-establishing it so that the universe itself will seem adorable and worthy of admiration. Then God, the Creator and Restorer of so great a work, will be frequented by the men of that day with constant proclamations of praise and blessings. (PS 26 : 1)

2. For this is the regeneration of the universe : the making again of all good things,

and the holiest and most awe-inspiring restoration [86] of Nature herself, worked out in the course of time (by God's Will) which is eternal. For the Will of God has no beginning, which is (always) itself and the same as as it has ever been beginningless; God's nature is a purpose of goodness; ... nor indeed does He will anything **haphazard**, ... but He thinks and wills all things good. (PS 26 : 2)

> When the world's decay has reached its utmost point, then comes round again the Age of Gold. God Himself comes forth to restore order to the shattered universe, and once again adorns it with a beauty which wins back the love and admiration of mankind once more, both for itself and for Him who has created it again in glorious splendour. God wills only good, and when the very nature of personality generates a sort of evil in His "absence"; He is bound to intervene and to bring back the disturbed balance upset by human faithlessness. This section seems replete with Iranian thought.

36. The Nobility of Man

1. When the Lord and Maker of all things, whom we have named God, had made the Second, a visible and sensible god, ... and it appeared to Him beautiful and wholly filled with all good things, then He delighted in it

and loved it dearly as His own child.[87] Therefore, He **first being** (wise)* and good, He wished there to be someone else who should be able to look upon that which He had made from Himself; and immediately He made Man, the imitator of (His) Reason and love. (PS 8 : 1-2)

2. Mind... is derived from the very Being of God,... so Mind is not separate from God's essential Being, but is rayed out[88] just like the light of the sun, (CH 12 : 1) and the soul... is led on its way (back) to Mind (by Him). (St. 25 : 4) This Mind is God in men;[89] and for this reason some men are divine, and (their) humanity is near to divinity; for the " Good Spirit "[90] said that the gods are immortal (men) and men are mortal gods. (CH 12 : 1)

3. Now Man is a godlike creature,[91]... and the true man is even above **the gods**, or at least equal in power with them. For no one of the celestials will ever come down to dwell on earth, forsaking the boundaries of heaven, but man goes up to heaven, and measures it, and accurately understands it—and more than

* *Or*: mighty.

all, he comes to be on high without even leaving the earth! Such is the greatness of his ecstasy! (CH 10 : 24-25)

4. Beyond all mortal races of living beings, these two things has God bestowed on man— mind and speech,[92] which are equal to immortality . . . If one uses these as he should, he will in no way differ from the immortals, or perhaps (he will differ only by being in a body), and when he quits the body he will be led by them both into the choir of the gods and of the blessed ones. (CH 12 : 12) Now Speech is an image (of the Mind), and (the) Mind, of God. (CH 12 : 12)

5. On this account . . . man is a great marvel,[93] a creature worthy of adoration and honour. . . . O how much more happily blended is the nature of man (than of others)! It is linked with the gods by kindred divinity. He looks down upon that part of him which is earthly within himself; he binds to himself with a bond of love all the rest with which he has learned that he is connected; he looks up to Heaven, he tends the earth. (PS 6 : 1) Without such beings God did not wish the universe to be complete. (PS 8 : 3)

6. So then he is set in the happier place of the Midst, so that he loves those who are below him and he himself is loved by his superiors.[94] To him all things lie open: with keenness of mind he goes down into the depths of the sea; the sky does not seem very high, for he measures it with the cleverness of intellect as though it were very near. With his quick (wit)[95] he penetrates the elements; no darkness of the air confuses the effort of his mind; the earth's density does not hinder his work; the profound depth of the sea does not blur his downward gaze. He is all and he is everywhere. (PS 6:2)

When God looked at the universe He had made He found it "very good"; being Himself good, and His nature being to *give*, He thereupon willed that some other being should share the enjoyment of this lovely creation, and so He made man, in whom He placed a reflection of His own power to understand and love the Good and Beautiful.

Of all creatures, it is only man who has true Mind, which comes from and is consubstantial with God's very nature. For, as we saw in § 2:4, Mind is emanated from God like rays of sunlight from the sun—nay, it is God Himself who, as the higher Mind in man, guides him homeward to his eternal Source. Those who are fully enlightened by Him share, then, more fully in His divinity. The "Good Spirit" here quoted is the teacher of "Hermes", that is Divine Mind, Poimandres, often identified with the Egyptian Chnūm. Actually, this gnōmon comes from the sayings of Heraclitus, regarded as inspired by Divine Mind.

Thus man, God's dwelling-place, is really himself divine, perhaps more so even than the star-gods, for while they are limited to heaven he can, even while in an earthly body, go up to heaven by the powers of his mind and share their bliss on high; so he can live in two worlds at once. S is quite mistaken when he thinks "Hermes" is saying here that man can know God only after "death"; he can know Him only when freed from the body, as in ecstasy, rapture, or samādhi, that is true —but this does not at all imply the loss, only the transcending, of the body.

Nor have other animals the gift of reasonable speech; it is man's prerogative alone, which lets him set in order, and so understand and share with others, the transcendent experiences of his soaring mind. Indeed these two gifts dower him with immortality even while still enfleshed; Mind reveals to him the Divine, and through Speech (*logos*) he hands his experience down to posterity. When the body drops away, this understanding vision leads him at once into the Divine Presence, where he becomes a "star" in heaven. As God is imaged in the mind and its thoughts, so are the mind's thoughts reflected in speech. Man's "word" is thus, like the holy "Word" of the Eternal, a true reflection of himself in manifestation.

So man enjoys true royalty; he is the link between God and the lower creation, and without his co-operation the whole universe would be incomplete—dare I say, valueless. Looking up to God with love, he becomes able to turn away from the passions of his body, of which he however takes all proper care as is his duty.

Love is the relationship between God and man, and between man and his inferior; it is the great power of man's mind—which is of God—that enables him to conquer and rule the sea and earth, the air and heaven itself—all this physical universe. His thoughts can roam anywhere, free in all time and space, just as he wills. He too is omnipresent like his Father.

37. The Chalice of Divine Mind

1. When the Creator had made the whole universe, not with hands but with a Word,[96]— so that thus you must understand that He is pre-existent and ever-being—He, the One and Only, made all and by His Will created the things that are. For this is His Body,[97] intangible, invisible, to be neither measured nor divided, nor like any other body, for it is neither fire nor water, nor air nor breath, but all are from it. Now, being good, He did (not) wish to reserve this to Himself alone, (but) to arrange the earth also in order. (CH 4 : 1-2)

2. So He sent down Man, a world of the divine body,[98] ... for man is a spectator of God's works, and (for this) was he born, to gaze in wonder[99] at (the universe) and to come to know the Maker.[100] Now the universe is (a divine creature), but man has this advantage over other living creatures, Speech and Mind;

now Speech... He imparted to all men, but Mind not yet...; (for) He willed... that this should be set up as a prize in the midst of the souls. (CH 4 : 2-3)

3. With this He filled a great Basin[101] and sent it down, appointing a herald whom He commanded to proclaim thus to the hearts of men: " Dip yourself often,[102] you who can, in this Basin; learning why you came into being, (and) believing firmly that you shall ascend to Him who sent the Basin down." (CH 4 : 4)

4. Now all who missed the point of the preaching, these are they who have Speech but have not received the Mind; and (these), not knowing why or by whom they have been made, ... are in the power of anger and incontinence, admiring what is not worth looking at, and devoting themselves to the pleasures and desires of their bodies, and believing that man has come into being for the sake of these things. (CH 4 : 4-5)

5. (But) all who gave heed to the preaching and dipped themselves in Mind, these shared in the Gnōsis and became perfect men, having received Mind.... As many as partook

of the gift from God, these ... in comparison with the (others) are immortals [103] before mortals, for, having embraced all things in their mind—those on earth, those in heaven, and if there be anything, above heaven—and raised themselves so high, they see the Good. Then seeing It they consider the time down here a misfortune (and), disdaining all things of the body, they press on to the One and Only. This ... is the Mind's wisdom,* a vision † of divine things and the perception of God. (CH 4 : 4-6)

By the mere expression of His thought through a creative Word God brought the whole universe into being as His Form or Body; He Himself has always been, before all time. Now this "body" of His is unlike all other bodies, limited in size, made of the elements, divisible; it is the ideal World Order, the universe which can be realised only by mind, the *noētos kosmos*. You cannot see or measure or break up this vast body of God's; it is not physical or tangible, but exists only on the subtle inner planes. God created man to share and enjoy this universe with Him, and by adding a mortal mind to the immortal universe He made it perfect and complete.

Man is indeed a microcosmic image of his Creator, endowed with mind to see and admire the macrocosm, and so to love its Maker. Alone of animals has he both speech and mind—though some men indeed have not yet

---

* *Or*: skill.

† The word *entoria* is not known elsewhere. It seems to mean an inner consciousness.

received the higher Mind (*Nous*) which can see God (cf. § 5 : 1); this comes in individuals who strive through virtues towards Self-Realisation. This Gnōsis of God, the One Self, burgeons out of the seed of admiring wonder at His works.

"Hermes" now enters into metaphor. God pours Mind, he tells us, into a great Font or Chalice, and proclaims through His prophet (" Hermes " himself ?) that all who can may plunge themselves into this Fullness of God's Mind, baptizing themselves in the Gnōsis of Him. This will teach them why they exist and implant a sure faith that they will inevitably go to God, the Source of Life and Light, because they have been saved from the darkness of ignorance. F has shown well that there is nothing here to make us suspect that " Hermes " is thinking of the Christian baptism, though his doctrine obviously belongs to the same line of thought as theirs. He speaks of the true baptismal rite, so constantly among early Christians associated with birth into a new life in the Divine Light—an idea very prominent among the Mandeans, or Baptists of St. John.

Some souls fail to benefit from this preaching of God's Gospel among men; they dare not leap into the unknown depths of the Chalice; so they remain in ignorance of God, the unhappy prey to passion, lost in a whirl of restless desires which can never give satisfaction to their hearts, which really long for the Infinite. But other souls are bolder; they plunge into the Chalice, merge themselves in God's very Being, and so become perfected initiates in this " Religion of the Mind "; they become like gods because they share the cosmic consciousness which is God's Life. So they see themselves in God, they see God and, eager to attain to Him, they lose all interest in worldly things and devote themselves to the constant practice of His vision and His service. We shall find, in §§ 42 and 45, an unravelling of the metaphor of this interesting and important section; it is the actual experience of God spoken of in halting ecstatic phrases by so many mystics everywhere, the glorious reality of which our baptisms and other rites are but a dim memory and shadow.

CHAPTER FIVE

THE WAY TO GOD

"Hermes" has spoken of God, of the Universe, of Man; and now he concludes his long "sermon" by telling us how Man through the Universe can become one with God, thus fulfilling the purpose of creation—the only pursuit therefore which can fulfil the unspoken need of our souls and so give us true satisfaction; he warns us also that in treading this path we must look for misunderstanding or cruelty from our fellows, who drug themselves with earthly substitutes. We can become immortal only by deliberately putting away all that is not immortal, all that belongs to the narrow personality and the body behind which it has hidden itself; we must step out of that bodily consciousness if we would waken to the consciousness of the Real; we must put on God's Being if we would grow like Him and so find eternal real happiness. And even in the ecstasy of God-Vision we must remember our joy is a pure unmerited gift, it is God's free grace has illumined us, it is by His power alone we can remain in touch with Him and share His life of bliss.

38. Man's Fullest Glory

1. Now it is impossible to be deeply devoted without philosophy; he who has

learnt what (existing things) are, and how they are arranged, and by whom, and why, will give thanks for all to the Creator as to a good Father and kindly Nurse and faithful Guardian. Feeling gratitude, he will become a devotee, and the devotee will **learn** also where and what the Real* is; then having learned (this) he will be even more devoted [1] and will never again be able to fall away from the Good.[2] (St. 2b : 2-3)

2. For when the soul has come to know her Forefather she has a wondrous yearning love (for Him)[3] and a forgetting of all evil things; this, . . . this is the goal of devotion, and if you attain to it you will live nobly and die happily, your soul not ignorant of whither she has to fly aloft. (St. 2b : 3-4) The Mind enters into the pious soul and leads her [4] up to the light of Gnōsis, and such a soul never grows weary of singing hymns and blessing (God) and doing all kinds of good to all men by word and deed in imitation of her Father.[5] (CH 10 : 21)

3. Since the world is God's work, he who lovingly guards † and adds to its beauty joins

---
* *Or* : truth.
† *Or* : Watches.

his work to the Will of God, while with the help of his (own) body by daily labour and care he builds up the shape which He has formed in His divine plan. (PS 11 : 4) The love of heaven and all who are therein is one continuous act of worship; this no other living creature does ... save man alone, and heaven and the celestials delight in the admiring wonder, the adoration, praise and worship of men.... (Indeed) the choir of Muses was sent down by the highest Godhead so that the earthly world should not seem too uncultured if it lacked the sweetness of rhythm, but rather that with the musical strains of men He, who is alone the all or the Father of all, might be praised, and thus not even on earth might the sweetness of harmony fail the heavenly praises. (PS 9 : 1-2)

4. Really, to know music is nothing but to know how things are connected* and how the Divine Reason has sorted (them) out; for the system of all separate things brought together into one by the Artist's skill makes up the sweetest and truest symphony in a divine song. (PS 13 : 2)

* Using Bradwardine's reading (*iunctarum*).

5. Some men, then, though they are very few, being gifted with a pure mind, have been entrusted with the noble task of looking up to Heaven: (PS 9 : 3) philosophy ... is only a ceaseless gaze and a holy reverence in coming to know God,[6] (PS 12 : 3) for to worship God with single mind and soul, and to revere His acts, and to give thanks to God's Will which alone is a fullness of goodness—this is philosophy untainted by any crude mental curiosity. (PS 14 : 1) But to all such as have sunk down to a lower intelligence through the mass of the body on account of the blending of their twofold nature, is assigned the duty of tending the elements and these lower things. (PS 9 : 3)

6. To God, (then), the Father of our souls, it is right that blessing be uplifted by ten thousand tongues and voices,[7] even though the words be unworthy (of Him), for it is beyond our power to speak (of Him).[8] Newborn babies cannot worthily praise the father, yet they give suitably according to their power and are excused. Indeed, this very thing is a glory to God that He transcends (the praise) of His children. The beginning, and the middle, and

the end of blessings is to confess that the Father is infinitely mighty and boundlessly unlimited. But we must ask pardon (for our inability), even though (children) do indeed find pardon from the father before the asking. (CH 18 : 12-13)

Love and Knowledge are not opposed to one another, but mutually interdependent. How can we love one whom we do not know, at least in part? And how can we learn without that yearning to know, which is true love? It is when we realize how wonderful is the universe, and how wisely and lovingly all, even to the tiniest hidden detail, has been designed, that in our hearts dawns a deep love and adoration for the Designer. This love deepens in turn our knowledge of all connected with the Beloved, and as our knowledge grows so too our love. Thus Devotion is seen to be the quickest way to Gnōsis of the Real.

Once she knows God is the only Reality, the soul can never again forget His glory in the foolish distractions of her earthly life. Thus, her eyes ever on Him who is all Perfection, she gains all the virtues without conscious effort, becoming that on which she thinks. Her mere yearning for Him avails; her righteous life ensures a happy and peaceful death, and after that she goes straight to her Beloved, on whom her heart has long been set.

Whoever works to help or beautify the world co-operates with its Creator, becomes His co-worker and His friend. All he does becomes an act of worship, wherein he joins the universal adoration of all Beauty and all Goodness. By turning all his activities, all his skills, to God's greater glory, he fulfils the purpose of his existence and ensures that our earth plays its part in the cosmic harmony. This is the highest and noblest thing a man can do.

Music is a correlative of devotion and philosophy; its study is the art of harmony, the science of co-operation, on which the universe is founded. For true philosophy is nothing but the love of God's wisdom and a single-minded devotion to Him. There may be few really to reach the heights: others must content themselves with the study and the service of earthly things, and so share in God's plan.

Our highest skill, our sweetest song, our tenderest thought can never be worthy of so infinitely adorable a God, any more than the tiny child can adequately understand or praise his father. We are God's infant children, and it is our joy and privilege to do what little we can for His greater glory, knowing that He remembers our frailties and makes allowances for them. Though His love does not require us to ask of Him our needs, yet our very asking deepens our intimacy with Him and warms up our affection; so He wills that we should pray to Him. I think that in this passage the Paganism of the West reached one of its highest flights.

39. Devotion and the Devotee

1. Devotion is the Gnōsis of God; the one who knows Him becomes full of all good things [9] and has thoughts divine and not like (those of) ordinary folk.* This is why those who are in Gnōsis do not please the crowd, nor the crowd them, (CH 9 : 4) (for) dissimilars[10] are never friends; (St. 11 : 4) they are thought

---

* *Lit*: The many.

mad [11] and bring ridicule on themselves, being hated and despised, and perhaps even sometimes killed. (CH 9 : 4)

2. But God's devotee will endure everything [12] because he has attained the Gnōsis, for to such a man all things are good, even if (they be) bad to others; when plotted against, he refers everything to the Gnōsis, and he alone changes evil into good.[13]. (CH 9 : 4)

Not only is devotion the quickest way to knowledge, it is itself the very union with God which is the aim of all true Knowledge. This union makes the devotee a saint, a citizen of Heaven. It therefore also makes him an alien, an exile, in the world; the true saint rarely meets with less than the contempt, envy, hatred of the world, for men dislike what is different from themselves. His ways, his acts, his thoughts and words, all spring from another source than theirs and rouse their ridicule and anger.

But even if men kill him for his virtues or for the ecstasy of inner life he has become, God's devotee draws endless strength and patience from the union within. He sees nothing anywhere but God; he sees only God in all, even in the wicked. Whatever pain or joy comes to him he welcomes as from the Beloved's own gentle hand, so even slander, torture, death, become for him God's richest blessings and add to his love for Him.

This is eternally true, in all lands, and we need not with R vainly try to date our document by it to the late 4th century, when the Christians actually persecuted Hermetists and other Pagans. It is as true today.

40. The Truth and the Way

1. What then is real? That which is undefiled, . . . the undivided,* the colourless, formless, naked, luminous, the self-attained, the changeless, and the good.[14] (CH 13 : 6)

2. Reality is nowhere on the earth, nor can it come into being; but some men can think (truly) about Reality to whom God may grant the power of divine vision. . . . For the Reality is itself the absolute Good, undefiled by matter and unencumbered by body, . . . unchanging and unalterable. (St. 2a : 6-9)

3. But you see . . . what things down here are like—incapable of receiving the Good,[15] transitory,[16] liable to pain and dissolution, changeable, ever varying and changing from one thing into another. What is not true even to itself, how can it be real? For all that varies is false, because it does not stay[17] in what it is but shows us ever different appearances. . . . The Real is what consists of itself alone and stays as it is by itself.[18] (St. 2a : 9-11)

* *Or*: Unbounded.

4. He who has not failed to know this perfectly can conceive of God, and, if one dare speak so boldly, he can become himself a seer [19] and gaze (on Him), and seeing (Him) be blessed.[20] . . . But it is not possible for one in a body to have this happiness; moreover down here he must train his soul so that she may not miss the way where it is possible to see Him. Men who love the body can never gaze upon the vision of the Beautiful and Good.[21] Now what is that beauty which has neither form nor colour? . . . God alone, or rather the Something which transcends the name of God. (St. 6 : 18-19)

5. Mortal cannot draw near to immortal, transitory to everlasting, nor corruptible to incorrupt.[22] (F 7) Out of the two natures, immortal and mortal, (God) has made one nature—that of man. (F 15) Thus has humanity been made in one part divine,[23] and in another part mortal while he (man) is in a body, but the right balance of the two, that is, of man, is reverence before all things, which leads to goodness. (PS 10 : 4—11 : 1)

6. But precisely this is seen to be perfect only when, fortified by virtue against desire,

he despises all alien things. All earthly . . . things are alien to all parts of kinship to God . . ., and they are rightly given the name of " possessions " . . . in that they are not born with us. For everything of this kind is alien to man, even the body; so that we should look down on not only those things which we seek after but (also) that from which the vice of seeking them comes to us . . . Man ought to go to this extent that, (strong) in contemplating the Divinity, he should look down on and despise the mortal part[24] which has been attached to him by the need of serving the lower world. (PS 11 : 1-2)

7. (So first you must forsake the body), for this alone is . . . the way to Reality,[25] whereon also our ancestors walked, and walking found the Good. Solemn this path and smooth,[26] but hard for a soul to tread while in a body; for first she must fight herself,[27] . . . and there is a conflict of one with two, the one speeding upward[28]* and the others dragging down. . . . So you must . . . first conquer in the struggle of life, and when you have

* *lit* : fleeing.

triumphed you may proceed homewards in this way. (St. 2b : 5-6, 8)

"Hermes" defines the Real in words which will sound familiar to students of Vedanta. As it is the quintessence of negativity, the Unmanifest, it is futile to seek the Real on earth, where all is fleeting, changing, illusory, false, unreal; yet it may be found by those who dwell on earth, if God gives them grace.

Realising this, you can think truly of God, see Him, and find happiness in His infinite perfection. But this cannot be done through the body or its senses, only by putting aside the body and all other things that you can feel; for these would blind your inner eyes to the subtle vision of the True and Beautiful and Good, who is more than our highest name for Him can tell.

Man is in part mortal and in part divine, and it is only through the divine immortal part of him, the higher Mind, that he can approach Divinity. He can do this even down here if he turns away from all that is unreal, all fleeting shadows of our world, and seeks out the eternal changeless God within, beyond, their vain appearances. But man is designed for something more than the mere finding of the Real; he is to be a bridge between the Real and the unreal, between the Creator and His world. It is when man treats all things with seemly reverence, remembering that all are parts of God's all-holy Body, that he becomes a creature delicately balanced between the "within" and the "without", able to build a bridge between the Most Highest and the lowest of the low, and so to fulfil God's Will for him.

Virtue can become perfect in us only when we renounce—that is, put in its proper place—all that is not God, all that is outside our inmost, deepest, most secret self. All these outer things have come to us only with the body, so that through them we might do service to the world; that is our duty, indeed, but it is a lower duty, meant for those who cannot aspire to the lonely heights of the "Cloud of Unknowing" where "the God who hides Himself" is found. The same idea is found in the *Gita* (12 : 10)

There is no other way of finding Him than this. We cannot climb the hill while walking downwards to the valley; we must turn our backs upon the green and fertile valley of sense, if we would tread the solitary rocky summit and breathe the pure wind that blows across the mountain heights. This is the old old way that men have taken through the ages, and at its end they have found God thereon. This path is swift and easy for the earnest, though it must always be hard for one surrounded by the delights of this visible world; for he must begin by overcoming their attraction, then kill out all desire for them in his own heart and mind, resist the downward pull of all his lower nature that seeks ever greater involvement into matter, and then, having subdued the foes within and "crucified the flesh", he can take his flight—"the alone to the Alone"—homeward to his eternal rendezvous with God.

41. The Divine Ecstasy

1. Truly the doctrine of the Godhead, to be understood by a divine effort of the mind, is most like a rushing torrent that plunges down from a height with headlong flow, so that it manages by swiftness of speed to outpace our attention—not only of the hearers but even of those who speak.[29] (PS 3 : 1) If

you do not follow * the speaker's words with closest attention, it † will fly past and flow beyond (you), or rather, it will flow back again [30] and mingle with the waters of its own source. (PS 19 : 1)

2. I have no more to say (of it) than this: I see in myself a certain direct ‡ vision which has come into being from God's grace,[31] and I have passed through out of myself [32] into a deathless body. I am not now the one [33] (I was) before, but I have been born (again) in Mind; . . . I am not now seen with those eyes . . . (as was) my former form . . . Would . . . that you also had passed through out of yourself like those who unsleeping are (yet) absorbed by dreams in sleep.[34] (CH 13 : 3-4)

3. So if anyone is a bodiless eye,[35] let him go out from the body to the vision of the Beautiful; let him fly up and away [36] and float on high, seeking to gaze not on form or colour but rather on That which made these, the Quiet and Serene, the Unchanging, . . . the

---

* *Or* : are not followed.
† *i.e.*, the doctrine.
‡ *lit.* : unmoulded, sincere.

One, the Self from Self, the Self in Self, the One like Itself (alone). (F 25)

4. *Tat*: O father, you have filled us with the good and most lovely vision, and by such a sight the eye of my mind has been almost blinded![37]

Hermes: No,[38] the vision of the Good is not fiery like the sun's ray, blazing down on (you) and forcing (you) to close the eyes; on the contrary, it shines (only) to the extent to which the **seer** can receive the inflow of the mental* radiance.[39] For it is swifter in descent on us, but harmless and overflowing with all immortality. Those who can drink in somewhat more of the vision are often and often lulled to sleep out of the body into the most lovely vision. (CH 10 : 4-5)

5. But now we are not yet tuned up to the vision, and so we have no power to unfold our mind's eyes and gaze upon the beauty of the Good, that imperishable and incomprehensible (Reality).[40] For you shall see It only when you have nothing to say about It,[41] for the Gnōsis of It is a divine Silence and a suspension of all the senses.[42] He who has perceived

---
* *Or*: intellectual.

This can perceive no other thing, nor can he who has gazed on This look on any other thing, nor hear of any other, nor move any part of the body; he forgets all the bodily senses and movements, and he is *still*.[43] Then, shining round all the mind, It floods the whole soul with light, drawing it out of the body, and changing the whole man into (pure) being.[44] For it is not possible . . . for a soul to be made God while in the body of a man.[45] (CH 10 : 5-6)

When the initiate, or the devotee, speaks of God, he is suddenly inspired by Divine Mind, so that almost in a rapture his human powers are swept away and he loses touch with his own words, uttering what the inspiration puts in his mouth.* So unless the hearer is equally inspired it is hard for him to follow what his teacher has said; his understanding is left behind while the higher part of his mind or intuition is also carried away by the rush of ecstasy. Spiritual things are really ineffable; it is only by great effort, aided by grace, that the lower mind can gain some feeble reflection of them through words, when it is intensely concentrated on the single aspiration.

This is the warning of " Hermes " that he is about to try to speak of his own state as one in active union with the All, with God—the Advaita Realisation. He throws himself into that " mood " or consciousness, so that his presence with them while in it may stir his disciples into a faint experience of its glory. Through

* The writer clearly speaks from experience here.

God's grace, he tells us, he has come to be wholly one sense—all his senses having merged into the one of mental vision. Thus he has " oozed " out of his physical body into the freedom of universal and eternal life. No longer is he the personality they once knew; that personality is transcended, lost in the Infinite Person who knows himself as one with all that is, one with God, who Himself is all. This is the " rebirth into Mind ", into God, which was the secret central to all initiation in Egypt and elsewhere, the highest mystery, which changed man into God. The *real* Hermes, he who can speak of this sublime experience, is in no way connected specially with the body the disciples see; he is the invisible, omnipresent, eternal Reality beyond Time and Form and Space, the Light that casts all bodies as its shadows. He longs for them also to share the glory of this " new " life, which he describes like Sri Ramaṇa Mahārishi as " sleep-waking ", vividly awake to the inner world, while seemingly asleep or in a trance to the physical exterior of things. Of this state little can usefully be said to those who have not known it for themselves—it would be talk of colours to a man born blind, of *swarams* to one always deaf. But it is a real state, known to many who live among us in the world today, though they instinctively obey the ancient rule and hide it behind a veil of silence. It is a certain high type of *samādhi*, and has been well described by St. Teresa and St. John of the Cross.

Though it is a gift of grace and cannot be induced at will, yet those who have learned to smoothe its way can help this ecstasy to manifest. By intense concentration on the God within, the Immanuel, with a vivid aspiration to merge into that eternal Reality we have so inadequately called God, the pure man can break out of the body and in a soaring rapture, a " flight of the spirit ", pass straight into union with That which is the All in all, the Self eternally existent beyond all that exists.

Tat, the beloved young disciple, so vividly follows his teacher's words that he is swept away into a staggering partial experience of the super-cosmic state. But "Hermes" reminds him that the beatific vision cannot arise from words alone, it is not taught by another but must awaken in the silence of the inner self—the God is born only in the darkness of the heart's cave. Nor is His coming violent and overwhelming, but sweetly gentle, humble, and subtly quiet, so that it is, like the Nativity in the Cave of Bethlehem, sometimes hardly known for what it is. Never does it overwhelm the devotee, for its power is perfectly adjusted to his power to bear the Light. Like a gentle and courteous Lover, God moves slowly with His human "brides", that they be not crushed by His infinity; as they grow more used to His loving visits and embraces, these become more frequent, more "natural", more full of all delight.

But we, "Hermes" tells us, are not yet in that blissful state of "betrothal" to the Universal, for it is beyond words (and we would try to speak of it), beyond all personal thought and feeling (and we would say "*I* have experienced it"), nor can we know it before a sweet silence and stillness have hushed the senses of the body into "sleep"—the "ligature" of Christian mystics. So supreme is this vision of the All that while it reigns no other consciousness can exist. God will have no rivals; when He speaks, all else are dumb; one who beholds Him is rapt out of himself and lost to the world. Nor of his own volition can he move the body or any part of it—for it is no more *his* body than is the tree, the mountain, or the sun. He bides in a joyous and solemn stillness while the Light ineffable floods his whole being and makes it into God. For him Time and Space have ceased to exist, the world has faded into nothingness, for he has now become the Eternal and Omnipresent. This can never be while he retains a consciousness of one body as peculiarly his own apart from every other body, but only when he is wholly merged in the blissful contemplation of God, who is the real Self of all, through which he becomes That, the Cosmic Soul, from which he came.

42. The Yoga of Egypt

1. Bid your soul go into any (land you choose), and it will be there quicker than your bidding; bid it pass on to the ocean, and there again it will be as quickly—not as moving from place to place but as being there;[46] bid it also soar up into the sky, and it will need no wings, but yet nothing can hinder it. . . . Cutting a way through all, it will soar up even to the last body; and if you should wish to break through [47] this whole also and to gaze on that which is outside—if indeed there be anything outside the universe— you have the right. (CH 11 : 18-19)

2. See what great power, what speed you have! And when you can do this, cannot God ? In this way, then, understand God[48] as having all things as thoughts in Himself—the universe, Himself, all. Unless therefore you make yourself equal to God,[49] you cannot understand God; for like is understood by like. (CH 11 : 20)

3. Expand yourself[50] to the same extent as the immeasurable Greatness; leap out of all body, and transcend all Time; become Eternity,[51]* and you shall perceive God. Realise that to you nothing is impossible; believe yourself immortal and able to grasp all things —every art, every science, and the way of life of every living creature.[52] Become higher than all height[53] and lower than all depth; gather in yourself[54] all the feelings of the created (elements), of fire, of water, dry and wet. (Perceive) that you are everywhere at the same time—on earth, at sea, in heaven; not yet born, in the womb, young, old, just dead, the after-death. Having perceived all these at once—times, places, facts, qualities, quantities —then you can perceive God.[55] (CH 11 : 20)

4. But if you imprison your soul in the body and insult it, saying, " I know nothing, can do nothing; I fear the sea,[56] I am unable to climb into the sky; I know not who I was, nor do I know who I shall be "[57]—then what have you to do with God? For you can (understand) nothing beautiful and good if you love the body and are bad. (CH 11 : 21)

* *Or*: Aeon.

5. For the utmost evil is the ignorance of God,[58] while to be able to know and will and hope is a Straight Path leading through the Good and easy for you to tread ;[59] it will meet you everywhere[60] and will everywhere be seen —both where and when you do not look for it, waking, sleeping, sailing, walking, by night, by day, speaking, keeping silence. For there is nothing which is not an image of (That)." (CH 11 : 21)

" Hermes " ends with an attempt to tell his hearers how they can enable this supreme realisation in themselves. The mind can in an instant flash from place to place, even to the limits of the universe or beyond, and can thus simultaneously enclose all places in itself. This is what God does. He holds the whole universe in His own Mind as thought images ; and if we are to know Him, to become one with Him, we must do the same ; we must enfold all things in ourselves at once.

It is a bold venture to which our Scripture leads us —self-identification with all life, in order to know its Source. We have to *be* all living things, all this world, the solar system, the whole scheme of " island-universes ", the past, the present, the future, the manifest and the yet concealed, joy and pain, heat and cold, high and low, the habits and thoughts of every creature—all, all, in our mind at once. Becoming all things, all life is ours, we are immortal, infinite, divine. Made all-inclusive like God Himself, we break into freedom from the limitations that held us to one little body at a certain place on earth and in a certain moment of time. In a flash we know God, and knowing Him we know all else as well ; our impetuous love hurls us into union with His immensity

But if we cry "Impossible!" or, more foolish still, "Blasphemy!" and make no effort to escape or transcend the narrow personality that falsely claims to be our very Self, then of course it will be impossible for us, and God will remain for us the Great Unknown. Then we can never hope for real happiness, which is to be had only in Him. But once we seek Him with faith and resolution, we shall find He makes it easy for us; He Himself comes to meet us; everything that happens in our life serves as a pointer along the way to Him; whatever we do or say, or even if we are inactive and silent, He comes to find and lead us home. For all things incarnate His love and speak to us of their Creator, if we will but listen to their voice.

43. Thanksgiving for the Gnosis

1. Now having come out of the sanctuary when they began to pray to God facing the south—because when anyone wishes to pray to God at sunset he ought to turn that side, just as to the east at sunrise—(PS 41 : 1)

2. So then, while they were uttering the prayer, Asclepius said in a low voice, " Tat, shall we suggest to your father that we should pray to God adding the usual incense and perfumes?"—The Thrice-Greatest heard him and, being distressed, said: " Hush, hush, Asclepius! for it is the greatest impiety to bring any such thing into the mind with regard to that One and Only Good. This and things

like it are unfit for Him, for He is full of all things that exist and has no lack of anything at all in the least. Let us rather adore Him by giving thanks, for His only sacrifice[61] is a blessing. (PS 41 : 2)

3. "We give Thee thanks, Most High, with a whole soul and heart straining up to Thee,[62] for it is by Thy grace alone we have received the light of Thy Gnōsis." (We have come to know) the ineffable Name[63] honoured by the title of 'God'[64] because Thou alone art Lord, and blessed by that of 'Father' because Thou hast shown to all a father's kindness and affection and love and the most sweetest of activity—freely granting us Mind, Speech, Gnōsis[65]—Mind, that we may know Thee; Speech, that we may call on Thee; and Gnōsis, that, having come to know Thee and been saved by Thy Light, we may rejoice. (PS 41 : 3)

4. "We rejoice that Thou hast shown us all Thyself; we rejoice that Thou hast deigned to make us God[66] by the **Gnosis** of Thyself * even while in clay; the only gratitude of man to Thee is to come to know Thy Greatness. We

* *Or* : by Thine Eternal Life.

have come to know Thee, O true Life of human life! We have come to know Thee, O greatest Light, the Torch of Gnōsis! We have come to know Thee, O all-prolific Womb,[67] pregnant (with the Father's) planting! We have come to know Thee, O Thou agelong Steadiness[68] of Him who movelessly revolves the All! (PS 41 : 4-5)

5. "Prostrating to Thee the (only) Good Being with this saying, we shall ask from Thy Goodness only this one grace[69] and no more: Grant that we may be held constant in the Gnōsis and Love of Thee[70] and may never[71] fall away* from such a kind of life!" (PS 41 : 5)

The teacher has now ended his long discourse; he and his three disciples emerge from the little shrine at sunset, to give thanks to God for this teaching whereby they can be born into a new immortal life. "Hermes" reproves Asclepius for suggesting that the usual ritual and incense (*Eg. kufi*) be offered with their worship, for it shows how little he has understood of God's self-sufficiency; the only gift that we can give to Him is the love and adoration of our hearts—and even that is not really our own. "We give Thee but Thine own, whate'er the gift may be." This ritual insistence upon a certain direction at the hour of worship (a *qibla*, to use the Muslim word) is clearly from another hand than the hymn in our § 24, and may well be later in date.

* *Or* : be separate.

"Hermes" then leads the disciples in a noble thanksgiving for the Divine Grace which has taught them how truly to know their kind and loving Father, by devoting to Him alone who is the Purpose of creation and its Fullness of Joy all the powers of their being. They thank God for revealing Himself to them and making them as it were at one with Him—which is the only real worship man can offer worthily to Him. After ecstatic cries of praise to the Life and Light from which all are born, the eternal Calm and Stillness in which all creation moves, they humbly offer their one prayer that they may abide unshaken in that knowledge and love of Him which they have now received. For, as Plato and Philo have told us, those who know God are both His lovers (*philotheoi*) and His beloved (*Theophileis*).

Of this noble prayer we have also a corrupt Greek version in the Magic Papyrus (*Pap. mag. Par. ii.* 11 254-302) used by a sorcerer as a spell in about A. D. 295. By this version we can in places correct the Old Latin translation of PS, which is here, as elsewhere, rather careless and uncomprehending. The date of this Greek copy suggests that the original, an esoteric text of small circulation, may well be at least two centuries older—which confirms other evidences collected by M.

CHAPTER SIX

THE REBIRTH OF TAT

Our last chapter shows us how after a brief explanation suited to his advanced stage Tat is initiated by his teacher into the Divine Union. We may notice the stress laid upon preliminary purgation, without which illumination must be largely illusory, and upon silence. The "Virgin Birth" takes place within the soul at God's Will and unites the soul to His Life, His Light. Knowing himself as one with the all, the initiate is immersed in heavenly joy, which expresses itself in thanksgiving to the One Source of all goodness, in whom he is now merged. Our "Gospel of Hermes" closes with a solemn warning against talking of these things with those who are unready themselves to undergo the purification essential before setting foot upon the higher rungs of the spiritual ladder.

44. Where, When, and How?

1. *Tat*: When I became your suppliant* while climbing up the Mountain, after you had talked with me as I asked to learn the teaching of Rebirth—because this alone of

---

* perhaps disciple, or *saraṇāgat*, a technical term.

THE REBIRTH OF TAT 157

all things I do not know—(you did not then think fit) to transmit it to men, and you said. . . : "As soon as you are alienated [1] from (the) world, (I shall hand it on)." Well, now I) have become ready, and I have made the thought in me foreign to the world's deceit; please fulfil now what is lacking in me,[2] as you said you would when promising to transmit Rebirth to me. (CH 13 : 1)

2. *Hermes*: This Race, my son, is not taught, but it is recalled [3] to memory by God when He so wills. (CH 13 : 2) I (would) beg you not to look into the origin of your family, for it is not lawful to narrate the birth of Gods. Nevertheless, (KK 64) as (I) myself share the nature of an Immortal and have travelled across the Plain of Truth,[4] I shall explain the facts to you in full detail. (St. 25 : 2) Attend, child, . . . for you are listening to a secret sight. (KK 32) (Now in this Birth), my son, it is Wisdom [5] understanding in Silence (that conceives), and the seed is the true Good which God's Will sows; . . . he who is born is a god, a . . . child of God [6] the All in all . . . (and he) is built up of all powers. The one who consummates the Rebirth is a

(certain) one, a man, a child of God, (acting) by God's Will. (CH 13 : 1-2)

The favourite disciple later approaches his teacher with a request for direct initiation into the divine mystery of "Rebirth", reminding him of an earlier promise to give this as soon as he ceased to be attached to worldly things. For while with half his mind he clings to creatures, no man can make the vast one-pointed effort that leaps into God or experience for himself the blessed Nativity in his soul. The "Mountain" to which Tat refers is clearly, as M points out, the "sacred mount of initiation" common to most Mystery cults of the age; the guess of S is puerile.

"Hermes" warns Tat against the motive of mere curiosity which cannot take the place of the required thirst for God-Knowledge (*mumukshatva*), and he reminds Tat also that the "Race" of God-knowers, of Gnōstics, is not taught externally by others; God's grace awakens the knowledge and love of Him in one who is properly prepared. Grace brings a catalyst into play, in the person of the initiator or Guru, when the aspirant is ready to be drawn into Divine Union. The time for this has now come, and "Hermes" will play the Guru's part in stirring that latent knowledge of God-consciousness into activity in Tat's mind.

These are the conditions: the soul to be initiated must be both wise and pure, and then when God so wills he meets an Initiate, a "child of God", who will guide him through the gates of "Rebirth" into the temple of the Light, so that he himself becomes a "child of God" in his turn. This true "Virgin Birth"—for it is spiritual, not carnal, as the Christian editor of the Attis-document in Hippolytus tells us—takes place in silence, for no words can convey the realisation of the Reality, just as in several Gnōstic systems Silence was the Mother of Creation. So also the Temple of Solomon, the pure dwelling-place for God, was built in silence, no sound of tools being heard during the construction of it. And the Babe is born naked, stripped of all egoism and all lower passions, composed wholly of spiritual "power", as God Himself is composed. (cf. § 2 : 2)

45. Initiation

1. The Mind is in God; (St. 11 : 2, 15) draw it into yourself, and it will come;[7] will, and it takes birth; suspend the senses of the body and the birth of the godhood takes place. (But first you must) purify yourself from the irrational torments of matter;[8] . . . one . . . torment is Ignorance, . . . and there are many others . . . (which) force the man who is confined in the prison of the body to suffer through feeling. But these at once depart from him on whom God has had mercy, and so the "Reason"-(body) is built up. (This is) the way of Rebirth. (CH 13 : 7)

2. And now, my child, be still, and keep solemn silence;[9] and thus will the grace from God not cease to come upon us.

*   *   *

Rejoice now, my child, you are being wholly purified by the powers of God,[10] (for they are here) to articulate the "Reason". Gnōsis of

God has come to us, and on its coming, my son, Ignorance has been driven out; ... together with Truth, the Good also has come into being along with Life and Light. .... (In this way) is the intuitive (essence) put together, and by the birth of this we have become gods.[11] Whoever, then, by means of grace has come to birth in God, abandoning bodily feeling, knows himself to be composed of (Life and Light), and he is full of joy. (CH 13 : 9-11)

3. *Tat*: Having been made steady[12] by God, father, I form* (mental) images not through the sight of eyes, but through (divine) powers with the (direct) help of intuition. Father, I see the All, myself, in the Mind. I am in heaven, on earth, in water, in air; I am in animals, in plants, in the womb, before conception, after delivery—everywhere![13]

Hermes: You have learned, my son, the way of Rebirth. ... What is seen (by you now) is no longer the three-dimensioned object, (but the bodiless)[14]. . . You have been born a God[15] and a son of the One, as I am myself. (CH 13 : 11-14)

* *Or* : I see not.

THE REBIRTH OF TAT

How to induce the "Divine Mood", Cosmic Consciousness, is now told. First of all, every passion and lower thought must be resolutely put away, beginning with the ignorance of God, which is the root of separate selfhood and bitterest enemy of the Real. And this implies a complete conquest of the lower nature, purging out all downward tendencies in order to soar up to God—the true "repentance" of the Gnōstics—for one who is not yet pure as the saints cannot see God. Then you must lull all the physical senses of the body to sleep; and this is done at once, without effort, as soon as God gives His grace; without that it is impossible. Next, consciously merge the self into God, the All, by an act of will—which may yet be as gentle and as simple as a tiny child cuddling down trustfully into its mother's arms.

Then a stillness, a pause, a waiting—the "Prayer of Quiet" or wordless aspiration, which swiftly merges into the "Prayer of Union", of which St. Teresa also speaks so well. Grace is already there, or the soul had never heard the call to this blessed communion; but now it flows incessantly, like the mother's milk into her thirsty child. God's power flows in, and swiftly builds up a new "body" for the young Initiate, in which he may live the new eternal life. First comes the Knowledge of Him as a taste of ineffable sweetness, a "kiss", a "most loving embrace", as the mystics call it,—and the old old ignorance of the eternal Beloved, the Desire of all the world, vanishes for evermore. With it goes all the taint of sinfulness, for all sin derives from our turning away from, denying, God. Goodness and the one Reality pour in, with eternal Divine Life and Light ineffable. God manifests His full glory in the soul, and she becomes irradiate with Him like the sunlit window of St. John of the Cross—a window still, and yet inseparable from the light. The "New Man" is still man, and yet is consubstantial with God, instinct with

His divinity, as he was always meant to be. Who but the "bride" can speak of the Lover's close embrace, and who will understand her even if she speaks?

After this silence, during which Grace swiftly unites Tat with God and moulds his new vehicle of Life and Light, he bursts forth in jubilation. He knows his real body is now the subtle form of light invisible to eyes of flesh; he knows that he sees no longer through those eyes but directly through the illumined "eyes of the heart"; he realises himself to be one with the whole universe, beyond Space and Time, lost in the infinity of the All. Then "Hermes" confirms that this is at last the real experience he sought; Tat has been "reborn", dipped in God's Chalice of the Mind, and he has no longer to rely on the spoken word of others to learn the Truth. If he will, he may now become a Guide to his brothers in the dark and lead them to the Light that he has found.

46. Preparation for the Secret Hymnody

1. *Tat*: Father, I wish to (learn) the art of blessing through a hymn [16] which, so you said, Poimandres foretold that (you would) hear from the Powers when you came to the Ogdoad.

Hermes: My son, you are making good speed for you have been purified (by) "striking the tent". Poimandres, the Supreme Mind, did not transmit to me more than had been written down, knowing that I should be able to grasp everything by myself, and to hear what I would, and to see all things. So He left it to me to make beautiful things. This is why the Powers in all sing also in me. (CH 13 : 15)

2. *Tat*: I desire to hear that (song), father, and wish to understand it.

Hermes: Be still, my child, and now hear the Hymn of Blessing suited to the Rebirth, which I had not thought good to make known to you so easily, for this is not taught save at the end of all, but is kept hidden in silence."[17] (CH 13 : 15-16)

> To receive, and then to give. He in whom God has taken up His dwelling always longs to show Him forth to the whole world so that all may share his overwhelming joy. Tat reminds his teacher of Divine Mind's promise in § 6 : 3 that entry into the sublime Eighth Sphere would teach a glorious hymn of praise to God, worthy of His infinite splendour. Now that Tat has reached that sphere above all earthly influences, he would claim the right worthily to adore the Almighty. With approval of his pupil's swift progress, earned by the earlier purgation in breaking from the body and its desire, "Hermes" tells him that this paean also is not taught by others; but the power worthily to praise and thank God rises spontaneously in one who has entered into His very Being. The Shepherd of Men knew that "Hermes" could directly intuit the proper Hymn, and left its composition in words to God's inspired Wisdom now enshrined in his heart. Having gone beyond all

discord, he can now hear the universal harmony and tune himself by that.

Asked then to sing his own universal hymn, as an example, the teacher tells his "son" to listen in reverent silence, for he is in his turn entitled to learn how the "powers" in him can join with those of the Ogdoad in their eternal adoration. This is the last lesson he has to learn, how to co-operate with the All in God's eternal work through his oneness with God's own nature.

47. The Secret Universal Hymnody

1. Let every **recess** * of the universe be opened unto me,

And let all Nature receive the utterance of my Hymn!

O Earth, be silent;[18] rustle not, ye trees;

And I will hymn the Lord who is the All and One.

Hush, ye skies, and be at rest, ye winds;

Let the deathless sphere receive my word.
(CH 13 : 17)

2. For I am about to hymn the One who founded all,

Who made Earth fast, and hung up (the) sky,

* *Or*: bolt.

THE REBIRTH OF TAT

Who **brought** the sweet water **in channels**
    to sustain all (the living),
(And) ordained that fire should appear for
    every use by gods and men.
Let us all with one accord give blessing
    unto Him
Who is high above the heavens,
. . . .
The Founder of the whole of Nature.
It is He who is the Eye of my mind,
Let Him accept the (voice) of my powers!
    (CH 13 : 17-18)

3. O ye powers that are in me,
Hymn ye the One and All!
Sing together with my Will,
All powers that are in me!
O holy Gnosis, by you illuminate
I sing through you the intellectual light!
. . . I rejoice in joy of Mind;
Ye powers, **rejoice** with me!
O good (that is within me), hymn the
    Good;
O Life and Light,[19] the blessing goes from
    you to you! (CH 13 : 18)

4. I give Thee thanks, O Father, Energy of
    (my) powers;

I give Thee thanks, O God, (Thou) Power
 of my energies !
Crying this, the powers that are in me
Fulfil Thy Will ;
Hymning the All . . .,
They (subserve) Thy Plan.
Thy Reason it is (in all) that (wholly) sings
 . . . to Thee through me ;[20] . . .
For (Thou), O Mind, dost play the shepherd
 to (my) speech.
Through me receive from all a reasonable
 offering,
(For) from Thee is the All,[21] (and) unto
 Thee the All ! (CH 13 : 18-19)
5. (The mind which is) in me, O Light,
 illumine ;
(This soul of mine), O Life, preserve ![22]
Creator, Thou art God,[23]
O God, inspire my spirit,—
Thy **Son*** cries this through Thy founda-
 tions,
Having found the blessing
From Thine Eternity.
What I sought I have seen ;
(What I have spoken of I possess).

* *Or* : Man.

THE REBIRTH OF TAT

Saved by Thy Plan, I am at peace;
It is by Thy Will (I have become a God).
(CH 13 : 19-20)

"Hermes" now sings his own inspired Hymn to the glory of God, the only real Initiator who has merged Tat into Himself in ecstasy. It begins with an invocation common to many early hymns, going back on one line of tradition to the "Song of Moses" and to Babylonian psalms, on another even to the Pyramid Texts of Egypt. The whole of Nature is called to share silently in his rejoicing to the Lord of All, the Creator and Giver of all, who is Himself the blazing spark of wisdom now inspiring the human soul that sings.

He then calls upon the whole of his own nature to co-operate with his will in adoring God and so to share in its active bliss while, urged by his own knowledge and love of God, he praises the radiant Sun of the inner world of Mind. He testifies that it is the same God "in" him who praises the God "outside", for without Him we can do nothing, and it is He alone who acts through us.

Then the Initiate's whole nature—mind, soul, heart, will, intelligence and body—thanks God for the light of Gnōsis, and in thus thanking Him they fulfil the end for which He created them. The words of "Hermes" are led as by a Shepherd (cf. § 1 : 1), inspired by mind, the sum of all his powers, and that mind is really the Divine Mind or Logos, to whom only self-surrender can be the appropriate sacrifice. Indeed, creation coming forth with the Outbreathed holy Logos (§ 1 : 3) is only perfected by the Inbreathing of the microcosmic logos in Man, returning to its eternal Source. It is the Divine Word that was in the beginning with God and came down to earth "and was made man", who gives to men the power and the right, if they trust in Him and follow

His Divine guidance, to become "the sons of God";
but this is a doctrine which merits, and has already
received, tomes of commentary in its honour. Acknowledging God as the Source of all he is and has, Man—
in the person of "Hermes"—now offers his whole self
to God his Father. This is the baptism of Light
(*phōtismos*) and the nourishment of the Infant God now
born in his heart—for which he sends up his fervent
prayer, a prayer for spiritual food and guidance. This
cry for light and food, for growth and the grace of wisdom, he utters through the "powers" God made and
gave to him. With it on his lips, he "passes on into
Life and Light" (§ 7 : 2), saved by God's redemptive
Plan—baptism in the light of Mind (cf. § 37)—from the
intoxication of error and the darkness of the flesh; he is
led rejoicing into God's eternal peace (§ 6 : 3).

The version of this Hymn adopted here differs
rather widely from that given by M, who did not try to
correct an extremely corrupted and interpolated text. I
have used the reconstruction by S, and also accepted his
very plausible and interesting suggestions based on early
Greek metres which he detected under the traditional
text. However, even this cannot claim to be a final
reading, though it may certainly be nearer the original
than what we have in our manuscripts. We have no
space here to examine S's reasons for the several emendations which we have incorporated in this reading.

48. The Neophyte's Joy

1. *Tat*: By repeating this blessing, Father,
you have put in my world also—

Hermes : Say " in the intellectual ", son.

Tat :—in the intellectual (world) a power
(drawn) out of your Hymn, and (through) your

adoration my mind has been further illumined. But moreover I also wish to present a blessing to God out of my own thoughts, ... not heedlessly, (for) I shall say what I behold in the Mind. (CH 13 : 20-21)
> 2. To Thee, O first Parent of (my) Coming-to-Birth, (I),
> Tat, to God send reasonable oblations (from my soul).
> O God, Thou art the Father;
> O Lord, Thou art the Mind;
> Receive from me the blessings which (Thou) dost will;
> For it is at Thy wish that all has been fulfilled (in me).[24] (CH 13 : 21)

3. *Hermes*: **Good,** my son, you have sent to God, the All-Father, an acceptable oblation; but add also " through the Word ".[25]

Tat: I thank you, father, (for) approving this essay (?) of mine. (CH 13 : 21)

4. Hermes: I am glad, my son, (that you) have produced fruit,[26] from the Real, the immortal products of virtue, (now that) you have mentally come to know yourself and our Father.[27] Having learned this from me, (now) promise silence (and) to reveal to no one [28]

the handing on of the Rebirth, so that we may not be deemed sacrilegious*. Enough has been said; for each of us has seen to (his own) needs—I as speaker, and you hearing. (CH 13 : 22)

Tat begins to thank "Hermes" for the new light thrown by this theurgic Hymn into his own mind, but is at once corrected for the slip—there is no longer any separate personal mind for Tat; it is merged in the Universal Mind. Accepting the gentle reproof, Tat now wishes to try his own hand at sharing in the cosmic harmony by uttering a hymn as a Prophet in his own right, according to the light and strength in him.

Acknowledging that his Gnōsis is due not so much to his teacher "Hermes" as directly to the Divine Source of all wisdom, who alone initiates, and by whose Will he has been "born again", Tat offers the sacrifice of his own heart and mind. For he knows well that this is the only form of worship God requires from man as a return for spiritual light and the perfecting of God's work in him.

The teacher approves this little essay, asking only for the due admission that all our "reasonable oblations" can go to the Good Father only through His sacred Word, the Logos, first "Son" of God, the mediator between man and the Supreme. (§ 16 : 2) At first blush, this looks like a Christian interpolation, but there is no real need for such an assumption; Philo, depending on the later Jewish "Wisdom Literature", often used the word "Logos" in much the same sense, though he wrote about A.D. 25, long before St. John's Gospel came into circulation.

* *lit* : maligners.

"Hermes" is delighted at his pupil's success in thus joining the immortal choir of the seraphic Powers of the Ogdoad in adoring God; his ability to do this is due to God's action on his purified and virtuous soul bursting into songs of jubilation. The young initiate must now promise to hide from others the high spiritual level he has reached, for if he boasted of his progress in the world and then erred in anything, mockery would descend on these holy things and Religion would be discredited. It is enough for them both, to have taught and to have learned, and there is no call for either to proclaim the mystery to others. They would never understand it, and would think Tat's asceticism a hatred of God's world, his solitude misanthropy, while really evil lies not in things but in their misuse and in giving them power over us. There is no real contrast between the secrecy here laid down and the open preaching in §§ 8 and 37; circumstances are different in the two cases. There an appeal is made to each individual in the crowd to turn from darkness and to seek God's Light, but the preacher makes no claim to any special and personal Gnōsis setting him on a higher level than his audience. Indeed, the true Gnōstic never does make such claims; his authority must be sought in his life, his very presence, the effect of his simple glance. If these proclaim the saint and true devotee of God, there is no need for words : if they do not, words will but repel.

49. The Last Words of "Hermes"

1. So far as possible,[29] then, this image of God has been outlined; and if you gaze on it attentively with the eyes of the heart . . . you will find the upward path, or rather the image itself will lead you on the road.[30] For

the Vision has something all its own; it holds and draws those who have succeeded in seeing (it), just as they say a magnet (draws) a lump of iron.[31] (CH 4 : 11)

2. But avoid close contact with the crowd,[32] (St. 11 : 4) for it is not attainable[33] for the uninitiated to be told such mysteries; (F 23) not that I want you to withhold for jealousy, but rather that you will seem ridiculous to the crowd . . . and these teachings will have exceedingly few (worthy) hearers, or perhaps not even a few.[34] (St. 11 : 4) (So) cover with silence the Divine Mysteries amid the secrets of the heart, and hide them with reserve. (PS 32 : 4)

"Hermes" sums up by saying that now, by word and by actual experience, his pupil has learned of God all that man can ever know while he remains a man. Contemplation on this "mental picture", this image of God in His universe, and the constant practice of this spiritual at-one-ment (*henōsis*) with the All, will perfect its kingdom in him and draw him closer and closer into the Divine, until at last he melts for ever into its glory. For one vision of God is enough, even if it be only for a moment, a flash, if it be but treasured in the heart. He who has once seen God can never look away from Him again, or lose himself any more in the pathless jungles of this lower world. The memory will lure him on and on until it is fulfilled in eternal union with God.

But, once more he repeats the warning, these mysteries are not to be revealed to all and sundry, nor are they to be spoken of at all to those unprepared to receive them with fitting reverence. It is not so much to save the Initiate himself from ridicule, still less is it that he should selfishly hug his own bliss to himself—for selfishness is impossible in one who has lost the ego in the ocean of God's love—but that very very few could benefit from such teaching. The truth would only harm them by driving them to the deadly sin of rejecting it with scorn, and thus turning them away from the one way of salvation. They would like swine trample upon the "pearls." and then "turn again and rend" the Prophet. So the "pearls" are to be kept safely in the secret casket of the heart, to be taken out and shown only to those who know how to value them. This reserve in the deeper spiritual truths, though alien to our modern pseudo-democratic idea of the equality of men, was common to *all* the older religions, and history has yet to show evidences that it was not based upon the wisdom culled from ages of experience.

NOTES

CHAPTER 1

1. *Uttara Gita* (1 : 52) says, "The yogis see the Self within when they shut out all their external senses." Wordsworth knew this; *Lines on Tintern Abbey* (41-49) speak of the mood wherein " we are laid asleep in body and become a living soul, while with an eye made quiet by the power of harmony and the deep power of joy we see into the life of things ". St. Teresa, *Interior Castle*, (5th Man., p. 93) says of this not so rare mystical experience, " The soul is . . . fast asleep as regards the world and itself," and in her *Life* (16 : 1) she calls it a " sleep of the powers of the soul, which are not wholly lost, nor yet understanding how they work ". Many mystics have added their own testimony.

2. Perhaps the name really means " Man-Shepherd " after all, as the early Hermetists evidently held. Cf. the Epitaph of Bishop Aberkios (cir. A.D. 190): " I am a disciple of a holy Shepherd . . . who has great eyes that oversee everything." In the 4000-year old Prophecy of the Egyptian Ipuwēr, it is said of Rē', the Sun-God of Light and Truth, " He is said to be the Shepherd of all men; there is no evil in His heart." This supports

Griffith's guess that the name is really Eg. Pe-eime-n-Rē' (The Knowing, or Gnōsis, of Rē'). The third guess, that the name represents the Eg. Pementre, the Witness, is also plausible. But Pagans and Christians agreed in giving to God the beautiful name of "Shepherd" (cf. *Ps.* 23 : 1 and *Jn.* 10 : 14).

3. Cf. the *Gospel of Eve*: "Wheresoever thou mayst be, I am there," and the Oxyrhynchus logion: "Wherever there is one alone, I say I am with him." The idea is a commonplace of mystical thought—Indian, Egyptian and Catholic, as well as Greek; we need not go to Plato for parallels.

4. Cf. *2 Enoch* (27 : 1-2) : "And I commanded that there should be taken from light and darkness, and I said, 'Be thick', and it became thus, and I spread it out with the light, and it became water." Also the Jewish Commentator (cir. A.D. 50) in the *Naassene Document*: "First Mind, the generative Law of all; second to the First-born was Liquid Chaos." This idea, seeming to derive from the Chaldean Tiamat myth, spread far and wide. Cf. *Gen.* 1 too.

5. The 12th c. *Precious Rosary* of the Tibetan, Dvagpo Lharje, (28 : 1) says : "The mind of all sentient beings is inseparable from the All-Mind." So also Fr. G. M. Dupont, S.J., in his *Foundations for a Devotion to the Blessed Trinity*, shows how all creation is *in* the Second Person, the Word of God; "The Word is the pattern upon which all things are made; . . . all things echo in time the Word spoken in eternity."

NOTES 177

6. Cf. *The Gnosis of the Light*, in the Cod. Bruc., (text of 2nd c.) (p. 2) : "He it is whose limbs make a myriad myriad Powers, and every Power is a being in itself."

7. The early Egyptian Gnōstic sect of Sethians said : "The Light-Ray . . . hastens towards the Word that comes down from above . . . more speedily than iron to the magnet," and the Valentinian *Gnostic Myth* (22 : 8), as given by Hippolytus, says : "The subtle portion . . . burst forth, arose, rushed upward above from below, with speed like that of poet's wing or of thought, and was at one with Non-Existent God. . . . The heavier sonship still remaining in the Seed . . . could not rush up aloft, . . . thus it was left behind." This text is also apparently Egyptian and of the 2nd c. ; the scholar will note its close parallelism with our passage.

8. Cf. Fr. Dupont (*op. cit.*) : "The unimaginable multitude of creatures issuing from God are all modelled on the unique divine thought, . . . the Divine nature itself ; (and thus) the Word . . . is the model, the exemplary cause of creation." Here Nature vainly tried to copy the perfect Ideal Archetype of a universe, and produced only the "Abortion". Merejkowsky, in his *La Mort des Dieux*, makes his Hermetist say : "All in the universe . . . are dreams of Nature thinking of God."

9. For the One Source of all must needs be Male-Female, Father-Mother, as in the *Stanzas of Dzyan*. So also the Jewish Commentator of the *Naassene Document* : "He tore asunder His Womb, and gave birth to His own Son." The Ancient Egyptians expressed this

with more brutal frankness. The idea survives even in the 13th c. St. Bonaventura, *Goad of Divine Love*, pages 6-7.

10. Hermaphrodite, bi-sexual. Cf. *Gen.* 1 : 27. Even in embryology, the sex is a late differentiation.

11. Cf. Plato's *Timaeus*, 37 C ; also PS 8 : " The Son is the universe ", and the *Gospel Myth* (22 : 1) " When, then, He saw His Son, He wondered at and loved him, and was struck with amazement, so marvellous seemed His Son's beauty to the Great Ruler." A truly Hermetic account !

12. Cf. *Gospel of Mary*, in Mead's *Fragments of a Faith Forgotten*, p. 586, " He nodded, and when He had thus nodded assent . . ." and *Chaldaean Oracles* (1 : 51) " His Will nodded assent."

13. Cf. Jew in *Naassene Document* : " In order that the great Man from above might be completely brought low, soul also was given to him." Mead has much of value to say on the widespread myth of First Man, the divine Adam of such Coptic apocrypha as *The Book of the Resurrection of Jesus the Christ* (see Budge's edition).

14. In an Orphic Fragment quoted by R. Eisler, the soul entering the unseen world is to say : " I am a child of Earth and starry Heaven, but my Race is of Heaven." This is just Hermes' position.

15. Cf. *Mk.* 12 : 25, and the *Gospel of the Egyptians* (quoted in ' 2 *Clement* ' 12 : 16) : Christ's Kingdom will come " when two shall be one, and that which is without as that which is within ; and the male with the

female, neither male nor female". Also the Pagan source of the *Naassene Document* (B. C. 50 ?) : " He is the Male-Female Man in all."

16. Cf. *Gen.* 2 : 21, and the *Mysteries of John the Apostle* (Budge: B. M. Ori. 7026), speaking of Adam and Eve: " Two bodies came from one body, but He did not separate them immediately." Cf. also *Gen.* 1 : 27 (Heb.) : " Male-Female created He him."

17. The same idea is in *Gen.* 9 : 1, 7 and in *Timaeus*, 42, where it is an address to the souls. We need not imagine direct quotation by " Hermes ".

18. Cf. *Wisdom*, 15 : 3 : " To know Thee is perfect righteousness; yea, to know Thy Power is the root of immortality."

19. Cf. §37 : 4, and PS 7 : 1 and 18 : 2.

20. Cf. §32 : 2. Fire is the punishment of souls also in the books of the Parsis, in the *Sibylline Oracles*, the *Gospels* and *Revelation*, and in the Qur'ān, as it is in most Eastern scriptures, such as the Buddhist and the Manichaean; it plays its part in old Egyptian books also.

21. Cf. § 29 : 4.

22. Cf. Plotinus, *Enneads* (1 : 6 : 7), and Porphyry's *Life of Plotinus*, 22, also the early agraphon : " when 'ye shall tread on the vesture of shame ". The Manichaean fragment from Turfān, S 9b, has : " Its pollution of death was removed, and it became liberated unto eternity and led on upward to Paradise, to that realm of the glorious." Cf. also §31 : 1.

23. The words of their song are given elsewhere as : " Come unto us, for we are thy fellow-members; we are

all one with thee." *The Book of the Resurrection of Jesus the Christ* says: "The angels of glory sang to Him as He passed on His way" (22b); Cf. *Pyramid Texts* 935, and 1197: "Our heart was not glad till thy coming, say they." In *Pyr.* 160 a mysterious Voice cries, "Lift him up to Thee, enfold Thou him in Thy embrace; he is Thy bodily son for ever," and promises (*Pyr.* 878) "O lofty one among the Undying Stars, thou perishest not eternally." The Jewish *Apocalypse of Baruch* (51 : 9-10) says: "Time shall no longer age them, . . . they shall be made like the Angels, and be made equal to the Stars," adding (104 : 6), "Ye shall become companions of the hosts of Heaven." Cf. also *Rev.* 22 : 5.

24. The Ogdoad, beyond the seven spheres of evolution ruled by the Planets, was a commonplace of thought in the first centuries. The *eighth* gate of Mithraists led to the Cave of Initiation, we are told; *Pistis Sophia* has also much on this subject; cf. also Theodotus in Clement of Alexandria's *Fragments,* 63, and Irenaeus *On the Heresies,* 1 : 30 : 12.

25. Cf. §2 : 2, and KK 125 : "Thus speaking, God became imperishable Mind."

26. Cf. Damascius, in Phot. Bibl. p. 3376, 23.

27. Cf. §8 : 3, and CH 10 : 15. Also the Hymn of Jesus in the Gnostic *Acts of John* (Mead): "I am Mind of all; fain would I be known," and the *Gnosis of the Light*: "It is His Will that the Universe should turn to Him."

28. The hymn was used by a 3rd c. Christian monk; see Berlin Pap. 9794. It would hardly have been a newly written composition at that time.

29. Cf. the Platonic use of drunkenness as an analogy in Plato's *Cleitophon*, 407 B, and the use in the 2nd c. Oxyrhynchus logion: "I found all men drunken."

30. *The Hymn of the Robe of Glory* (Mead), perhaps by Bardaisan, 2nd c.: "I sank into a deep sleep from their poisonous food."

31. The word *agnōsia*, opposite of *Gnōsis*, means estrangement, and thus rejection of God; cf. § 29 : 12.

32. Cf. the Manichaean fragments, S 49 ff, and M 4: "Awake, shining soul, out of the sleep of drunkenness wherein thou hast fallen asleep," and the *Chaldaean Oracles*, vol. 1, p. 30, "Not knowing that God is wholly good. O wretched slaves, be sober!" (K. 15)

33. The word is *exousia*, the authority to teach, handed on by the teacher to a qualified disciple. Cf. *Jn.* 1 : 12.

34. Cf. the Christian 2 *Esdras* (2 : 34): "Look for your Shepherd, he shall give you eternal rest."

35. Cf. *Mk.* 4 : 4.

36. Cf. *Jn.* 4 : 10-14 and 7 : 37-38, also *1 Cor.* 3 : 6, the *Odes of Solomon* (a very primitive Christian baptismal hymnal) and the Mandaean book, *Genzā*.

CHAPTER 2

1. Cf. Plato's *Timaeus*, 28 C

2. Cf. § 41 : 4-5, and St. Francis de Sales in *Divine Love*, 5 : 1, " If we saw Him as He really is, we should die of love for Him."

3. Cf. the *Gospel Myth*, 22 : 1 : "... so vast and wise a God that the creation is unable to speak of Him, or even to have room for Him in thought." Also J. Macbeth Bain in *The Christ of the Holy Grail*, (p. 13) : " The One whom we are naming ' the Christos ', ' the Holy One ', is really unnameable, Whom to seek to describe is almost a profanity." And, " When the inspired soul is most fully conscious of the realisation of the Holy One in the great joy of the illumining inflow, it bows in silence. It can utter no sound. And this bowing in silence is the only mode of deep utterance, and is therefore the best word." Cf. also § 41 : 5.

4. Cf. Proclus, *Hymn to the Transcendent* : " How shall words hymn Thee, Thee whom speech never attains ? . . . How name I Thee who alone art without a Name ? "

5. Cf. Justin's *Apology*, 1 : 10 : 1, and Clement of Alexandria's *Stromata*, 5 : 12 : 82 ; also *The Gnosis of the Light* (p. 1) : " This is that Ingenerable and Eternal One who has no name and who has all names."

6. Cf. the inspired *Hymn* of the Egyptian King Akhenaton (B.C. 1375) : " Thou art the Mother and the Father of all that Thou hast made," and the *Responses* of Abammon, (often miscalled Iamblichus), (32 : 4-5) : " He is the Source and God of Gods."

7. Cf. *The Gnosis of the Light*, (p. 2) : " He who has given all things from within Himself."

NOTES 183

8. Cf. *Mt.* 19 : 17 and *Lk.* 18 : 18 ; also the earlier form, long retained by the Fathers: " There is (but) one good, God the Father."

9. Cf. Methodius *con. Porphyrium* (ed. Bonnwetsch, p. 347): " For when He wills the good, He being Himself the Good remains in Himself."

10. Valentinians gave Him a *syzugon* (cf. Irenæus, 1 : 1 : 1)—Silence, Grace, Understanding. Cf. § 22 : 2.

11. This is wholly opposed to the dualism of the Semitic and Aryan peoples, setting up a devil as in eternal revolt against God. He is *alone.*

12. All the world vainly longs for the Good, but as God desires only the Good, which is already in Himself, His desire is at once fulfilled.

13. Cf. the Arabic Hermeticum, *de Castigatione Animarum* (*DCA*) (translated from Latin by Scott in his *Hermetica*), (4 : 1b): " If anything ' pure ' is found in the world, that thing is not really pure ; for there can be no real purity in anything that is not everlasting."

14. Cf. *Jn.* 15 : 19, and the Oxyrhynchus logion: " Unless you fast to the world, you shall in no way find the Kingdom of God."

15. In *Repub.* 6 : 508 D, Plato tells us that God is the Sun of the ideal and spiritual world. The idea was also fundamental in Christian thought from the beginnings ; cf. *Rev.* 22 : 5.

16. " All things that you see before you in this world are nothing but dreams," says the Hermetist in *DCA* 13 : 8, and again in 1 : 6 : " All the shapes and images which you see with your bodily eyes ... are mere

semblances and copies of the forms which have real existence in the thought-world." Here we have an extreme form of the *māyā*-doctrine of Vedānta: cf. Asvaghosa's *The Awakening of Faith* : " All existence is like a reflection in a mirror, without substance, only a phantom of the mind," and Asanga's teaching in *Tibetan Yoga and Secret Doctrines* : " Man, held in bondage by the hypnotic glamour of appearances, is wrapt in an unbroken sleep of Ignorance, dreaming dreams which he thinks real." But " Hermes " shows elsewhere that God's world *is* a reality for us so long as we hold the body ; it is only in comparison with God Himself that it is false, illusory. Christians hold the same view.

17. The epithets of the Beautiful are found also in Plato's *Phaedrus*, 250 C, D.

18. Cf. Dr. Tauler's *The Inner Way*, (p. 47) : " He who desired to have all the world with God would have nothing more than if he had God alone," and H. P. Blavatsky's *Practical Occultism* : " Desire God, and not anything that He can give."

19. Cf. §§ 8 : 1 and 38 : 2-3. Note the wise balance here between Knowledge and Devotion. The love of God and the knowing of Him are really inseparable. Cf. the Note 2 to this Chapter.

20. Cf. Dietrich's *Abraxas*, (p. 176). Plato taught that God is bodiless, while the Stoics said that He assumes all bodies. As in " Hermes " the whole universe is God's body, he inclines rather to the Stoic view. Cf. also the Hermes-Prayer in Mead's *Thrice-Greatest Hermes* (*TGH*), vol. i, p. 90 : " Thou who alone . . .

dost transform Thyself in holy forms, making to be from things that are not, and from the things that are, making the not to be." The doctrine has a strongly Egyptian background and colour, though not unknown in Asia.

21. Cf. Swāmi Rāmdās, *At the Feet of God* (p. 47): "God alone has assumed the form of the universe—all creatures, all beings and things in it." God having taken all forms cannot be identified with any one form, so St. John of the Cross, *The Ascent of Mount Carmel* (3 : 1) has; "God is without form or image on which the memory may dwell." This seems to contradict our text, but the reconciliation is obvious.

22. God is the Idea, the Model, whereon all forms are based—an idea found also in Plato's *Republic*, 2 : 380.

23. Cf. PS 8 : 1, "He is the object of the senses of those who see," for He is the only reality behind all sensible things.

24. The universe is not He, but a reflection of His activity from which He is not separate; thus *Gita*, 10 : 42: "Having pervaded this whole universe with one fragment of Myself, I remain." Immanent, yes; but transcendent too.

25. Cf. the Hymn in § 24 : 1-3.

26. A technical term of the Gnōsis; *lit.* "fullness" —God in all and all in God. Cf. CH 16 : 19, "The all is parts of God."

27. Cf. the Akhenaton *Hymn*: "Thou didst create the earth according to Thy will when Thou wast alone."

28. Cf. PS 2 : 1 : "All are one, and one is all, inasmuch as all were in the Creator before He created all." This is also the Catholic doctrine; all creation was eternally latent in God's Thought and Will.

29. Cf. § 15 : 1. His activity is timeless, unceasing. Cf. also the *Gospel of Thomas* : "He remains what He is, making all things, and is naught of the things which are."

30. Cf. CH 10 : 14 : "And the universe, son of God, was born."

31. Cf. Plato's *Timaeus*, 37 E, and Philo's *Quod Deus Im.* 6 : "God is also the artificer of Time, for He is Father of its father; and Time's father is the universe ... This, then, the younger son, the sensible, being set in movement, has caused Time's nature to appear and disappear." It is by movements in the visible universe that we measure time.

32. Cf. *Iswar Gita*, 9 : 18 : "He is the Soul of all beings," and the *Bhāgavatam*, 11 : 2 : 41 : "Knowing all things to be the body of Hari," and 4 : 29 : 51 : "Hari is the Self of all embodied existences."

33. It is ever-changing, and yet immortal in God's Mind. Cf. CH 10 : 10.

34. Cf. CH 11 : 6 : "He who makes is in them all," and *Chaldaean Oracles*, ii, p. 31 : "The Father of men and gods placed mind in soul and soul in inert body," (Kroll, 47); also *Wisdom*, 12 : 1 : "Thy incorruptible Spirit is in all things," and Mother Julian of Norwich in her *Revelations of Divine Love*, p. 11 : "I saw that He is in all things."

NOTES 187

35. Cf. *Timaeus*, 34b.

36. Cf. *The Mysteries of John the Apostle*, p. 4; "Before even God created the heavens and the earth, water was in existence." Epiphanius, in his book on the *Heresies* (25 : 5), quotes from a Nicolaitan scripture of perhaps 1st. c. A.D.: "There was Darkness and Abyss and Water: and Spirit in the midst of them made separation of them." This was associated with the Myth of Man, in the Jewish stratum of the *Naassene Document*, as taught by the earliest Christian Gnostics condemned in *Rev.* 2 : 15 by about A.D. 90. Berossus has the Phoenician version: "In the beginning all was Darkness and Water." Several Oriental cosmogonies, followed by many Gnōstics, began in this way: it is a very ancient form.

37. Cf. Fr. Dupont (*op. cit.*) "The Father utters His Word, and in His Word all else ..., the totality of the Godhead."

38. In *Gen.* 1 : 7 the 'firmament' divides the upper and lower waters. So, in the ancient Egyptian cosmogony of Ōnu, Shōw, hot air, separates Nūt, sky, from Geb, earth, in the heart of the primeval and universal flood—Nūn. (See the Pyramid Texts).

39. Cf. the myths of Phaethon and the Orphic Phanēs.

40. This idea is adopted by Cornelius Labeo (cir. A.D. 126), and it is also found in the *Gnosis of the Light* (Mead: *Fragments of a Faith Forgotten* (FFF), p. 548): "The hair of His head is the number of the hidden worlds." But this enters deeper into the mysteries.

41. God is here pictured as the universal monarch, Cf. KK 50 and St. 24 : 1.

42. In *Abraxas*, p. 182 ff, an Egypto-Greek text tells us that God creates by a sevenfold peal of laughter that awakens the new day. All true creation is an act of joy, as the Montessorians have found !

43. Cf. *Ps.* 33 : 6.

44. Cf. *Wisdom* 7 : 17-22 and 9 : 9. Nature, or Wisdom, is born out of God's Will, as also in the Gnōstic *Acts of Thomas* : " The Maiden is Light's Daughter." (FFF, p. 419)

CHAPTER 3

1. Cf. the *Hymn of Cleanthes* preserved in Stobaeus, 1 : 1 : 12.

2. Cf. § 37 : 2.

3. Cf. *Wisdom*, 2 : 23 : " God created man to be immortal, and made him to be an image of His own eternity."

4. Later Platonists too held that the universe is also an image of God, as well as His son. Produced by Him, it reflects His qualities, as a poem the poet's.

5. As opposed to the demoniac power used in magic, as *Clementine Homilies*, 2 : 27, has it. These Clementine books (2nd c. ?) show many resemblances to Hermetic teaching.

6. Cf. *Philippians*, 2 : 13, and Philo, *de Cherubim*, 13 : 43.

7. Cf. Algernon Blackwood, *The Centaur*, p. 119 : " The archetypal world, Soul of the Earth, swam close about him, enormous and utterly simple."

NOTES

8. Cf. § 34 : 5.

9. Cf. Pap. Mag. Berl. Parthey 1 : 26, where Chnūm, as Lord of the Nile, is called a " good farmer ".

10. Cf. § 22 : 1. Basilides, together with many Platonists, taught that God is beyond feelings and thoughts, ever unmoved, and changeless in Himself. But this makes it impossible to reach Him, so " Hermes " rejects the doctrine.

11. Cf. the Valentinian Psalm in FFF, p. 307 : " All things dependent on Spirit I see." (from Hippolytus, 6 : 32)

12. It is the fate of the wise to be mocked by fools ; cf. *Mk.* 14 : 65.

13. Cf. * 41 : 1, and Plotinus, *Enneads,* 6 : 9 : 4 : " as showing the way to one who desires to look at something ". The lower mind and reason are not to be despised ; they come from God, and logically followed with courage and sincerity will always point the way towards their Source.

14. Cf. Plato's *Timaeus*, 34 B.

15. Cf. CH 9 : 7 : " Now bodies . . . some are of earth, of water some, some are of air, and some of fire." All space is filled with matter derived from the four " elements ", mixed together in varying proportions.

16. Cf. *The Gnosis of the Light*, (p. 23) : " Nothing can contain Thee, who art the space for all," and (p. 1) : " He beholds all beings of the universe within Himself." This was the vision of Arjuna in the *Gita*, c. 11.

17. Cf. *Devikālottaram*, 65 : 57 : " All the creation is in Me, and I am they."

18. Cf. Plato's *Republic*, 508 E ff., and Irenaeus, 2 : 12 : 2, where he speaks of the Valentinian doctrine of the first pair of Aeons rayed out by God being Truth and Gnōsis.

19. Cf. *Avadhūta Gita*, 7 : 7 : " The one eternal Reality exists everywhere."

20. Cf. *2 Enoch*, 43 : 3, (A.D. about 50) : " There is no other except the Lord," and Swāmī Rāmdās (*op. cit.*) : " Can we see God ? Yes—see Him in His works—in His manifestation He pervades all. There is no place where He is not. Every object is no other than He." (p. 13)

21. Cf. Blackwood (*op. cit.*) p. 29 : " The universe lies in every human heart."

22. Cf. *Wisdom*, 1 : 13 : " God made not death ; " and PS 29 : 3 : " Nothing in the universe is mortal."

23. Cf. Blackwood (*op. cit.*, p. 59) : " The universe is everywhere consciously alive, and the earth is the body of a living Entity." This was also Fechner's teaching.

24. Cf. *Romans*, 11 : 36.

25. Cf. §§ 2 : 2 and 45 : 3. The mental world can be seen only though the mental eye ; it is Mind who speaks here, in the form of the Teacher.

26. Cf. CH. 10 : 18.

27. The influence of the Moon on mind and matter was long held a superstition, and like many other such is now being vindicated by agricultural research. Cf. also Firmicus, *Math.* 4 : 1.

28. Cf. Diodorus, 3 : 44 : 3, and Plutarch, who says that from the Moon Earth would seem " a muddy sediment at the bottom of the universe ".

29. Most Gnōstics held that the Creator or Demiurge is distinct from the Supreme God, and the so-called Carpocratians thought creation was carried out by lesser angels under God's direction. (Hippolytus, 7 : 20)

30. Cf. St. 5 : 2, and *Timaeus*, 41 C.

31. Cf. the Akhenaton *Hymn* : " The world is in Thy hand . . . Men live through Thee." Also the Babylonian Hymn to the World-God in *Alt. Ori. Text. und Bilder*, p. 80 : " Compassionate and gracious Father, who holds in His hand the life of the entire world," and " Where Thine eye (gazes) steadily there harmony (remains)." The idea was a favourite with the Hebrews.

32. Cf. 2 *Esdras*, 6 : 6 : " Then did I consider these things, and they were all made through Me alone, and through no other."

33. Cf. PS 3 : 1 : " Now lend me the whole of thyself."

34. Cf. § 11 : 1. " Hermes " was as true a monotheist as the Prophet Muḥammed or the Deuteronomist.

35. Cf. CH 16 : 19 : " Thus making all, He makes Himself ; nor can He ever cease, for He Himself is ceaseless."

36. Cf. St. Augustine, quoted by Dean Inge in *Personal Idealism and Mysticism*, p. 79 : " If God were to cease speaking the Word even for a moment, heaven and earth would vanish." So also Dr. John Tauler, *The Inner Way*, p. 47 : " Creatures . . . have their being in God ; if God turned away for a moment, they would cease to exist." It is

only God whose existence is wholly independent, self-sustained.

37. Cf. the gradual degeneration of the soul in § 29 : 11. Sin is a kind of "rust" that forms on things with the passing of time ; it is inherent in the nature of matter itself. So Tennyson, *The Passing of Arthur*: "lest one good custom should corrupt the world".

38. Cf. the *Apocalyse of Baruch*, 98 : 4 : "Sin has not been sent upon the earth, but man himself has created it," and *The Mysteries of John the Apostle*, p. 17 : "Sin is a stranger to God ; ... it is man who himself commits sin." So also the 13th c. St. Bonaventura, *Goad of Divine Love*, p. 236, testifies : "All evil is only from thyself, and all good from God alone." The Areopagite, with Hermetic antecedents, ascribes sin to the absence of positive Good, that is, of God ; in His presence all sin vanishes. Cf. *Ecclus*, 39 : 33 : "The works of God are all good."

39. A constant refrain of Egyptian texts : e.g., *The Great Hymn to Amon* (Cairo Pap. 17), "Thou sole and only One."

40. Cf. *The Gnosis of the Light*, p. 13 : "It is because of Thy image that we have seen Thee, that we have run to Thee."

41. Cf. Dionysius, *The Divine Names*, (5 : 8) : "He is all things as Cause of all, . . . and He is none of them all."

42. An anti-Christian interpolator here added "nor spirit", perhaps in answer to *Jn.* 4 : 24. Cf. Abammon's *Responses*, 8 : 1 ff., and Irenaeus on the Valentinians

(1 : 24 : 3) : "Mind was born from the unborn Father." We need not vex ourselves with the apparent contradiction here of § 3 : 1 ; paradox is the only possible way to speak of ineffables. Rather should we try to resolve the problem by a higher synthesis, realising the many layers of truth in the word "Mind".

43. Cf. *Gita*, 8 : 18 : "From the unmanifest stream forth all the manifest at the coming of day."

44. Cf. Phosilampes in the *Gnosis of the Light* : "Through Him is the existent and the non-existent through which the Hidden which is and the Manifest which is not exists." Also see Simon's *Great Announcement*, preserved in Hippolytus 6 : 4. Even Scott (*Hermetica*, vol. 1, p. 158) says: "There are no really existent 'external objects'; there is nothing but perceptions and God who causes the perceptions"—a fair statement of the Advaita position. Both Numenius and Plotinus speak of the importance of Indian philosophy in their day (3rd c.); and Berkeley was also very greatly influenced by it.

45. Tennyson in *The Higher Pantheism* says that we see God and not those objects that we think we see. Cf. 2 *Enoch*, 48 : 5 : "Being Himself invisible, He made from the invisible all visible things."

46. Cf. *Jn.* 14 : 21, and St. Teresa, *Interior Castle* (p. 176) : "His Majesty grants such favours to whom He chooses; yet if we sought Him as He seeks us, He would give them to us all." Also cf. *Exodus* 33 : 19.

47. Cf. § 30 : 3. God can only be seen by the light of Spiritual Mind. Cf. the Akhenaton *Hymn*, "They see by means of Thee," and *Rev.* 21 : 23.

48. Cf. the *Sybilline Oracles*, 3 : 18, "The Eternal Himself revealed Himself, who is and was, and ever shall be; for who being mortal can behold God with his eyes?" Cf. *Exod.* 33 : 20 and *Jn.* 1 : 18.

49. Cf. § 49 : 2 and CH 4 : 3 : "Grudging comes not from Him"; also *Timaeus*, 29 E ; " He was good, and to the good there can never at any time by any grudging of aught." Cf. also St. Teresa, *The Way of Perfection*, 16 : 8 : "There is no fear of His failing to do His part if we do ours," and in her *Life*, 13 : 15 : " He never fails us if we do what we can." The saintly Fr. Dominic Barberi, C.P., said : "We must do all we can, and God will do all we cannot."

50. Cf. the Tamil *Yoga Aphorisms* of a woman-saint, Avvayar, 1 ; 10 : 8, who bids us "lovingly contemplate all as God in manifestation," and Blackwood *op. cit.* p. 29) : " He plunged into that archetypal world that stands so close behind all sensible appearances, . . . he sailed away into some giant swimming mood of beauty." It is the ecstasy of the true Nature-poets, and, of course, wholly pagan.

51. Cf. § 3 : 1, and *Ps.* 139 : 13-16. Every man is, in small, the All-Man, Son of God, ever-remaining in Heaven. "As above, so below."

52. Cf. §§ 21 ; 4 and 22 : 1.

53. Cf. Dionysius (*op. cit.* 4 : 7, 10) : "Even the non-existent participates in the Beautiful and Good. . . .

All things non-existing are super-essentially in the Beautiful and Good," because latent in God's mind.

54. Cf. PS 2 : 1 : "All things have been in the Creator before they were created," and Schmidt's *Kopt.-Gnos. Schriften*, i, p. 358 : "Thou art the Demiurge of those things which have not yet manifested themselves ; for Thou alone knowest these, we know them not." Also cf. Simon's *Great Announcement* : "Himself producing Himself by means of Himself, He manifested to Himself His own thought."

55. Cf. Swāmi Rāmdās, *Sayings*, p. 74 : "God is the manifest and the unmanifest."

56. Cf. *Wisdom*, 13 : 5 : "By the greatness and beauty of the creatures proportionably the maker of them is seen."

57. Cf. *Martyrdom of Peter* : "Thou who art to be understood by spirit alone.... Thou art the all, and the all is in Thee. Yea, all that is is Thou, and there is nothing else that is but Thee alone." The same thought is to be found in *Parapūja*, in Swāmi Sivānanda's *Stotra Ratnamāla*.

58. Cf. *Kopt.-Gnos. Schr.* vol. 1, p. 366 : "He has no name, and all names belong to Him." Cf. also our own § 9 : 3-4.

59. Cf. *Uttara Gita*, 3 : 9 : "Wherever the mind goes it sees the Supreme Spirit there, because all and everything is full of the One Brahman," and *Bhāgavatam*, 4 : 31 : 18 : "So you should direct worship and contemplation to Hari as one with you," and "When and where you have faith, there worship Me, for I am

present in all beings as well as in your own self, being the Self of all," (11 : 27 : 48). Cf. also the Tibetan book. *Jetsün Kahbum*, 12 : "In whatever place you pray with sincerity and eagerness, there will I be in front of each of you."

60. Cf. *Kopt.-Gnos. Schr.* vol. 1, p. 334 (4), also Robert Eisler in *Weltenmantel und Himmelzelt*, p. 471 n. 3 : "The Holy One is the place of the world; the world is not the place of the Holy One," and on p. 744 : "God pervades the world; He is the Space which supports it, the extension which upholds it." Cf. also Philo in *de Somn.* 1 : 11 : 62, and Arnobius *adv. Nationes,* 1 : 31 : "For Thou art the First Cause, the place of things and spaces, the foundation of all things that exist."

61. Cf. § 10 : 2.

62. Cf. Fr. de Caussade, S. J., *Letters*, part 1 : "God alone exists by Himself and owes nothing to any but Himself."

63. Cf. Philo's *Leg. Alleg.* 3 : 70 : 195. This is typically Egyptian, and Indian. Cf. *Gospel of Eve*: "I am thou, and thou art I," and the *Ātmapanchakam* in *Stotra Ratnamāla* : "There is really no universe other than Myself." The idea is prominent in the popular Hermes-Prayers of Hellenistic age : cf. TGH vol. 1, pp. 85 : "For Thou art I, and I am Thou," and 89 : "For Thou art I, and I am Thou; Thy Name is mine, and mine is Thine; for that I am Thy likeness." It survives among the Christian mystics, *e.g.* Bl. Angela de Foligno in Algar Thorold's *Catholic Mysticism,* p. 150 : "Thou art I, and I am Thou," while St. John

of the Cross elaborates it in his *Spiritual Canticle*, 36 : 5 : "Thus I shall be Thou in Thy beauty, and Thou wilt be I in Thy beauty, because Thy beauty itself will be my beauty." It can be traced right back to the Pyramid Texts.

64. Cf. Tukaram's *Abhangas*, 1128 : "If I mean to worship Thee such worship becomes impossible as Thou art identical with all means of worship. . . . If I am to sing a song, Thou art Thyself that song. . . . There is no place where I could dance now." (Quoted in Ranade's *History of Mysticism in Maharashtra* ; an excellent book.)

65. Cf. Swāmi Rāmdās, *Sayings*, p. 90 : "God only is, and He is all." Also cf. Fr. Lallemant, S. J., *Spiritual Doctrine*, 2 : 6 ; 2 : 3—"All that is not God is nothing," Dr. Tauler (*op. cit.* p. 47) "All creatures are absolutely nothing," and Fr. de Caussade, *Letters*, part 5 : "God alone is all, and all else is nothing."

CHAPTER 4

1. Cf. the process in the embryology of *Pistis Sophia*, pp. 344-350.

2. Nature is the Mother of all that are born ; cf. Plato's *Phaedo* 86 A—D, and St. 15 : 2.

3. Some Platonists taught that desire is the sole cause of birth, but "Hermes" agrees with the Stoics in ascribing it to destiny, or *karma*. Cf. Plutarch, *Fragments*, 5 : 9 (TGH, vol. 3, p. 67) : "The intercourse and the conjunction of the soul with body is contrary to nature."

4. Cf. *Ecclus.* 44 : 8-9.

5. Cf. Plato in *Timaeus*, 69 B, and *Phaedo*, 66 and 105 E. This teaching on the cause of death is found again in Carrington, *Death : Its Causes and Phenomena* (1913). The student will find modern psychic research throws much light on the subject of this section. When the passions are subdued, the soul is freed from the body, even if the latter for some time continues its own activities. Jivanmukti.

6. Cf. Stobaeus, *Ecl.* 1 : 61.

7. Cf. Plato's *Phaedo*, 67 D.

8. Cf. the " Wedding Song of Sophia " in the Gnostic *Acts of Thomas*, " They shall be clad in kingly vestments and put on robes of light," and in the " Hymn of the Robe of Glory " (FFF p. 412-3, amended by Bevan): " My bright embroidered robe, which was shining with glorious colours, ... was made ready in its home on high." This is the " wedding garment " of *Mt.* 22 : 11, without which none can enter the Kingdom.

9. Cf. CH 10 : 21 : "When mind becomes a spirit, the law requires it to take a fiery body to execute God's decrees." This is the true starry, or ."astral " body of Philoponus, Plotinus 4 : 3 : 4, 9 and 15, Origen in *de Principiis*, 2 : 2, Plutarch in *Fac. in orbe lunae*, 28 ; 943 ff., Edward Carpenter in *Drama of Love and Death*, p. 264, and *1 Cor.* 15 : 35-50. It is in this radiant fiery body the soul passes through its purgatory, " tried as by fire ", as the Apostle puts it.

10. St Teresa, *Interior Castle*, p. 274, says of God's devotees that "they fear death no more than they would

a delicious trance ". Thousands who have watched a happy deathbed can say the same.

11. Originally Osiris, Judge of the Dead, then Pluto; in no sense an evil spirit or devil.

12. Cf. Vision of Thespesius (or "Aridaeus", edited by Mead) given by Plutarch, and Plato's *Gorg.* 524 D : " When a man is stripped of the body, all the natural or acquired affections of the soul are laid open to view." This truth is greatly stressed by Swedenborg, *Heaven and Hell*, and in all modern spiritualist literature. It is, indeed, universal in religion.

13. Cf. Empedocles in TGH, vol. 2, p. 362 : " Thrice ten thousand seasons shall he wander apart from the blessed, being born meanwhile in all sorts of mortal forms, changing one bitter path of life for another."

14. Cf. the three degrees of punishment in the Vision of Thespesius : bodily on earth, purgatorial, and hellish ; also Plutarch, pp. 564 F and 567 A. Plato's *Phaedo*, 107C has it : " The shades of notorious criminals who had been punished in earth life were not so hardly dealt with ; . . . whereas those who had passed their lives in undetected vice, under cloak and show of virtue, were . . . forced with labour and pain to turn their souls inside out." That is why Jesus also was more severe with hypocrisy than with any other vice.

15. Cf. Origen *contra Celsum*, 8 : 27 : " He who holds God above all things through devotion to Him is gracious." This is the constant theme of the Hindu devotees. All good qualities follow devotion to God.

16. Cf. *Heb.* 11 : 1, and St. Thomas Aquinas's famous hymn : " Faith, our outward sense befriending, makes the inward vision clear."

17. Cf. 1 *Enoch*, 38 : 4 : " The Lord of Spirits has caused His light to appear on the face of the holy, righteous and elect," also *2 Esdras*, 7 : 55 : " The faces of those who have used abstinence shall shine above the stars," and *Apocalypse of Baruch*, 51 : 10 : " They shall be changed . . . from beauty into loveliness, and from light into the splendour of glory." Cf. also *Daniel* 12 : 3 and *Proverbs*, 4 : 18. This is the *tejas* of the Hindus.

18. A similar idea is found in § 3 : 4, and in *Mk.* 12 : 25, *Lk.* 20 : 35 and several Gnostic books.

19. The Greeks said Plato's doctrine of reincarnation came from the Egyptians ; it appears also in the pagan source of the *Naassene Document*, 3,—where it is associated by a commentator with the *Gospel according to the Egyptians*, while calling it also a Chaldaean belief. It may well have come in this detailed form from India, about B.C. 450, and so through Egypt.

20. Cf. § 36 : 4, and the " Hymn of Jesus " in the Gnostic *Acts of John* (FFF, pp. 431-435).

21. Cf. 1 *Cor.* 15 : 40-41.

22. Cf. Porphyry *ad Marcellam*, 20, " For God-knowledge " (*i.e.* Gnosis) " makes speech scanty ; " Swāmi Rāmdās, *At the Feet of God*, p. 36 : " He must talk very little, . . . he must never enter into any controversy or discussion ; " the ancient Egyptian *Maxims of Ani* : " Be not of many words, for in silence thou shalt

gain good. . . . Pray thou with a desiring heart whose every word is hidden, and He will supply thy need and hear thy speech and receive thy offering." St. John of the Cross, *Minor Prose Writings*, p. 150 says : " The soul which is ready to talk and converse with creatures is not very ready to converse with God."

23. Cf. *1 Cor.* 9 : 26, where the same Greek word is used.

24. Cf. St. Teresa, *The Way of Perfection*, 18 : 1 : " God gives by far the heaviest crosses to His favourites." and St. Jean Vianney in Henri Ghéon, *The Secret of the Curé d'Ars*, p. 115 : " Let us love the Cross ; . . . it is God's gift to His friends." The value of suffering to a spritual life is recognized also by Confucius and the Vaishnavas.

25. Cf. *Timaeus,* 86 B : " (considering) pleasures and griefs exceed the greatest of diseases in the soul."

26. Cf. § 32 : 2. The word implies estrangement from, rejection of, God.

27. Cf. *Phaedo*, 81 D, and Porphyry, *de Antro*, 64 : 15.

28. Cf. *The Mysteries of John the Apostle*, p. 18 ; " When men die, each one of them is taken to the place of which he is worthy ; " the idea of a predestined place for each soul is also found in *Jn.* 14 : 2 and *2 Enoch* 49 : " Even to each one there is a place prepared for the repose of that soul ; " Swedenborg worked out the idea very fully in his *Heaven and Hell*.

29. Cf. *2 Enoch*, 44 : 5 : " (Everyone) shall learn his own measure, and shall take his reward according to his measure." Cf. also GI, 50 : 4.

30. Cf. Plotinus, *Enneads*, 8 : 4 : "Everyone has all things in himself and again sees all things in another, so that all things are everywhere, and all in all, and each in all, and infinite the glory. For each of them is great, since the small also is great" (*ap.* Mead). Cf. also *The Gnosis of the Light*, in FFF, p. 557.

31. Cf. § 36 : 5-6 and PS 23 : 1 : "the relationship and intercourse of men and gods".

32. Cf. *1 Cor.* 13 : 12.

33. Cf. *Heb.* 4 : 13, and *1 Enoch*, 9 : 5 : "All things are naked and open in Thy sight."

34. Cf. § 7 : 3.

35. Cf. Mother Julian, (*op. cit.*, p. 47) : "If he saw God continually, he would have no ... yearning that tends towards sin."

36. Cf. Basilides's poem, as quoted in FFF, pp. 274-5.

37. Iamblichus, quoted in Stobaeus, 1 : 49 : 40, distinguishes between the soul fresh from earth's stains and that just coming from the beatific sight of God in Heaven.

38. Cf. Paul's account in *Rom.* 7 : 18-25, and *2 Esdras*, 9 : 15 : "The corruptible body presses down the soul;" also the Manichaean text, M. 7, "From the Light and Gods am I, and become a stranger from them." Earth is always a Babylonian exile to the soul who knows her real home is Heaven.

39. This paragraph may well be compared with Wordsworth's *Ode on Intimations of Immortality*.

40. Cf. the *Shikand-Gumānig Vizar* on the teachngs of Māni : "He had bound and imprisoned Life and

Light in the body;" their release is told of in our § 45 : 2.

41. Mother Julian (*op. cit.* p. 47) says: "In such a time he is in tempest and in sorrow and woe, because he sees not God." *Cf. the turmoil* described in Plato's *Timaeus*, also §§ 28 : 1 and 32 : 2.

42. Cf. DCA, 7 : 5 : "Souls foul and unclean in their very nature can be made bright again only by being plunged in misery and remaining long in that condition, and undergoing it again and again." Hell is not eternal or punitive, as some have taught; it is curative, and lasts until the cure is complete.

43. Mother Julian (*op. cit.* p. 76) says: "It is the greatest pain that the soul can have to turn from God at any time by sin." For all joy is in Him, and he who turns away from the light will see only darkness ahead.

44. Cf. *Ecclus.*, 42 : 20 : "No knowledge is lacking to Him, and not a thing escapes Him." A favourite refrain of the Qur'ān.

45. The law of Karma, as taught also in *Gal.* 6 : 7 and *Col.* 3 : 25.

46. Philo, DVC, tells us how the Therapeuts (Hermetists?) were "taught ever more and more to see . . . that which is." Cf. also § 40 : 2.

47. Cf. §§ 3 : 3, 31 : 2 and 37 : 5.

48. Cf. § 25 : 1-2.

49. Cf. § 28 : 3 and CH 12 : 9.

50. In the Ptolemaic Kyme hymn, Isis speaking as the Divine Power says (line 54) : "It is I who conquer Destiny, Fate obeys me."

51. In condemning the use of magic to conquer fate, Zosimus quotes Hermes's lost book *The Inner Door*.

52. Cf. Boethius, *Philosophic Consolations*, 4 : 6.

53. Cf. Stobaeus, 11 : 2 : 20. Scott here changes the text and reads: "(Yet men's evil actions are) involuntary "—"(*to de kakon akousion*)"—saying that once man chooses evil he thereafter loses the power of choice and is swept on in the same path. Mead reads *hekousiōs* for *akousiōs*, and gets a simpler meaning, which I have preferred.

54. Cf. Plato's *Republic*, 10 : 617 E and 2 : 379 C.

55. Cf. § 29 : 3.

56. Cf. DCA 2 : 8: "If you desire true pleasures and unceasing joys, you must put off your unclean garment," and DCA 7 : 2: "Cast off the burden of your body . . . and clothe yourself in garments congruous with your true being." Bardaisan tells us in the *Hymn of the Robe of Glory* how the prodigal prince "stripped off their filthy and unclean garb and left it in their country," *i.e.* Egypt, the physical world of matter.

57. Cf. *Gal.* 5 : 17, *Rom.* 7 ; 5 and 8 : 1-13, also *Cod. Bruc.* in FFF, p. 520, ff, and in *Phaedo*, 64 ff. The phrase is common in all spiritual and ascetic literature, and has to be understood with commonsense.

58. Cf. Plato's *Republic*, 10 : 617 E.

59. Cf. *Chaldaean* Oracles, vol. 2, 52, "Thou oughtest to hasten to the Light and to the Father's rays, whence a soul richly arrayed with Mind has been sent to thee," (Kroll 52), and *idem*: "For divine things are not

accessible to mortals who fix their minds on body; it is they who strip themselves naked (of this thing) that speed aloft to the Height."

60. Cf. *Mk.* 10 : 24.

61. Cf. DCA, 11 : 6, " Put away from you, then, and be on your guard against everything that you feel with your bodily senses to be pleasant; lay hold on and make use of everything that your Mind finds to be pleasant." Cf. also, *1 Enoch,* 108 : 8, " Love . . . not any of the good things which are in the world," and St. John of the Cross, *The Ascent of Mount Carmel,* 2 : 15." Learn to be interiorly empty of all things," and in 3 : 6, " The soul, if it is to draw near to God, must empty itself of everything that is not God." This is a fundamental of Western Mysticism, as it is of Eastern too.

62. Cf. Fr. A. Poulain, *The Graces of Interior Prayer,* " (Perfection is) an endless road along which we continue to advance."

63. Cf. Dionysius, *The Divine Names,* 4 : 14 : " The Divine Love indicates distinctly its own unending and unbeginning as it were a sort of everlasting circle," and the Jewish writer in the *Naassene Document,* 25, " The beginning of perfection is the gnōsis of man, but gnōsis of God is perfect perfection."

64. Cf. DCA 6 : 5-7.

65. Cf. CH 9 : 3 and our § 29 : 4, 12; also *Phaedo,* 81 B ff, and 82 E. There are two self-inflicted punishments: the vain desire for sensual pleasure, and later on the new imprisonment in a body.

66. It was a controversial point whether rebirth into animal bodies was really a metaphor, or to be taken literally. The general opinion was that Plato and others meant by it only a more brutish body to fit the degraded soul. Cf. *Chaldaean Oracles*, 2 : 86, "(The soul) completes its life again in men and not in beasts . . . This is the law from the Blessed Ones that naught can break." (Kroll 62, quoted by Proclus)

67. Cf. the Jewish writer in the *Naassene Document*, "He distributes beauty and bloom to all that exist, according to each one's nature and peculiarity."

68. Cf. CH 18 : 8 ff.

69. Cf. *1 Enoch*, 18 : 13-16 and 21 : 3-6.

70. Cf. St. 24 : 11. India likewise claims to be the *Puṇyabhūmi*, land of merit, and China once called herself "the Celestial Kingdom".

71. Cf. *Col.* 3 : 1I, and the *Sybilline Oracles*, 5 : 484-500. Even the ancient Egyptian Prophet Ipuwēr (cir. B.C. 2000) has : "Foreign enemies shall enter, and the established order of things shall be completely overturned," Cf. the Hebrew prophecies about Egypt in *Isa.* 19, *Jer.* 46 and *Ezek.* 29-32. Such are timeless; it is futile to use them in dating books unless the details are far more precise than we have here.

72. Cf. *Apocalypse of Elias*, 26 : "He will count the holy places and weigh the idolatrous statues of the heathen, he will number their treasures." Khēʻ-kheper-rēʻ-sonbu, a near-contemporary of Ipuwēr, bewails : "The plans of the Gods are violated, their dispositions

are disregarded," (see Breasted, *Development of Religion and Thought in Ancient Egypt*, p. 200).

73. A similar apostrophe to Egypt is found in the Ptolemaic Isis stele at Kume, line 60 : " Rejoice, O Egypt, who has given me birth."

74. Cf. *Exodus*, 7 : 17-21, and *Apocalypse of Elias*, 30 : " In those days blood will flow from Kos to Memphis ; the River of Egypt will become bloody, so that for three days none can drink of it," and *idem*, 27, " In those days the towns of Egypt will mourn." Ipuwēr, 2 : 6, says, " Blood is everywhere ; there is no lack (?) of death," and goes on, " Indeed, many dead are buried in the river ; the stream is a tomb, and the embalming-place has become a stream." (Breasted, pp. 206, 208)

75. Philo, DVC, p. 892, has : " They who are in every way the most highly advanced lead out a colony, as it were, to the Therapeutic fatherland," *i.e.*, near Lake Maryūt in North Egypt.

76. Many Christians held the world itself to be evil (cf. *Eph.* 6 : 12) and hated the cosmic powers worshipped by the pagans. Valentinus (Hippolytus, 6 : 33) speaks of " the devil, the ruler of this world ", and *Pistis Sophia*, p. 164, has " Renounce the love of the world." Cf. also *Jn.* 2 : 15-17. The authentic voice of the Jews on this is heard in *2 Enoch*, 52 : 6 : " Cursed is he who brings the Lord's creation into contempt," and also in *Gen.* 1 : 31.

77. Cf. *Timaeus*, 29 E, and Ipuwēr, 4 : 2-3, " Indeed, great and small say, ' I would that I might die.'

Little children say, 'Would there were none to keep me alive'." (Breasted, p. 209) The beautiful *Dialogue of a Man with his Soul* says: "Death is before me today like the odour of myrrh, like sitting under the sail on a windy day . . . Death is before me today as a man longs to see his house when he has spent years in captivity." Such weariness of life is well-known in all lands. (Breasted, p. 195).

78. Cf. *Codex Theodosiani*, 16 : 10 : 2, "Let the madness of sacrifices be abolished." In the same way pagans thought the Christian martyrs mad—and still do! But as Fr. Lallemant, S. J. says in his *Spiritual Doctrine*, 4 : 4 : 1 : "There is a madness which is a true wisdom before God," and S'ri Rāmakrishṇa said somewhere, "If you must be mad, be mad after God!" Pagan martyrologies also exist; men were ready to die for the "Religion of the Mind", and many did, in the ages of wild fanaticism.

79. Cf. §§ 8 : 4 and 39 : 1.

80. The word *angelos* occurs in Lactantius in this sense of "demon", and it was also in the *Book of Ostanes*, often named along with Hermes and Zoroaster as scripture. Cornelius Labeo (died A.D. 120) depends upon Hermes in this doctrine. Cf. also the story in KK 54.

81. Cf. §§ 32 : 2 and 38 : 2.

82. Cf. Philo, *de Providentiā*, 1 : 18, and Seneca, *Consol. ad Marc.* 26 : 6.

83. Cf. *1 Enoch*, 80 : 2-3, and *Apocalypse of Baruch*, 85 : 10 : "The youth of the world is past," *2 Esdras*,

14 : 10, "The world has lost his youth and the times begin to wax old," while Cyprian, in A.D. 251 says, "You must know the world has now grown old." This typically Jewish-Christian concept is also found in *Rev.* 22 : 20 and *1 Jn.* 2 : 18; it clashes with the whole pagan idea of §21, and is here probably a 3rd. c. interpolation, though it may come in from Irān.

84. Cf. *2 Enoch*, 80 : 2-7 and *Sybilline Oracles*, 5 : 512-531. St. Augustine (*Civitas Dei*, 2 : 3) says: "The common saying—The rain has failed, the Christians are the cause." Later on, the Christians ascribed all troubles to the survival of paganism. Both believed that Nature depended on the due performance of rites. Even Mencius, in far China, in his book, 6 : 9, says: "The world fell into decay and principles faded out. Perverse speech and violent deeds waxed rife once more. There were instances of ministers who murdered their kings, and of sons who murdered their fathers." For close parallels, see Breasted, pp. 193-4, 200-210.

85. Cf. *Gita* 4 : 7, "Wherever there is decay of righteousness ... then I Myself come forth for the protection of the good and the destruction of evildoers."

86. Cf. §§ 6 : 1, and *Mt.* 19 : 28 for the same Greek word. Marcus Aurelius in 11 : 1 has "the periodical rebirth of the all". The idea of cyclic ages, of *manvantaras* followed by *pralayas*, is also Indian as well as Stoic. That God should restore the world is implied in most religious thought, because He is good and cannot bear evil. Cf. Mother Julian (*op. cit.* p. 6): "Our natural will is to have God, and the Good Will

of God is to have us." And His Will must eventually prevail.

87. Part of this passage derives from Plato's *Timaeus* 92 C, 29 E-31 B, and 37 C; it is probably later than CH 9. Philo also says that God's knowledge brought forth "the one lovable sensible son, the world".

88. Cf. Plotinus, *Enneads*, 5 : 1 : 6-7, and § 19 : 3.

89. The "Immanuel". Cf. also the whole book *Christ in You*", and the books of J. Macbeth Bain; also Swāmi Rāmdās, *At the Feet of God*, p. 3 : "We are a slender touch of thought of the Universal Mind."

90. This is, in fact, a Stoic adaptation of a saying of Heraclitus (cir. B.C. 510); cf. Plotinus. *Enneads*, 4 : 7 : 10, and CH 10 : 25 : "Man on earth is a god subject to death, while God in Heaven is man immune from death."

91. Cf. Macarius, *Homilies*, 15 : 22, and *Hermippus*, 1 : 6 : 40.

92. The word *logos* means : reason, word, speech; it is built up in man at his "Rebirth" (cf. §45 : 1) The Egyptian idea in the *Ptah-document* (B. M. Stela No. 797—Breasted, pp. 43-47) is that a perfect mind is expressed through thought in perfect words; this is what was meant by the common Egyptian phrase conferred upon the "dead": *me'e-khrow*, "true of speech"—one who perfectly expresses in act and word a perfect thought. Cf. CH 12 : 14 "The *logos* is image and mind of God."

93. Cf. PS 23 : 2 : "He deserves our wonder, in that he is greatest of them all."

94. Cf. Philo, *Fragments*, 662 M : " For it is necessary to be . . . sociable, world-loving, God-loving, so that he may be also beloved of God."

95. Cf. *2 Enoch*, 30 : 8, " (Man draws) his intelligence from the swiftness of the angels and from cloud." With this passage also cf. *Hermippus*, 1 : 6 : 40, and §§ 36 : 3 and 42 : 1.

96. Cf. *Ecclus*. 1 : 4, " Wisdom was created before all," and 42 : 15, " By the Word of God are His works ; " also *Gen*. 1 : 3, *Ps*. 33 : 6, and *Jn*. 1 : 1-3. The idea goes back along one line to the Pyramid Texts, but is inherent in the Magic that preceded most Religion everywhere.

97. Cf. CH 14 : 7, " This is, as it were, His body—the making." God's body is the all, produced by His Will to be His instrument. There is no need whatever to follow S in his changes of our text. God is still the " Bodiless ", because He transcends all.

98. Man is a microcosmic image of the universe, and so of God. Cf. §§ 16 : 7 and PS 8.

99. Cf. the *Logia Jesou* ; wonder is a beginning of gnōsis, for it awakens love and a yearning for the beloved.

100. Cf. *The Gnosis of the Light*, p. 15 : " We live that we may know Him, the Mystery of Silence."

101. Cf. the Jewish commentator in the *Naassene Document*, " Anacreon's Cup . . . tells him with speechless sound of what Race he must be born if he hear the Hidden Mystery in silence."

102. An Egyptian idea, in no way due to Christian influence as some suppose : Cf. *Pyramid Texts*, 1979 :

"Thou hast come forth from the Lake of Life, purified in the celestial lake, and becoming Opener of Ways," and *The Book of the Dead*, ch. 17: "My sin is expelled, my iniquity is removed; I have cleansed myself in those two great pools which are in Heracleopolis." Cf. also 2 *Kings* 5 : 10 and *Ps.* 51 : 2 and 7.

103. Cf. the "Mandaean Chrism" in the sacred book *Genzā*, 22: "We sign in the name of the Life, from the great Mixing-Bowl" (*krater*: the same word as in our text) "on high, boundless and infinite, with joy, joy, joy!" For the early association of the Christian rite of baptism with Life, Joy and Light, cf. the *Odes of Solomon*, and Rendel Harris's notes thereon.

CHAPTER 5

1. Cf. Brother Lawrence, *The Practice of the Presence of God*, (Letter 15) : " The deeper and more extensive our knowledge shall be, the greater will be our love."

2. Cf. Clement Alex., *Stromata*, 4 : 22 : 139, and *Gita*, 8 : 22 : " He ... may be reached by unswerving devotion to Him alone in whom all beings abide, by whom all this is pervaded." This is also the constant theme of *Bhāgavatam*. Cf. St. John of the Cross, *The Dark Night of the Soul*, 2 : 18, " It is love only that unites the soul and God," and *The Spiritual Canticle*, 38 : 5, " It is impossible to attain to the perfect love of God without the perfect vision of God." This is why right belief is so important, neither knowledge nor love alone; it is the interplay of the two that engenders the

Divine union. See also St. Bernard and St. Francis de Sales on this subject.

3. Cf. *Ekāgratamān Ishwar*, " Religion is falling in love with God," and *Nārada Bhakti Sūtras*, 19, " Love ... is feeling the greatest misery in forgetting God." St. John of the Cross, *The Spiritual Canticle*, 6 : 2, says, " The more the soul knows God, the more grows her desire and anguish to see Him," and again in 9 : 7, " For the wages ... of love are nought else ... than greater love, until it attains to perfection of love ... in order to find complete refreshment there." The prodigal in *The Hymn of the Robe of Glory* tells us, " My free soul longed for its natural state," which Sri Ramaṇa Mahārishi assures us is that of conscious union with the Supreme Self, God. From ancient Egypt, cf. *B. M. Ostr. 5656 A*, " O Amon-Rē', I love Thee, and I have filled my heart with Thee," and the *Hymn* of Akhenaton, " Thou art in my heart ; There is no other that knows Thee save Thy son." Cf. *Jn*. 1 : 12 and *Mt*. 11 : 27 ; it is the *son* alone who can know the full Godhead. Nay, all religious literature is full of such expressions, we need quote no more ; it is the crown, the aim, of all philosophy and religion.

4. Cf. §§ 8 : 3, 18 : 4 and 49 : 1. Sri Rāmakrishṇa says, " It is He Himself who leads you unto Him," and many Hindu texts and saints have said that God Himself takes the form of the Teacher, to guide the aspirant to all Truth through the Mind. Cf. *Jn*. 14 : 26.

5. Cf. CH 16 : 11 : " The duty of mankind is to give worship," and Marcus Aurelius, 5 : 33, " What is

enough ? What else but to serve and praise the Gods and to do good to men ?" Cf. *Lk.* 10 : 27, and Dvagpo Lharje, in the Tibetan book, *The Precious Rosary*, 25 : 6, " For him who is endowed with the fullness of compassion, it is the same whether he practise meditation in solitude or work for the good of others in society."

6. Cf. Avvayar's *Yoga Aphorisms*, 1 : 2 : 9, " The object of this body is to seek resolutely the Lord within ; " also Brother Lawrence (*op. cit.* Conv. 2) : " Our only business is to love and delight ourselves in God," and St. Jean Vianney, in Abbé Monnin's *Secret of the Curé d'Ars*., p. 263, " It is in order to love God that we are on earth."

7. Cf. St. Teresa's *Life*, 16 : 6, " It wishes it were all tongue in order that it may praise our Lord."

8. Cf. *Apocalypse of Baruch*, 54 : 8, " If my members were mouths, and the hairs of my head voices, even so I could not give Thee the meed of praise, nor laud Thee as is befitting, nor could I recount Thy praise, nor tell the glory or Thy beauty."

9. Cf. PS 1 : " And if you understand this, you will see (God), you will be overflowing in the whole mind with all good things," also *Jn.* 15 : 18-19. United with the Source of all Good, the soul is changed to Good.

10. Cf. *Wisdom*, 2 : 15, " He is grievous unto us even to behold, for his life is not like other men's, his ways are of another fashion."

11. Cf. Plato' *Phaedrus*, 249 D, " He is scolded by the many as though he were beside himself."

12. Cf. *Jn.* 16 : 33, *1 Cor.* 13 : 7, and Abammon's *Responses*, 10 : 2a : " He whose thoughts are fixed on the Gods will not care what men say about him." Also Fr. Lallemant's *Spiritual Doctrine,* 4 : 5 : 2 : 1, " He who possesses God is not troubled by anything ; for God is all to Him, and all the rest is nothing to him."

13. Cf. *Rom.* 12 : 21 and 8 : 38, also *Testament of Benjamin*, 4 : 3, " By doing good he overcomes evil," and Plotinus, 4 : 3 : 16, " And if he who suffers (injustice) is a good man, the end of these things turns into good." In his letter to the Romans, Ignatius prayed eagerly for martyrdom, for out of such evils comes the greatest good ; Asvaghosa, *The Awakening of Faith*, has : " They regard themselves as manifestation of the absolute undifferentiated Reality ; then with the aid of the great wisdom they put an end to ignorance, they see the Divine."

14. Cf. *Sarvasāra Upanishad*, " Brahman is that which is free from all vehicles " (naked), " the absolute Consciousness without specialties, which is secondless Be-ness, which is Bliss free from illusion. . . . It is itself differenceless " (undivided), " and is seen as the seat of all. It is the pure, the noumenal, the true and the indestructible." *Nirālamba Upanishad*, " full of all potencies, without beginning or end, that is described as pure, beneficial, peaceful, unqualified and indescribable." *The Apocalypse of Abraham*, 17, adds, " Thou art self-originated, incorruptible, spotless, self-complete, self-illuminating." Cf. also Dionysius, *The Divine Names*.

15. Cf. § 11 : 2-5.

16. Cf. *Varāha Upanishad*, "The whole of the universe is caused by thought alone," and *Tripura Rahasya*, 11 : 68, "The world is nothing but an image thrown on the screen of consciousness."

17. Cf. St. Teresa, *Interior Castle*, p. 107: "It wearies of everything, realising that no true rest can be found in creatures," and St. Bernard's hymn, "From the best bliss that earth imparts we turn unfilled to God again." St. Augustine, *Confessions*, 1 : 1, "Our hearts are restless till they find their rest in Thee."

18. Cf. Dionysius, *op cit.*, 4 : 23, "To be ever the same is a characteristic of the Good."

19. Cf. *Chaldaean Oracles*, 2 : 50, "Let the immortal depths of thy soul be opened, and open all thy eyes at once to the Above," (Kroll 51).

20. Cf. *Ekāgratamān Ishwar*, "We shall find Him through a self . . . stripped bare of everything but a humble and passionately seeking heart."

21. Cf. *Acts of John* (FFF p. 450): "As we are we we can never embrace Thy perfect Greatness—Greatness that can be contemplated by the pure alone, for it is imaged in Thy Man alone,"—cf. also *Mt.* 5 : 8. As St. John of the Cross says in *The Ascent of Mount Carmel*, 1 : 5, "God will never dwell there where aught is present beside Himself." So also DCA, 1 : 4 : "Free yourself from the pollution of the physical world, and to that end humble yourself, and seek and strive earnestly to attain to Him who is the Source and Father of Good. . . . that so you may come to partake of Life

and enjoy happiness and bliss." Cf. also St. Teresa, *Relations*, 8 : 17, "When the soul sees itself hindered and kept back from entering, as it desires, on the fruition of God, it conceives a great loathing for the body, on which it looks as a thick wall which hinders it from that fruition which it then seems to have entered upon within itself."

22. Cf. Molinos, *The Spiritual Guide*, P 9 : " God is above all creatures, and the soul cannot see Him nor converse with Him unless she lifts herself above all." Lactantius glosses this passage in " Hermes " : " come close to and follow with the intelligence."

23. Cf. DCA, 12 : 5, " All things that you ought to get knowledge of are in your possession and within you," and *idem*, 12 : 7, " Call yourself back then to yourself, O soul, and seek in yourself all that you ought to gain knowledge of." So the ancient gnōmon : " Know thyself "; cf. *Lk.* 17 : 21.

24. Cf. Fr. de Caussade, in *Abandon*, 4, " The more you are stripped of all and separated from yourself, the more you will possess God," and in his *Letters*, part 3, " When a heart is empty God fills it." Brother Lawrence, *op. cit.*, Letter 5 : " The heart must be empty of all other things." So St. John of the Cross, *The Ascent of Mount Carmel*, 3 : 1, " That union can never take place without a total separation from these forms which are not God." Cf. also Blackwood, *op. cit.*, p. 251, " Once sweep aside the trash and rubbish men seek outside themselves today, and the wings of their smothered souls would stir again. . . . Self would disappear,

and with it this false sense of separateness. The greater consciousness would awake in them;" also on p. 195, "The personal life must slip aside, be trampled on, submerged, before there can be room for the Divine Presences." Cf. *Mk.* 8 : 34. Ven. Louis de Blois said, "A soul cannot arrive at this intimate union with God unless it hath become entirely pure and simple and thus hath a likeness to God."

25. Cf. St. John of the Cross, *The Ascent of Mount Carmel*, 2 : 7, "If we cling to anything whatever . . . , we shall miss our way and never be able to ascend by the narrow path," for as Sankarāchārya says in *Viveka Chudāmani*, 300, "The real nature of the Supreme Self . . . can be reached by the very pure-minded and virtuous, in the state of transcendental peace resulting from intense and keen attentiveness." Patanjali, *Yoga Sūtra*, 1 : 16, "Dispassion, carried to the utmost, is indifference regarding all else than soul, and this indifference arises from a knowledge of soul as distinguished from all else."

26. Cf. Swāmi Rāmdās, *At the Feet of God*, p. 9 : "The royal road is straight and short—it is easy to tread. No thorns—no obstacles beset the smooth and flowery way." There is no need for S's suggested change.

27. Cf. *Chaldaean Oracles*, 2 : 51, "The mortal soul once endowed with Mind must put bridle on his soul, in order that it may not plunge, into the ill-starred Earth but may win to freedom." (Kroll 32). This struggle between the higher and the lower in man is described in all religions.

28. Cf. St. Augustine, *Civitas Dei*, 10 : 29, " Whether the body is to be fled from so that the mind may be able to remain with God in blessedness "—the problem solved by all ascetics in their own way.

29. Cf. Blackwood, *op. cit.*, p. 212 : " Far beyond words it lies, as difficult of full recovery as the dreams of deep sleep," and *Chaldaean Oracles*, 1 : 23, " There is no need of strain in understanding This ; but thou shouldst have the vision of thy soul in purity turned from aught else, so as to make thy mind empty and attentive (only) to that End of Understanding . . . . for It subsists beyond the mind." (Kroll, 11) Cf. also Philo, DVC, p. 901, " For when in giving an interpretation one continues to speak rapidly without pausing for breath, the mind of the hearers is left behind, unable to keep up the pace."

30. Cf. Plotinus : " If he passes out of himself like an image to its prototype, he has reached the end of his journey. This may be called the flight of the alone to the Alone." St. Teresa's *Life*, 18 : 4, " The soul sometimes leaps forth out of itself like a fire." This is rapture, *not* death, as S seems to imagine. Without it, man cannot see God.

31. Cf. PS 10 : 1 and CH 10 : 17.

32. Without this, no mystical state is possible ; He has to lift man into that high state of purity, that loving gaze, wherein God may be seen.

33. Cf. *Acts of John*, " I am not what I seem to be, but thou shalt see what I am when thou comest."

Only when man reaches the Ogdoad where God dwells alone can he know truly God's all-holy nature.

34. Cf. §§ 1 : 1 and 7 : 1, also St. Teresa's *Life*, 16 : 10, "I seem to be dreaming the things I see." Sri Ramana Mahārshi calls this "sleep-waking". It is a state which arises naturally when the Reality behind all phenomena has once been glimpsed, for all else is seen then as unreal shadows.

35. Cf. *The Repose of John*, p. 7. "Thou didst graciously bestow upon me other eyes which do not make themselves visible."

36. Cf. Rúysbroeck, *Flowers of a Mystic Garden*, "Some ineffable operation like the embrace of God lifts him upon the heights of beatitude." Many mystics speak of this "embrace" of God which raises man to the Heights.

37. Cf. St. Teresa's *Life*, 20 : 37, "The soul is utterly blinded, absorbed, amazed, dizzy at the vision of so much grandeur;" she speaks of a "heavenly madness" (16 : 8), when she says "(I was) beside myself, drunk with love", (16 : 3)—the drunkenness whereof the Sūfis have so much to say. So also Philo, DVC, p. 57, speaks of the Therapeuts as "drinking the pure wine of the love of God".

38. Cf. Dvágpo Lharje, *The Precious Rosary*, 11 : 5, "A mere glimpse of Reality may be mistaken for complete realisation." St. John of the Cross also warns us of this danger, which often leads to spiritual pride.

39. Cf. Dionysius, *The Divine Names*, 4 : 1, "The Good . . . by Its very existence sends to all things

that be the rays of Its whole goodness, according to their capacity." The large cup holds much water.

40. Cf. § 12 : 2.

41. Cf. St. Teresa's *Life*, 18 : 14, " It is useless to try to speak, because it is not possible to conceive a word, nor, if it were conceived, is there strength sufficient to utter it."

42. This is the " Prayer of Quiet " of the mystics; this holy Silence is the Mother of the Virgin-born " Man, Son of God ".

43. Cf. *Hermippus*, 2 : 20 : 187, " Having abandoned all the bodily senses and movements, he is still." This is the " Ligature " wherein even conscious prayer ceases; and mind and body become like a stone, lost in God. Fr. Poulain, *The Spiritual Journals of Lucie Christine*, p. 63, " The faculties cannot act or make those movements by which they ordinarily go to God, because they are fixed in Him, and He holds them in the embraces of His love."

44. Cf. Coffin Texts from Ancient Egypt (cir. B.C. 1900) in *Annales du Service*, V, 235; " I am the soul of the God, Self-generator . . .; I have become He. I am He before whom the sky is silent . . .; He has made me into His heart, He has fashioned me into His soul; I was not born with a birth," with which may be compared the *Pyramid Texts*, 253-255, " The Gods are silent before thee, the Nine Gods have laid their hands upon their mouth." Cf. St. Teresa's *Life*, 21 : 13, " God is the Soul of that soul now," and St. Catherine of Siena, *Dialogues*, p. 149, " Love

transforms the lover into the object loved "—a truth fundamental also in Hindu faith.

45. Cf. *Rom.* 8 : 8.

46. Mind is itself instantaneously present anywhere it is turned ; cf. § 36 : 6, also Lactantius, *de Opif. Dei*, 16 : 9-10, *Iliad*, 15 : 80 and *Odyssey*, 7 : 36. Of the discarnate spirit the same is said by Tanquerey in his *Synopsis Theologiae Dogmaticae*, sect. 901, where the quality is called " agility ".

47. Man, liberated from his self-chosen bondage to Nature, now breaks through upward, into the Ogdoad, as in § 3 : 2 he broke through downward. Cf. St. Teresa's *Life*, 20 : 12, " The soul . . . rises upwards above itself and above all created things."

48. Cf. the beautiful passage in Plotinus, *Enneads*, 6 : 5 : 7 and 12, also Richard Jeffries, *The Story of my Heart*, pp. 8 ff and 38 : " Having drunk deeply of the heaven above, and felt the most glorious beauty of the day, . . . I now became lost and absorbed into the being or existence of the universe. I felt down deep into the earth under, and high above into the sky, and farther still into the sun and stars, still farther beyond the stars into the hollow of space, and losing thus my separateness of being, came to seem like a part of the whole. . . . I cannot understand Time. It is Eternity now. I am in the midst of it. . . . Nothing has to come ; it is now. . . . To the soul there is no past and no future ; all is and will be ever, in now . . . . My soul has never been, and never can be, dipped in Time." Also Edward Carpenter, *The Art of Creation*,

p. 230: "It is the great deliverance from the prison-life of the separate self, and comes to the latter sometimes with the force and swiftness of a revelation. . . . Or again a strange sense of Extension comes on me, and of presence in distant space and time . . . through all forms and ranges of being." (Cf. also *The Book of the Twelve Bēguines*, 14 : 2.

49. Cf. St. John of the Cross, *The Spiritual Canticle*, 39 : 6, "(Souls in bliss) are truly gods by participation, equals of God and His companions." *Idem*, 22 : 5 and 24 : 5, "a true embrace, by means of which the soul lives the life of God (pervaded with) the delight of the glory of God . . . , wherein the soul is made equal with God through love." Also, *The Book of the Twelve Bēguines*, 14 : 2, "He realiseth himself as uplifted in one Height with God," and 16 : 2, "There are we emptied of ourselves and of every creature, and made One with God in Love."

50. Cf. *Uttara Gita*, 1 ; 9, "Conceive . . . the manifested sky . . . as one undivided Brahman, then merge the self into it, and it into your own self."

51. In the *Naassene Document, aiōn*, eternity, is a name for the Cosmic Man. The seeker is to identify himself thus with the perfect Man, Son of God, as first planned by God, and thus return to his inheritance in Heaven. A close parallel to our text is found in F. Ll. Griffith, *Stories of the High Priests of Memphis*, p. 92.

52. The word *ethos* is very rare in this sense: from it we derive our word *ēthics*. Cf. § 45 : 3. Richard Jeffries, *op. cit.*, says: "I prayed . . . that I might

take from all their energy, grandeur and beauty, and gather it into me," and Carpenter, *op. cit.*, says, "The Self, hitherto deeming itself a separate atom, suddenly becomes aware of its inner unity with these other human beings, animals, plants, even. It is as if a veil had been drawn aside. A deep understanding, knowledge, flows in."

53. Cf. Pyramid Texts, 733. "Thou purifiest thyself, thou ascendest to Ré'; the sky is not empty of thee . . . for ever," and Note 49 above.

54. Cf. Patanjali, *Yoga Sūtras*, 4 : 22, " The mind, when united with the soul and fully conversant with knowledge, embraces universally all objects." Cf. also, Tukārām's *Abhangas*, 3370: "You are really as large as the universe itself," and Sankarāchārya's *Viveka Chudāmani*, 31, "Devotion after all is enquiry into one's own self." Cf. also Clifford Bax's *Marriage of the Soul*, "Oh, I have reached the boundaries of my soul. I am becoming all things."

55. Cf. Dionysius. *op. cit.*, 5 : 10, " He is Eternity itself . . . and the measure of existing things," and St. John of the Cross, *Spiritual Canticle*, 14 : 5, "(When), as in this case, the soul is united with God, it feels that all things are God."

56. Cf. St. Teresa's *Interior Castle*, p. 52 : "We are afraid of everything and therefore fear to make progress."

57. Cf. the pagan source of the *Naassene Document*, "I become what I will, and I am what I am," and Zosimus (ap. Scott, *Hermetica*, iv, 106) : " He

becomes all things that He will . . . and appears to each as He desires." This is a typically Egyptian and Indian thought, that man becomes what he thinks upon; it is almost the keynote of Upanishadic ethics. Cf. also *Exodus*, 3 : 14. Cf. also, the *Chaldaean Oracles*, 29 : 93, " Believe thyself to be out of body, and thou art," (Kroll 64).

58. Cf. §§ 4 : 4 and 29 : 12, also St. John of the Cross, *Spiritual Canticle* 26 : 13, " Where God is not known, naught is known." The Upanishads also tell us that the Brahman is that which being known all is known.

59. Cf. § 38 : 2.

60. Cf. St. Teresa, *The Way of Perfection*, 21 : 1, " He will never fail you but will help you in all your troubles, and you will find Him everywhere," and Dr. John Tauler, *The Inner Way*, p. 145, " The man who lays hold on God and desires Him only, . . . all things will be but the road to God for him." Samartha Rāmadās, *Dasābodh*, 14 : 3, " He cannot see men, for wherever his eye is cast he sees only God." Fr. de Caussade, *Letters*, part 2 : " Let us be well persuaded that God may be found everywhere without any effort, because He is always present to those who seek Him with their whole heart," Mother Julian, *op. cit.*, p. 35, " The fullness of joy is to behold God in all," and St. Thérèse de Lisieux in *The Secret of St. Thérèse de l'Enfant Jésus*, by Carmelites, p. 53 : " We ought to see Him only in all things." It is the crown of the Vaishṇava life also.

61. Cf. Cicero *de Naturā Deorum*, 2 : 71, " so that we may revere Them always with pure, concentrated and incorrupt mind and voice." Seneca goes farther than this : " He who has imitated has worshipped Them enough." Apollonius and Porphyry taught the same. Cf. also, *Ps.* 50 : 8-15, 51 : 16-17 and 141 : 2, *Isa.* 1 : 11-17, *Rom.* 12 : 1 and *Heb.* 13 : 15. Like all ancient cults, the Egyptian attached great importance to due ritual and offerings ; Hermes was ahead of his fellows.

62. Cf. § 7 : 2. This is the Sursum Corda of all true worship ; St. Thérèse says in " *A Little White Flower,* p. 176 : " For me, prayer is an uplifting of the heart, a glance towards Heaven."

63. Cf. § 9 : 3-4.

64. Cf. § 10 : 2-3.

65. Cf. §§ 18 : 1 and 36 : 2. Gnōsis follows on the right use of Mind and Reason (or Speech ?), guided by God's grace. There are three stages in Prayer : *noēsai*, thinking of God, *epikalesai*, adoring Him, and *epignōnai*, merging in Him with love. Cf. also §§ 28 : 3-5 and 45 : 2. *The Book of the Twelve Béguines*, 14 : 2, has, " When we know and understand, then are we blessed and made one with God in love," and in 11 : " Then the pure and single eyes are strengthened by the inpouring of that clear Light of the Father, and they behold His Face, in a simple seeing."

66. Cf. Clement Alex., *Stromata*, 4 : 23 : 149, " In this way it is possible for the Gnōstic already " (*i.e.*, even in this life) " to become God," and thus what the Hindus call a Jivanmukta.

67. Cf. § 3 : 1 and *Chaldaean Oracles*, 1 : 57, "Source of sources, Womb that holds all things together," (Kroll 19).

68. Cf. § 19 : 3 and St. Ambrose's *Hymn* : "O Strength and Stay, upholding all creation, who ever dost Thyself unmoved abide."

69. Cf. St. Teresa's *Relations*, 5 : 1 : "But let no one think that of himself he can abide in the light, for that depends on (God's) grace."

70. Cf. Clement Alex., *Stromata*, 7 : 1 : 2, "The worship beseeming God includes both loving God and being loved by Him." St. Thérèse de Lisieux speaks much of this one real worship.

CHAPTER 6

1. Cf. §§ 4 : 2 and 42 : 4, also *1 Jn*. 2 : 15, and *Pistis Sophia*, 125, "Strive thereafter to renounce the whole world and all the matter therein, that ye may receive the Mystery of the Light."

2. Cf. the 2nd. c. *Mithriac Ritual* (Mead), "Translate me, now held ... by my lower nature, unto the generation that is free from death ... in order that I may become reborn in Mind." Shinran Shōnin, 13th c. Japanese Buddhist, says in *Buddhist Psalms*, p. 51, "When the new birth through the clearness of the Divine Promise is attained in the Eternal Kingdom, it is not like unto the birth of this world." Jesus teaches this Rebirth in *Jn.* 3 : 3-8.

3. This is Plato's *anamnēsis*, to be self-realized, by one who is "carried away by heavenly love"

(Philo, DVC, 891). Cf. the Jewish writer in the *Naassene Document*, "One is the Race without a King which is born above."

4. Cf. *The Book of the Dead*, ch. 17. "Proceeding upon the Road which I have known upon the Island of the Truthful, I have reached 'the land of the Celestial Horizon-dwellers, and I have ascended through its holy Doorway. O you who are in the Presence, give your hands to me; I am the soul that comes into existence among you." The phrase is found in Plato's *Phaedrus*, 248b. We may note also the Jew in the *Naassene Document*, 28, "For this is the Gate of Heaven, and this is the House of God where the good God dwells alone, into which no impure shall come, but it is kept under guard for the spiritual alone; where when they come they must cast away their garments and all become bridegrooms, obtaining their true manhood through the Virginal Spirit. For this is the Virgin big with child, conceiving and bearing a Son . . ." to which the Christian Gnostic commentator adds, "not psychic, not fleshly, but a blessed Aeon of Aeons." With this cf. § 42 : 3, "Become Eternity (Aeon)" after stripping off the body and its desires. The Mystery is fundamental in all the Mediterranean cults, and is, as here, usually touched on with reverent vagueness only; one of the mystics speaks of it thus: "Naked seek the naked Jesus".

5. Cf. Jacob Boehme, as quoted in Evelyn Underhill, *Mysticism*, (1913), p. 147 : "The mother of the New Man is the Virgin Sophia, the Divine Wisdom or Mirror

of the Being of God." It is extraordinary how tenacious such thoughts are in the religious mind of humanity.

6. Cf. *Pyramid Texts*, 886-7 and 273 : " My Father art Thou, O Rē', . . . King Wonas is a great god," and Sri Ramaṇa Mahārshi, *Anubandhan*, 12, " He alone is born who returns to his primal source, . . . born every moment of his life anew and afresh."[1]

7. Cf. St. Teresa, *The Way of Perfection*, 28 : 2, " We are not forced to take wings to find Him, but have only to seek solitude and to look within ourselves," and *idem*, 32 : 10, " If made with due determination, it cannot fail to draw the Almighty to become one with our baseness, to transform us into Himself and to unite the creature with the Creator."

8. Cf. St. John of the Cross, *The Living Flame of Love*, 2 : 26, " (Without purity) the joy and knowledge of God cannot be established in the soul." An interpolator in our Hermetic text named eleven other torments —all arising from ignorance of, *i.e.*, separation from, God : grief, incontinence, desire, injustice, greed, deceitfulness, envy, fraud, anger, rashness, malice. These twelve vices are associated with the twelve Zodiacal Signs ; cf. CH. 13 : 12.

9. Cf. Molinos, *The Spiritual Guide*, 1 : 129, " Rest in this Mystical Silence, and open the door, so that God may give Himself to you, unite Himself with you and change you into Himself ; " also the Hymn in the Gnostic *Acts of Thomas*, (FFF p. 404) " Come, O Silence, thou Revealer of the mighty things of all the Greatness,"—the latter term being the customary Jewish

"Power", used to avoid the actual ineffable Name of God. Also cf. the Marcosian *Ritual of Illumination*, preserved by Irenaeus, "Make thyself ready . . . that thou mayst be what I am, and I what thou art." The beautiful little Egyptian mystic poem in *Pap. Sallier*, 1 : 8 : 2-3, has : "Thou sweet Well for him who thirsts in the desert; closed to him who speaks, but open to him who is silent. When he who is silent comes, lo, he finds the Well." Dionysius, *The Divine Names*, 1 : 5, "It is during cessation of every mental energy that such a union as this of the deified minds towards the super-Divine Light takes place." Many later Western mystics have explained this more fully.

10. An interpolator names them : Gnōsis, Joy, Self-Control, Continence, Righteousness, Unselfishness Truth, the Good, Life and Light. These ten make up the Gnōstic "Robe of Glory"; expanded, they become the 33 Aeons in the supreme Plērōma of the Godhead, the infinite Powers in Eternal Light, as in our § 2 : 2. Cf. *Pyramid Texts*, "Thou hast power over the Powers that are in thee," (2011) with which cf. our § 47 : 3.

11. Cf. *Pyramid Texts*, 703-704 : "King Atōti is Thou, Thou art King Atōti ; . . . Thou shinest in King Atōti and King Atōti shines in Thee." This kind of identification of the initiate with God is found throughout Egyptian religious texts.

12. Cf. *Gal.* 6 : 15 and 2 *Cor.* 5 : 17.

13. Cf. § 24. The initiate himself, like God, is now omnipresent. This state of "Omnidentity" or "Cosmic

Consciousness" is well described in the books of Dr. Bucke and Dr. Winslow Hall; it is known to many who have never heard of others sharing their experience. Cf. Blackwood, *op. cit.*, p. 134, " Dispersed about the whole Earth I felt, deliciously extended and alive," and, *idem*, p. 70, " The boundaries of his personality were enormously extending. . . . It was as though his self were passing outwards into hundreds of thousands and becoming countless as the sand. He was everywhere; in everything, shining, singing, dancing." Tennyson writes: " The individuality itself seemed to dissolve and fade away into boundless being. . . where death was an almost laughable impossibility, the loss of personality. . . seeming no extinction but the only true life. . . . The state is utterly beyond words." Edward Carpenter, *Towards Democracy*, " . . . a sense that one is those objects and things and persons that one perceives, and even that one is the whole universe." This Advaita experience is well described in the *Ashtāvakra Gita*. Cf. also the note 48 on Chapter 5 of this book.

14. Cf. Fr. Germanus, C. P., in his *Life of (St) Gemma Galgani*, pp. 224-5, and St. Teresa, *Interior Castle*, 5 : 93, " In fact it has died entirely to this world, to live more truly than ever in God."

15. Cf. *Pyramid Texts*, 763, " Thy soul stands among the gods, among the glorious ones ", and St. John of the Cross, *The Dark Night of the Soul*, 2 : 20, " (In) the beatific vision. . . (the) soul becomes wholly assimilated unto God."

16. Cf. Clement Alex. *Exx. ex Theodote*, 80, "Him whom Christ brings to rebirth He changes into Life, into the Ogdoad," and the Magic Pap. Leyden, Pap. W. 139 : 45 and 141 : 5.

17. Cf. Philostratus, *Life of Apollonius of Tyana*, 1 : 1 : "It would have been hard for them to keep silence, had they not first learned that it was just this silence which spoke to them." As in India, all Western Mysteries involved secrecy. An ancient Jewish complaint against Jesus was that he "burned his food in public", *i.e.*, betrayed the hidden things.

18. Cf. *Deut.* 32 : 1, *Isa.* 1 : 2, and Philo, *in Flaccum*, 14 : 123 : also the *Pyramid Texts*, 2063-4, "The sky burns for thee, and the earth shakes because of thee before the Divine Birth ; when the two mountains separate, the God comes into being, the God takes possession of his body."

19. Cf. § 45 : 2. Life and Light are similarly placed together in *Jn.* 1 : 4 and in most Gnōstic and Mandaean systems.

20. Cf. Sarapion of Thmuis, *Eucharistic Prayer*, (A.D. 350) : "The Lord Jesus and Holy Spirit shall speak in us and hymn Thee through us," and St. Gemma Galgani in Fr. Germanus's *Life*, p. 221, "When we praise Thee, O Lord, it is not we, it is Thou who praisest Thyself in Thyself." See also *1 Cor.* 1 : 24.

21. Cf. *Gita*, 10 : 20, "I am the beginning, middle and end of all things." Cf. also Heraclitus, "From all, one ; and from one, all," and Marcus Aurelius, 4 : 23.

"From thee all, in thee all, unto thee all," speaking of Nature. Cf. also *Rom.* 11 : 36 and *1 Cor.* 8 : 6.

22. Cf. *Pyramid Texts*, 1461, "Thy body is in King Piōpi, O Rē'; preserve alive Thy body in King Piōpi, O Rē'."

23. The Will of God and the All (*i.e.* universe) are identical and inseparable. Cf. §§ 23 : 9 and 24 : 4, also Clement Alex., *Paed.* 1 : 6 : 37, "His Will is work, and this is named Universe."

24. This is the cry of the Triumphant Christ, "It is finished!" Cf. Blackwood, *op. cit.*, p. 199 : "He saw himself . . . whole; he knew himself divine."

25. It is the Divine "Word" or "Reason" (logos) which is implanted by God in the sea of man's mind to make it fruitful; cf. § 16 : 2, also *1 Pet.* 2 : 5 establishing a universal Christian practice in prayer. Cf. also Serapion of Thmuis, (in *Texte und Ut. N.F. II.* 3b, p. 22) : "For the Father's Will is His Word. . . . While the Word dwells apart in the Mind, then there is silence. But when the Mind wills to shine upon the All, the Word comes forth to illuminate the All." Thus every true and enlightening saying is a part, an expression of the eternal Word of God.

26. Cf. *Mt.* 3 : 8 and *1 Jn.* 3 : 9 and *Jn.* 15 : 5, a Jewish metaphor, taking virtue to be the fruit of gnōsis, while Plato held it to be a cause of gnōsis. Both are true; without virtue and purity we cannot know God; nor can we know and love God without producing purity and virtue in ourselves.

27. Cf. § 4 : 2, and the Oxyrhynchus logion. "(try then) to know yourselves, and you shall know you are sons of the (Heavenly) Father," also Mother Julian, *op. cit.*, p. 46, "And when we truly and clearly see and know what our self is, then shall we truly and clearly see and know our Lord God in fullness of joy."

28. Cf. the 2nd c. Rabbi Akiba, in *Pirqe Abōth*: "Silence is a fence for wisdom," and the *Chaldaean Oracles*, 2 : 64 : "Keep silence, thou who art admitted to the sacred rites," (Kroll 55) and the "Hymn of Jesus" in the *Acts of John*, "Keep silence on My mysteries."

29. Cf. *The Book of the Twelve Bèguines*, 11, "This Light and this Vision give to the contemplating spirit a conscious certainty that she seeth God, so far as man may see Him in this mortal life."

30. Cf. §§ 8 : 3 and 18 : 4, also *The Book of the Twelve Béguines*, 11, "And so, in like manner, if thou followest the bright rays that stream from the Face of God upon thy clear gaze, they will lead thee into the source of thy created being, wherein thou shalt find no other thing but God alone."

31. This simile is used also in Plato's *Ion*, 533 D, Plutarch, *On Isis and Osiris*, in the *Naassene Document*, and in many mystic books.

32. Cf. Porphyry, *ad Marcellam*, 14 : "You must avoid all body-lovers as atheist and polluted."

33. Cf. *The Book of the Resurrection of Jesus the Christ*, p. 14 A, "Do not let this book come into the hands of any man who is an unbeliever or a heretic.

... Reveal them not to any impure man, but keep them safely." Also Dionysius, *To Titus*, says: "Things all holy are not within the reach of the profane, but are manifested to those who are genuine lovers of piety," and *The Apocryphon of John* has: "All those who are in the heavenly paradise are sealed with silence."

34. Cf. PS 22 : 1, "The pious are not numerous, however; nay, they are very few, so that they may be counted even in the world," and *Gita*, 7 : 3, "Among thousands of men scarce one strives for perfection; of the successful strivers scarce one knows Me in essence," and Shinran Shonin, in *Buddhist Psalms*, 208, "Not one man is there of thousands who may be born into the Land of Purity.... There is not even one among tens of thousands who may enter it." Cf. also Fr. Lallemant, *op. cit.* 4 : 2 : 2 : 2, "There are hardly any persons who constantly hold themselves in God's paths;" and this is why Dvagpo Lharje says in his *Precious Rosary*, 21 : 4 : "For a religious devotee to preach the Doctrine to the multitude instead of meditating upon it in solitude is a grievous mistake."

SOURCES OF "THE GOSPEL OF HERMES"

A. Corpus Hermeticum (CH)

CH 1. (*Poimandres*) : *1 in GH 1 : 1, **2-3 in GH 1 : 1, *4 in GH 1 : 2, *5 in GH 1 : 3, *6 in GH 2 : 1, *7 in GH 2 : 2, *8 in GH 2 : 3, *9 in GH 2 : 4, *10 in GH 2 : 4, *11 in GH 2 : 5, *12 in GH 3 : 1, *13 in GH 3 : 1-2, *14 in 3 : 3, *15 in 3 : 4, **16-17 in 3 : 5, *18 in 4 : 1, *19 in 4 : 2, *20 in 4 : 3, *21 in 4 : 4-5, *22 in 5 : 1-2, *23 in 5 : 3, *24 in 6 : 1, *25 in 6 : 2, *26 in 6 : 3-4, *27 in 8 : 1-2, *28 in 8 : 3, *29 in 8 : 4, *30 in 7 : 1, *31 in 7 : 2-3, and *32 in GH 7 : 2

CH 2. Introduction to the Gnosis of the Nature of All Things : *4 in GH 13 : 1, *10 in 19 : 1, *11 in 19 : 2, *12 in 19 : 3 and 22 : 4, *13 in 22 : 4, *14 in 10 : 2 and 22 : 4, * 15 in 10 : 2, *16 in 10 : 2-3, and *17 in GH 10 : 1

CH 3. The Sacred Sermon : *1 in GH 16 : 1-2, *2 and *3 in 16 : 3, *3 in 17 : 2 and 25 : 1, *4 in GH 25 : 3

CH. 4. The Chalice, or the Oneness : *1 in GH 37 : 1, *2 in 37 : 1-2, *3 in 37 : 2, *4 in 37 : 3-4, *5 in 37 : 4, *6 in 37 : 5 and 31 : 2, *7 in 31 : 5, *8 in 31 : 1 and 4, *9 in 31 : 3-4, *10 in 16 : 1 and *11 in 11 : 2 and 49 : 1

Footnote : On the following pages, please read * as § before paragraph numbers.

SOURCES OF "THE GOSPEL OF HERMES" 237

CH 5. (Unmanifest God Most Manifest) : **1* in GH 23 : 1, **2* in 23 : 1-3, **3* in 23 : 4, **5* in 23 : 5, ***6-7* in 23 : 6, **8* in 23 : 7, **9* in 23 : 7-8, **10* in GH 23 : 9 and 24 : 1 and **11* in 24 : 2-4

CH 6. (Good is in God Alone) : **1* in GH 11 : 1-2, **2* in 11 : 2-3, **3* in 11 : 3-4, **4* in 11 : 5 and 12 : 1, **5* in 12 : 2-3, **6* in 11 : 4 and 12 : 3

CH 7. (Ignorance of God is the Greatest Evil) : **1* in GH 8 : 2-3, **2* in 8 : 3 and 31 : 1, and **3* in 31 : 1

CH 8. (Nothing is Destroyed) : **1* in GH 20 : 4, **2* in 15 : 1, **5* in 10 : 1 and 17 : 2

CH 9. On Thought and Feeling : **1-3* in GH 18 : 1, **4* in 39 : 1-2, **5* in 22 : 3, **6* in 18 : 2, **8* in 15 : 1, **9* in 18 : 1 and 3, **10* in GH 18 : 4

CH 10. The Key : **2* in 14 : 4. **3* in 13 : 1 and 14 : 4, **4* in 14 : 4, and 41 : 4, **5* in 41 : 4-5, **6* in 41 : 5, **7* in 29 : 2, **8* in 29 : 12, ***9-10* in 29 : 3, **12, 14* in 17 : 1, **15* in 29 : 10-11, **16, 18* in 27 : 4, **19* in 27 : 3 and 32 : 1, **20* in 32 : 2, **21* in 32 : 2 and 38 : 2, **22-23* in 29 : 9, **24-25* in 36 : 3

CH 11. Clear Mind, or Mind to Hermes : **2* in 15 : 1, **3* in 15 : 2, **4* in 15 : 3, **5* in 22 : 3, **6* in 17 : 2 and 21 : 1, **7* in 21 : 1-2, **8* in 21 : 2-3, **9* in 21 : 3 ***11-12* in 21 : 4, **13* in 21 : 4 and 22 : 1, **14* in 22 : 2 and 27 : 2, **15* in 27 : 2, **16* in 13 : 2, **17* in 22 : 1, **18* in 13 : 1 and 42 : 1, **19* in 13 : 1 and 42 : 1, **20* in 42 : 2-3, **21* in 42 : 4-5 and **22* in 24 : 4

CH 12. On the Human Mind : and : On Life : **1* in GH 18 : 1 and 36 : 2, **3-4* in 29 : 4, **5* in 30 : 4, **8* in 27 : 3, **10* in 29 : 4, **11* in 27 : 4, **12* in 36 : 4, **15* in 20 : 3, *16 in 20 : 3 and 27 : 1, *19 in 27 : 3, *21 in 20 : 1, *22 in 20 : 2, *23 in 20 : 2 and 21 : 4

CH 13. *Hidden Teaching in the Mountain*: *1 in GH 44 : 1, *2 in 44 : 2, **3-4 in 41 : 2, *6 in 41 : 2, *7 in 45 : 1, *9 in 45 : 2 and 10, *11 in 45 : 2-3, **12-13 in 45 : 3, *15 in 46 : 1-2, *16 in 46 : 2, *17 in 47 : 1-2, *18 in 47 : 2-4, *19 in 47 : 4-5, *20 in 47 : 5 and 48 : 1, *21 in 48 : 1-3, and *22 in 48 : 4

CH 14. *A letter to Asclepius*; *3 in 14 : 4, *4 in 10 : 1 and 3, *5 in 14 : 3, *7 in 14 ; 3, 17 : 2 and 22 : 3

CH 16. *Asclepius to King Ammon*: *3 in GH 14 : 3, *7 and 8 in 16 : 4, *9 in 27 : 1, *11 in 29 : 13, **13-14 in 30 : 2, **15-16 in 30 : 2-3, *17 in 18 : 3, and *18 in 15 : 1

CH 18. (*The Encomium of Kings*): *3 in 18 : 3, *10 in 33 : 2, **12-13 in 38 : 6, *14 in 29 : 9, **15-16 in 33 : 2

B. The Perfect Sermon (PS)

*1 in GH 9 : 1, *3 in 41 : 1, *6 in 36 : 5-6, *8 in 36 : 1 and 5, *9 in 17 : 2 and 38 : 3 and 5, *10 in 17 : 2, *11 in 38 : 3 and 40 : 6, *12 in 18 : 4, 27 : 5, 28 : 5 and 38 : 5, *13 in 38 : 4, *14 in 16 : 1-2 and 38 : 5, *19 in 18 : 4 and 41 : 1, *20 in 9 : 3-4, *21 in 26 : 1, *22 in 29 : 9, *24 in 34 : 1-4, *25 in 34 : 4-8, *26 in 34 : 8 and 35 : 1-2, *27 in 27 : 1 and 5, *28 in   1-2, *29 in 28 : 3-5, *31 in 14 : 1-2, *32 in 14 : 2, 18 : 4 and 49 : 2, *33 in 19 ; 1-2, *34 in 20 : 1-2, *35 in 25 ; 1 and *41 in GH 43 : 1-5

SOURCES OF "THE GOSPEL OF HERMES" 239

C. Kore Kosmou (World-Virgin) (KK)=St. 23

*4 in GH 16 ; 7, *9 in 16 : 6, *10 in 16 : 7, *16 in 29 : 2, *27 in 16 ; 7, *29 in 16 : 7, *32 in 44 : 2, *51 in 17 : 2, *62 in 29 : 13, and *64 in 44 : 2

D. Other Extracts from Stobaeus (St)

St. 1. Hermes to Tat (On God's Ineffability): **1-2 in GH 9 : 2

St. 2a. (On Truth): **6-8 in GH 40 : 2, *9 in 40 : 2-3, **10-11 in 40 : 3, **12-13 and 16 in GH 13 : 2

St. 2b. (On Devotion and Philosophy): *2 in 38 : 1, *3 in 38 : 1-2, *4 in 38 : 2, and **5-6 and 8 in 40 : 7

St. 6. On the (Decans and) Stars: **18-19 in GH 40 : 4

St. 7. (On Justice): *3 in GH 30 : 1

St. 8. (On Fate and Providence): *5 in 30 : 1

St. 11. (The Opposites): *2 (15) in GH 45 : 1, *4 in 39 : 1 and 49 : 2, *5 in 27 : 5

St. 12-14. (On Providence and Fate) in GH 30 : 4-5:

St. 15. (On Soul): **3-4 in 25 : 1, *6 in 25 : 3

St. 16 (On Soul): *1 in GH 29 : 1

St. 18. (On the Power of Choice): **3-4 in GH 30 : 6

St. 20. (On Soul): *1 in GH 29 : 1, **5-7 in 25 : 2

St. 24. (Second Book of Kore Kosmou ?): *3 in GH 33 : 1, *4 in 33 : 1 and 29 : 13, *8 in 29 : 2

St. 25. (Sermon of Isis to Horus): *2 in GH 44 : 2, *4 in 25 : 3 and 36 : 2, ** 5-8 in 29 : 7, *9 in 29 : 5, ** 10-11 and 13 in 29 : 5

St. 26. (On Incarnation): **1* in GH 29 : 6, **2* in 29 : 8, **4* in 32 ; 3

E. Fragments and Citations (F)

F 1 in GH 28 : 1, *F 3* in 9 : 4, *F 7 and 15* in 40 : 5, *F 17* in 29 : 3, *F 21* in 30 : 4, *F 23* in 49 : 2, *F 25* in 41 : 3, *F 27 and 30* in 16 : 2, *F 31-32* in 16 : 4-5, and *F 33* in GH 16 : 4.

INDEX

ADORATION of God, 5-8, 17, 20, 21, 23, 28, 33-35, 38, 43, 46-48
Aeon, (see Eternity)
Air, 1, 5, 23, 29, 34, 36, 37, 45
Ammon, 9
Angels, evil, 34, good, 29
Animals, 2, 29, 32, 38, 42, 45
Apostleship, 6-8, 37
Artist, 23, 38
Asceticism, 31, 37, 40, 44
Asclepius, 9, 43
Attention, 9, 41, 44, 49
Authority, 7, 30, 33, 42, 46
Avenging Spirit, 5

BAD Deeds, 28
Baptism, 37
Births, 4, 11, 13, 23, 25, 29, 30, 33, 41, 42, 44, 45, 48
Blood, 34
Boat swept away, 8
Bodiless, the, 13, 19, 23, 29, 31, 45
BODY, formation of, 25; prison for soul, 4, 25, 37, 40, 42, 45, but not for child's, 29; dropped at death, 6, 27, 28; full of soul, 15; force of God, 20; instrument of feeling, 29; mind has fiery, 27; seat of sex, 29; fruit of bad actions, 29, 30, 32; cannot see God, 40, 41; to be renounced, 31, 42; God has, 37
Breath, 1, 3, 16, 22, 25, 37

CAGE, 29
Chain of births and deaths, 29
Chalice of Mind, 37
Change, 1, 11, 13, 14, 22, 25, 27, 29, 39-41, 45
Chaos, 1
Charioteer, 16
Chief Spirit, 28
Choice, 8, 30, 31, 42
Choral Dance, 29, 36

Conflict, Inner, 40
Confusion, 34, 35
Consort, 11, 22
Covenant, 4
Creative Mind, 2
Creatures, 2, 22
Cruelty, 34

DARKNESS, 1, 4, 8, 16, 28, 34, 36
Death, 4-6, 8, 20, 27-30, 34, 36, 38, 42
Deification, 6, 31, 33, 41, 43-45, 47
Destiny, 2, 4, 25, 28, 30
Devil, no, 11
Devotee, 27, 28, 34, 38, 39
Devotion, 8, 12, 27, 28, 31, 34, 38, 39
Doctor, 29
Doctrine, 9, 18, 41, 44, 49
Drunkenness, 8

EARTH, 5. 16, 21, 23, 27, 28, 33, 34, 36, 38, 40, 42, 45
Ecstasy, 1, 7, 36, 41
Egypt, 34
Eighth Sphere, 6, 46
Elements, 1, 2, 16, 19, 25, 27, 36, 38, 42
Error, 8, 28-30, 35
Eternity, 14, 15. 20, 28, 42, 47
Eyes, of body, 7, 21, 23, 28, 41, 45, of heart or mind, 8, 23, 31, 41, 47, 44

FAITH, 18, 28, 37, 42
Falling away from God, 7, 30, 38, 43
Fame, 25
Father, the, 4, 7, 9, 10, 14, 15, 20, 23, 28, 29, 35, 38, 43, 47, 48
Feeling, 18, 26-29, 45
Few are wise, 38, 49
Fire, 1, 3, 16, 21, 23, 27, 32, 37, 41, 47
Foreigners, 33, 34
Forgetfulness, 25, 29, 38, 41
Forgiveness, 29, 38

GARDENER, 18
Gnōsis, 1, 6-8. 11, 12, 29-31, 37-39, 41, 43, 45, 47
GOD: *His Nature* : Holy 7; no evil in, 17, 31 ; The One and All, 9, 14, 21, 23, 28, 31, 37, 38, 41, 43, 47 ; includes all, 11, 13, 19, 20, 23, 24, 42, 43 ; is eye of mind, 47 ; is Mind, 2 ; feels and thinks, 18 ; greater than names, 9, 23 ; not taught by words, 29, 31 ; wills to be known, 7, 8, 23, 28, 29 ; and to share creation, 37 ; is revealed by bodies, 13, 22, 23, 42 ;

INDEX   243

    pervades all, 20, 22, 23 and is all, 18, 20, 22, 24 ; source of all, 10, 11, 15, 16, 20, 22, 23 ; origin and goal, 47 ;
    His Qualities : the Good, 10-14, 24, 28, 35, 38, 40, 43, 47 ; the Beautiful, 12, 41 ; Unmanifest, 23 ; Invisible, 23, 31, 37 ; Unimaginable, 23 ; Ineffable, 9, 31 ; beyond all praise, 7, 38 ; Intangible, 19, 37 ; Formless, 13, 31 ; Infinite, 31 ; Eternal, 16, 24, 31, 37 ; Incorruptible, 20 ; Omnipotent, 28 ; Omnipresent, 1, 20, 24, 28 ; Omniscient, 28 ; Incomparable, 22 ; Impassive, 19 ; Inerrant, 19 ; Self-embracing, 19 ; Steady, 14, 23, 43 ; Conceivable, 40 ; Perceptible, 1, 2, 14, 40 ;
    His Activities : Cause of Life, 21, 22 ; Creates through Will and Word, 2, 13, 37 ; Makes all, 14, 16, 21-23, 36 ; gives all, 10, 24 ; moves all, 14, 23, 43 ; protects all, 18, 29 ; ever-working, 22, 23 ; opposes error, 33 ; grants vision, and Divine Mind, 16, 37, 40 ; reminds Race of Rebirth, 37, 44 ; steadies soul, 45 ; leads soul, 36 ; only work is creation, 22, 34, 38 ; settles orbits, 2, 23, 25 ;
    Relation with Creatures : Inseparable from universe, 14, 20, 22 ; all depend on Him, 17 ; all obey Him, 17 ; He loves creation, 3, 36 ; man should adore Him, 17 ; friend of man, 27, 30 ; He defends His devotee, 28 ; is just to all, 28 ; love for Him, 29, 38 ; He shows Himself to His lovers, 28, 43 ; who desire to see Him, 23 ; how to know Him, 42 ; His two Gifts, 36 ; His Law, 29, 30, 32, 33 ; prayer to Him 7, 24, 43, 47, 48.
Godlessness, 29
Gods, the, 10, 16, 20, 25, 29 (angels), 30, 33, 34, 36, 38, 44
Good, the, 11, 12, 19, 24, 29, 31, 37, 38, 40, 42-45, 47
Good Deeds, 22, 34, 38
Good Spirit, the, 36
Grace, 3, 7, 23, 41, 43, 45

HARMONY, 3, 4, 6, 25, 29, 31, 36, 38
Heart, 31, 43, 49
Heaven, or Sky, 16, 17, 21, 23, 28, 34, 36, 38, 41, 42, 45, 47
Hell, 5, 28, 29
Hermes, 9, 30, 43, 44, 47, 48

IGNORANCE, 4, 8, 23, 27, 29, 37, 42
Illusion, 11, 12, 44
Image, 17, 23, 33, 34, 36, 42, 49
Imagination, 23
Immortality, 3, 8, 15, 28, 29, 34, 36, 41
Immortals, 21, 36, 37, 40, 42, 44
Impiety, 10, 23, 29, 32, 34, 43
Impulses, 29
Incense, 43
Incredulity, (see Mockery)

Indian, 34
Infant, 29, 38

JOY, 6, 43, 45, 47, 48
Judgment, 27, 28
Justice, 28-30

KINGLY souls, 29, 33

LABOUR, 38
Life, 2, 6, 7, 15, 18, 21, 22, 25, 27, 29, 34, 38, 40, 42, 43, 45, 47
Light, 1, 2, 7, 8, 21, 22, 28, 34, 41, 43, 45, 47
Love-charm, 29

MAGNET, 49
Maker, the, 9, 10, 13, 14, 21-23, 29, 35-38, 47
Male-female, 2, 3, 29
MAN : is Son of God, 3, 4, and His image, 3, 17 ; kindred to the gods, 29, 36 ; is destined ruler of creation, 3 ; honourable, 36 and crown of creation, 36 ; has mighty powers, 36, 42 ; best of creatures, 17, 27 ; can unite with God, 6, 27, 29 ; some are divine, 36 ; can be reborn as god, 45 ; alone can worship God, 38 ; is everywhere, 36 ; a link in chain of love, 36 ; why he was made, 36 ; his work, 17, 28, 37 ; God's Man, 7, 47 ; is known by God, 29 ; desires to create, 3 ; wills to look down, 3 ; is caught by Nature in body, 3, 45 ; becomes soul-mind, 3 ; is under destiny, 30 ; twofold in nature, 3, 40 ; is evil, 17 ; delights in evil 27 ; uses fire and water, 47 ; liable to err, 30 ; few are Gnostics, 30, 38, 49 ; has many activities, 21 ; his lot on earth, 25.
Materiality, source of evil, 11, 12, 22, 29
Matter, 2, 15, 16, 20, 28, 40, 45
Memory, 32, 44
Merging into God, 6, 28
Mind, Human, 3, 15, 17, 18, 22, 23, 26, 28-30, 32, 34, 36-38, 41, 43, 47, 48
MIND : SUPREME : is the First God, 2, 24, 48 ; is in Him, 45 ; as His Power, 27 ; is from His Being, 36, and inseparate from Him, 34 ; is Father of the Word, 2 ; Life and Light, 2-4, 7 ; Space, 19 ; is Poimandres, 7, 46 ; continuous with Human Mind, 18 ; wills creation of animals, 2 ; falls in love with Man, 3 ; enters pious souls, 5, 31, 38, 45 ; teaches men to know God, 1, 43 ; guides his speech, 47 ; protects devotees, 5 ; devotee born again in, 41 ; devotee sees all in, 45 ; and merges in, 27, 28 ; is God in men, 36 ; and prize to aim at, 37 ; this is Religion of, 34
Mockery, 8, 18, 27, 34, 39, 49
Model, 25, 32

Moistness, 1, 4
Moon, 21, 23, 29
Mortals, 3, 21, 23, 27, 30, 36, 37, 40
Mountain, 44
Muses, 38
Music, 38
Mysteries, 49

NAME, 9, 23, 33, 40, 43
Nature, 2, 3, 7, 14, 16, 25, 26, 29, 30, 32, 34-36, 38, 40, 47
Necessity, 16, 29, 30, 40
Nurse, 38

OFFERINGS, 7, 23, 47, 48
Ogdoad, 6, 46
Oil, 29
Olympus, 29
Orbits, 2, 23, 25, 34

PASSIONS, 5, 11, 27, 29, 30, 34, 37
Patience, 39
Peace, 33, 47
Persecution, 34, 39
Philosophy, 38, 41
Plain of Truth, 7, 44
Planes, 27, 29, 33
Pleasure, 29, 31, 37
Poimandres, 1, 2, 4, 6, 7, 46
Possession, 30
Possessions, 40
Powers, 2, 6, 7, 45-47
Prayer, 7, 23, 43
Preaching, 8, 37
Processions, 31
Providence, 29, 30
Punishment, 28, 29, 32-34
Purgation, 6, 27, 35, 45, 46
Purpose of creation, 14, 16, 22, 35, 36

RACE, the, 7, 8, 44
Rational part of soul, 30
Ray of God, 23, 28, 30, 36
Real, the, 13, 40, 48
Reason, 28, 30, 38, 45, 47
Rebirth, 44-46, 48
Reincarnation, 29, 32
Religion, 34
Renewal, 27, 35

Repentance, 8
Reverence, 9, 21, 28, 29, 34, 38, 40
Rivers, 23, 34

SALVATION, 8, 29, 30, 43, 47
Sanctuary, 9, 34, 43
Scythian, 34
Sea, 16, 23, 34, 36, 42
Seed, 18, 25, 43, 44
Self, the, 19, 41
Senses, the, 1, 4-6, 21, 41, 45
Seven Men, the, 3
Seven Rulers, the, 2, 3, 16
Sexes, 4, 26, 29
Silence, 7, 9, 29, 34, 41, 42, 44-49
Similarities, 39, 42
Sin-stains, 28, 29
Skill, 23, 32, 38
Sleep, 1, 7, 8, 41, 42
Soaring up, 23, 41, 42
Soul, 15, 21, 25, 27-30, 32, 34, 38, 40-43, 47, 48
Speech, 18, 29, 36, 37, 42
Spirits, 18, 28-30
Spiritual Guide, the, 8, 36, 44
Stars, 21, 23, 25, 28, 30, 34
Statue and Picture, 23
Storms, 28
Straight Path, the, 42
" Striking the Tent ", 46
Sun, 16, 23, 28, 30, 36, 41
Suppliant, 44

TAT, 9, 43-48
Temple, 8
Tending the earth, 17, 28, 36, 38, 40
Thought, 18, 19, 22, 23, 38, 42, 44
Time, 14, 15, 35, 37, 42
Tombs, 34
Torrent, 8, 41
Trees, 47
Truth, 18, 22, 25, 28, 31, 38, 40, 45

UNBELIEF, 28, 31
Universal Soul, 29
UNIVERSE: derived from Light, 2; as God's son, 14, 15, and image, 17, 23, 40; a divine creature, 20, 37, and visible god, 36; inseparable from God, 14, 23, exists only in Him, 22, 42; is eternal and deathless, 15, 20, though ever changing, 27;

INDEX 247

full of life, 17, 20; and light, 21; is wholly full, 18; was made by a word at God's Will, 37; partly good, 11, 17; yet full of evil, 11; all-formed, 13; on the whole good, 34; is body of God, 37; and loved by Him, 36; all is good in His sight, 36; is His instrument, 18; to be revered, 17, 34; though understood only by God, 20; feels and also thinks, 18; generous in gifts, 34; perfected by man, 36; ruled by Sun, 16; nothing outside it, 42; Egypt is its shrine, 34; no longer admired, 34; grows old, 34; restored by God, 35; its beauty 21.
Unseen, 27, 31

VICES, 28, 40
Virtue, 40, 48
Virtuous Men, 5, 10, 23, 28, 34
Vision, 1, 2, 7, 23, 30, 37, 40, 41, 44, 49

WATER, 1-3, 5, 8, 16, 29, 37, 45, 47
Waves, 28, 34
Way Down, the, 29
Way Up, the, 6, 12, 27-29, 31, 36, 40, 42, 49
Weariness, 34, 38
Wicked Men, 5, 28, 29, 34
Will, 2, 14, 16, 18, 20, 23, 34-38, 44, 45, 47, 48
Winds, 28, 29, 47
Womb, 23, 25, 42, 43, 45
Word, 1, 2, 16, 37, 48

ZONES, 6

BOOKS ON THE HERMETICA

F. Patricius (Card. Francesco Patrizzi) : in Nove de universis philosophia (Ferrara, 1591); *Gustav Parthey*, Hermetis Trismegisti Poemander (Berlin, 1854); *Dr. Everard*, The Divine Pymander of Hermes Mercurius Trismegistus (London, 1650) : *L. Ménard*, Etude sur l'Origine des livres hermétiques et translation d'Hermés Trismegistus (Paris, 1866) ; *R. Pietschmann*, Hermes Trismegistos nach ägyptisch-griechisch-orientalisch überlieferungen (Leipzig, 1875) ; *Chambers* : Hermes Trismegistus ; *R. Reitzenstein* (R), Poimandres, in Studien zur griechisch-ägyptischen und frühchristlichen Literatur, (Leipzig, 1904) ; *G. R. S. Mead* (M), Thrice Greatest Hermes (London 1906) ; *W. Scott* (S), Hermetica (Oxford, 1924) ; F. Braüninger, Untersuchungen zu den Schriften des Hermes Trismegistos (Gräfenhainigen, 1926).

OTHER BOOKS FOR STUDY

K. Narayansvami Aiyar, Thirty Minor Upanishads ; *Anonymous*, Ashtavakra Gita, The Acts of John ; *Rev. H. N. Bate*, The Sibylline Oracles ; *Algernon Blackwood*, The Centaur ; *Patrick Boylan*, Thoth, the Hermes of Egypt ; *Dr. James H. Breasted*, The Development of Religion and Thought in

BOOKS ON THE HERMETICA

Ancient Egypt: *Dr. R. M. Bucke,* Cosmic Consciousness; *Sir E. A. Wallis Budge,* Coptic Apocrypha in the Dialect of Upper Egypt; *Edward Carpenter,* The Drama of Love and Death; *H. Carrington and Meader,* Death: Its Causes and Phenomena; *Cicero,* de Natura Deorum; *Clemens Alexandrinus,* Stromata: *Dr. Albrecht Dietrich,* Abraxas; *Dionysius the Areopagite,* The Divine Names, Mystic Theology; *Fr. Germanus, C. P.,* The Life of (St.) Gemma Galgani; *F. Ll. Griffith,* Stories of the High Priests of Memphis; *Dr. W. Winslow Hall,* Recorded Illuminates; *Hippolytus,* The Refutation of All Heresies (sp. Naassene Attis-Document, Simon's Great Announcement, and the Gospel Myth) (trans: Rev. J. H. Macmahon); *Dr. R. E. Hume,* The Thirteen Principal Upanishads; *Irenaeus of Lyons,* Against Heresies (trans: Rev. John Keble); *Richard Jeffreys,* The Story of my Heart; *St. John of the Cross,* The Ascent of Mount Carmel, The Spiritual Canticle; *Mother Julian of Norwich,* Revelations of Divine Love; *Lactantius,* de Opif. Dei; *Fr. Lallemant, S. J.,* Spiritual Doctrine; *Lamplugh,* The Gnosis of the Light; *Sarma K. Lakshman,* Guru-Ramana-Vachana-Mala; *Mark Lidzbarski,* das Johnnesbuch der Mandäer; *G. R. S. Mead,* Chaldaean Oracles, Hymn of Jesus, The Hymn of the Robe of Glory, Fragments of a Faith Forgotten, Pistis Sophia; *Dmitry Merejkowsky,* La Mort des Dieux; *Swami Nikhilananda,* Dṛg Dṛs'ya Viveka; *Sir W. M. Flinders Petrie, F.R.S.,* Personal Religion in Egypt before Christianity; *Philo Iudaeus,* de Vita Contemplativā; *Plato,* Phaedo, Republic,

Timaeus; *Plotinus*, The Enneads; *Plutarch*, On Isis and Osiris; *Fr. A. Poulain, S. J.*, The Graces of Interior Prayer; *Sri Sankaracharya*, Viveka Chudāmani; *Fr. G. B. Scaramelli, S. J.*, Mystical Theology; *Emanuel Swedenborg*, Heaven and Hell; *Carl Schmidt*. Koptisch-Gnostische Schriften, I; *St. Teresa of Avila*, Life, The Interior Castle; *Evelyn Underhill*, Mysticism; *Dr. Evans-Wentz*, Tibetan Yoga and Secret Doctrines.

OTHER BOOKS REFERRED TO

Hebrew: Genesis, Exodus, Deuteronomy, 2 Kings, Psalms, Proverbs, Isaiah, Jeremiah, Ezekiel, Daniel, Wisdom, Ecclesiasticus, 1 and 2 Enoch, Testament of Benjamin, Apocalypse of Abraham, Apocalypse of Baruch; *Philo*, Quod Deus Im., de Cherubim, in Flaccum, de Somn., Leg. Alleg., de Providen.; Pirqe Aboth (Rabbi Akiba).

Classical: *Dr. Robert Eisler*, Orpheus the Fisher, Weltenmantel und Himmelzelt: *Porphyry*, Vita Plotini, de Antro, ad Marcellam; *Abammon*, Responses; *Proclus*, Hymn to the Transcendent; *Firmicus*, Math., *L. Apuleius*, The Golden Ass; *Plutarch*, Fragmenta, Fac. in orbe lunae; Hymn of Isis at Kumae; *Boethius*, Philosophic Consolations; *Cornelius Labeo; Diodorus; Seneca*, Consol. ad Marc.; *Marcus Aurelius*; *Homer*, Iliad, Odyssey; *Philostratus*, Apollonius Tyaneus.

Christian: Scriptural: Matthew, Mark, Luke, John, Romans, 1 and 2 Corinthians, Galatians, Ephesians,

Philippians, Colossians, Hebrews, 1 Peter, 1 John, Revelations; *Gospels of* Eve, Mary, Thomas, the Egyptians; Apocalypse of Elias, 2. Esdras, Odes of Solomon, Martyrdom of Peter, The Repose of John, The Apocryphon of John, The Book of the Resurrection of Jesus the Christ;

Fathers: *Justin*, Apologies; Epitaph of Bishop Aberkios, *Clemens Alexandrinus*, Fragments, Paed.; Oxyrhynchus Logia Iesou; *Methodius*, con. Porphyrium (Bonnwetsch); *Epiphanius* on the Heretics; *Arnobius*, adv. Nationes; *Origen*, de Principiis, contra Celsum; Codex Theodosianus; *Cyprian*; *St. Augustine*, City of God, Confessions; *Macarius*, Homilies; *Palladius*, The Paradise of the Holy Fathers (trans: Budge); *St. Ambrose*, Hymns; *St. Thomas Aquinas*, Hymns; *Sarapion of Thmuis*, Eucharistic Prayer; *Dionysius*, To Titus; The Mysteries of John the Apostle.

Mystical: *Anonymous*, Christ in You; *J. Macbeth Bain*, The Christ of the Holy Graal; *St. Bernard*, On the Love of God; *Ven. Louis de Blois*, Writings; *St. Bonaventura*, The Goad of Divine Love; *St. Catherine of Siena*, Dialogues; *Fr. de Caussade*, S. J., Abandon, Lettres; *Fr. G. M. Dupont*, S. J., Foundations for a Devotion to the Blessed Trinity; *St. Francis de Sales*, Divine Love; *Dean Inge*, Personal Idealism and Mysticism; *St. John of the Cross*, The Dark Night of the Soul, The Living Flame of Love, Minor Prose Writings; *Abbé Monnin*, The Spirit of the Curé d'Ars; *Miguel de Molinos*, The Spiritual Guide; *Fr. A. Poulain*, S. J., The Spiritual Journals of Lucie

Christine; *John Ruysbroeck*, Flowers of a Mystic Garden; *Henry Suso*, Life; *Dr. John Tauler*, The Inner Way; *St. Teresa of Avila*, The Way of Perfection, Relations; *St. Thérèse de Lisieux*, A Little White Flower; *Algar Thorold*, Catholic Mysticism.

Other: *Fr. Tanquerey*, Synopsis Theologiae Dogmaticae; *Fr. Dominic Barberi*; *Tennyson*, Poems (The Passing of Arthur, The Higher Pantheism); *Wordsworth*, Poems (Ode on Intimations of Immortality, Lines on Tintern Abbey): *Clifford Bax*, The Marriage of the Soul; *Edward Carpenter*, Towards Democracy; *H. P. Blavatsky*, Practical Occultism.

Egyptian: The Hymns of Akhenaton the King-*Budge*, The Book of the Dead, Legends of the Gods; Coffin Texts; *Adolf Erman*, Gespräch eines Lebensmüden mit seiner Seele, Aegyptische Religion; *Hugo Gressmann*, Altorientalische Texte und Bilder; The Great Hymn to Amon; The Prophecy of Ipuwer; Maxims of Ani; *Dr. Kurt Sethe*, Altaegyptische Pyramidentexte; the Mystic Poem in Sallier Papyrus.

Indian: *Anonymous*, Ashtavakra Gita, Avadhuta Gita, Bhagavadgita, Bhāgavata Purāṇa, Devikalottaram, Ekagratamān Ishwar; Tripura Rahasya; *Asvaghosha*, The Awakening of Faith; *Avvayar*, Yoga Aphorisms; "*M*", The Gospel of Sri Ramakrishna; *Patanjali*, Yoga Aphorisms; *Samartha Ramadas*, Dasabodh; *Swami Ramdas*, Sayings, At the Feet of God; *Ramana Maharshi*, Anubandhan, Who am I?; *Sisirkumar Ghose*, Lord Gauranga; *Swami Sivananda Saraswati*, Stotra Ratnamāla; *Tukārām*, Abhangas.

BOOKS ON THE HERMETICA 253

Various : Genza, Turfān Inscriptions, de Castigatione Animarum, Jetsün Kahbum, Shikand Gumānig Vizar, The Book of Mencius, The Book of Ostanes, Hermippus, *Mead*, The Gnostic Crucifixion, The Mithriac Ritual.

PARALLELS WITH THE GOSPEL OF ISLAM

Gospel of Hermes	Gospel of Islam	Gospel of Hermes	Gospel of Islam
1 : 1	4—5 : 1	27 : 5	52 : 6
2 : 3	8 : 1	28 : 1 51 : 1	53—54 : 2-3
4 : 1	10 : 2	28 : 1-2,5	50 : 1-2, 4
4 : 2	17 : 2—54	28 : 3	64
5 : 1	96-98	28 : 3-4	50 : 5
5 : 2	60 : 1	28 : 5	68 : 3
5 : 3	54 : 1, 3—55 : 1	29 : 3	98 : 2, 4
6 : 3	12 : 3—56 : 1, 7	29 : 5	56 : 5
6 : 4	31	29 : 8	54
7 : 3	8 : 1	29 : 9	16 : 5
8	25—32	29 : 13	13 : 2—51
9 : 2-3	97 : 2	30 : 4	91 : 2
9 : 4	1 : 1	30 : 3, 6	64
10 : 1	65 : 3	31 : 1	91 : 2
10 : 2	11 : 5	31 : 4	93 : 2
10 : 3	2 : 1, 3	32	54
11 : 1	2 : 5—68 : 3	34 : 6	61 : 3—62 : 3
12 : 3	16 : 4	34 : 7	94 : 2
14 : 1	6 ; 2	34 : 8	48—52
15 : 1	8 : 1	35 : 1	19 : 2
16 : 5	10 : 4	36 : 1	7 : 3
16 : 8	7 : 3—18 : 1	36 : 6	10 : 5-6
17 : 1	71	37 : 1	1 : 2
17 : 2	7 : 3	37 : 3	92 : 1
18 : 1	94 : 2	37 : 3-5 29 : 3—32—39 : 2
21 : 1	7 : 4	38 : 2-3	56 : 5, 7
21 : 2	9 : 2	39 : 2	91 : 2—96-8
21 : 3	1 : 2	40 : 1	34 : 3
21 : 4	8 : 3	40 : 7	O. P.
22 : 2	6 : 1	43 : 1	93 : 1
22 : 3	1 : 2	43 : 3	O. P.
23 : 4-5	9 : 2—10 : 5	45 : 2	68 : 3
23 : 6	14 : 1-2	47 : 2	7 : 5, 10 : 1, 5, 11 : 4
25 : 1-3	14 : 1	47 : 5	99—C. P.
26	84 : 1	49 : 1	92 : 1

These lists of parallels may be taken as a suggestive aid in comparative study, but must not be taken as exhaustive.

PARALLELS WITH THE GOSPEL OF CHINA

Gospel of Hermes	Gospel of China	Gospel of Hermes	Gospel of China
1 : 1	13 : 3	32 : 2	17 : 6
3 : 1	37 : 3	33	17 : 1, 4-5—39
4 : 4	40 : 3	34 : 6	36 : 2
5 : 1	23 : 1	35 : 1	38 : 5
6 : 2-3	10 : 1	35 : 2	15 : 1, 5
6 : 4	25 : 1—43 : 6	36 : 3	16 : 6
8 : 2	30 : 3	36 : 3-4	16—25 : 1-3
9 : 2	24 : 1	36 : 5	37 : 3
18 : 1-2	14 : 4	36 : 6	16 : 10
18 : 3	15 : 3	37 : 4	20 : 1
18 : 4	42 : 4	38 : 1	29 : 1—31 : 1-2
21 : 1-2	16 : 8	38 : 2	16 : 2, 29 : 3, 41 : 2
21 : 3	17 : 3	38 : 4	3
22 : 2	16 : 9	38 : 5	16 : 2
23 : 4-5	16 : 8	39 : 1	27 : 1—31 ; 1
27 : 1-2	34 : 3	39 : 2	14 : 3—24 : 1—
27 : 3	31 : 1		40 : 2-3, 43 : 4-5
27 : 5	32 : 6—42 : 4	40 : 2	41 : 2
28 : 1	38 : 1—39 : 9	40 : 2-3	41 : 3
28 : 4	43 : 1-2	40 : 4	41 : 4—42 : 4
28 : 5	36 : 1—37 : 4	40 : 6	22 : 3
29 : 1, 3	10 : 1	40 : 7	20 : 1
29 : 4	29 : 5—36 : 3	41 : 1	43 : 3
29 : 9	17 : 3	42 : 3	13 : 3
29 : 11	44 : 2	42 : 4	24 : 1
29 : 12	38 : 1	42 : 5	41 : 2—43 : 2
29 : 13	36 : 2	44 : 1	41 : 4
30	33 : 3	45 : 1-2	11 : 4
30 : 2	14 : 4	45 : 3	12 : 2
30 : 3	37 : 3	47 : 1	11 : 4-5
30 : 4	36 : 1	49 : 2	12 : 2—13 : 1—
31 : 3	24 : 1		22 : 6, 35 : 6

PARALLELS WITH THE GOSPEL OF JESUS

Gospel of Hermes	Gospel of Jesus	Gospel of Hermes	Gospel of Jesus
3 : 4	103 : 2—106 : 2	30 : 3	7 : 2
5 : 3	13 : 1-5—103 : 2—106 : 2	30 : 4-5	44 : 2
6 : 2	13 : 1—5	31 : 1	44 : 2
6 : 3	16 : 4	31 : 2	83
6 : 4	61	31 : 3	80
7 : 2	42 : 2—49 : 1—95	33	105 : 2
7 : 3	48	34 : 2	110 : 1
8 : 1	1 : 1—6 : 1	34 : 3	101
8 : 2-3	1 : 2	36 : 2, 4	61
8 : 2	16 ; 3	37 : 3	1 : 1—6 : 1
8 : 3	11—35 : 1—42 : 2	37 : 4	2
8 : 3-4	63	37 : 4-5	30
8 : 4	37—46—60	38 : 3	14 : 1
9 : 1	94	38 : 5	31 : 5-6
10 : 1-2	72	38 : 6	72
10 : 2	49 : 1—69 : 1	39	70
11 : 1	5 : 2—13 : 5—16 : 4	39 : 1	27 : 1—38 : 1
11 : 4	78 : 1	39 : 2	13 : 5
11 : 5	79	40 : 5-7	67 : 1—68
16 : 8	42 : 2	40 : 6	74 : 1—90
20 : 1	73 : 1	40 : 7	107 : 2
21 : 3	69 : 3	41 ; 5	67 : 1—68
22 : 2	69 ; 3	42 : 2	74 : 2
27 : 3	14 : 1	42 : 3, 5	103 ; 1
27 : 5	120 : 2	43	48
28 : 1	12—47 : 2—50 : 3	43 : 2	14 : 2
28 : 2	118 : 6—120 : 2	43 : 3	42 : 2
28 : 3	7 : 2	43 : 5	49 : 1
28 : 5	61—79	44	75
29 : 4	16 : 2—47 : 2	45 : 1	23
29 : 8	12	45 : 3	104 : 2
29 : 9	42 : 2—50 : 3	47 : 2	74 : 2
29 : 11	73 : 2—75	47 : 5	42 : 2
29 : 12	28	48 : 2	42 : 2
29 : 13	15 : 1-2—17 : 3—27 : 3 and 51	48 : 4	1 : 2—25—45—54—56—57 : 2 and 97 : 1-2
30 : 2	28	49 : 2	107 : 2

PARALLELS WITH THE GOSPEL OF ZARATHUSHTRA

Gospel of Hermes	Gospel of Zarathushtra	Gospel of Hermes	Gospel of Zarathushtra
1 : 1	27 : 2, 54 : 1, 65	16 : 3	22 : 1
1 : 2	27 : 4, 45 : 3, 5, 55 : 3	16 : 4	20 : 4, 22 : 1, 3
1 : 3	3 : 1	16 : 5	7 : 1
2 : 1	56 : 1	16 : 8	31 : 4, 45 : 3, 61 : 1, 66 : 1
2 : 3	7 : 8	17 : 2	7 : 8, 33 : 4, 45 : 3, 54 : 5
2 : 5	66 : 3	18 : 1	56 : 1, 69 : 1
3 : 1	7 : 8	18 : 3	46 : 1
3 : 2	24 : 1	20 : 1	7 : 8, 45 : 3
3 : 4	36 : 2, 40 : 1	21 : 1	45 : 3
4 : 1	32 : 2	21 : 2-4	66 : 3-5
4 : 3	36 : 1-3, 45 : 1	22 : 1	2 : 2, 54 : 2
5 : 1-2	46 : 2, 61 : 2, 3, 74 : 4	22 : 3	7 : 8
5 : 3	41 : 2-4, 58 : 2, 63 : 1	22 : 4	60 : 3
6 : 1	66 : 1-2	23 : 1	17 : 2
6 : 2	44 : 1	23 : 2	53 : 1, 61 : 1, 62 : 2
6 : 3	44 : 2-5, 78 : 3, 5	23 : 4	52 : 3, 66 : 3-5
6 : 4	3 : 5, 28 : 4	23 : 6	26 : 2, 36 : 2
7 : 2	53 : 1, 61 : 4, 63 : 3	23 : 8	55 : 2
7 : 3	29 : 6	23 : 9	51 : 5
8 : 1-2	30 : 2-3, 54 : 1, 65 : 4, 69 : 1	24	61 : 1, 68 : 6
		25	36 : 2
		26	81 : 3
8 : 3	31 : 4, 36 : 3	27 : 1	36 : 2, 39 : 1
8 : 4	30 : 4	27 : 3	32 : 1, 36 : 1, 53 : 1
9 : 2	51 : 5		60 : 3, 66 : 1
10 : 1	6 : 1-2	27 : 5	36 : 2-3, 44 : 1
10 : 3	66 : 1	28 : 1-2	36 : 1, 38 : 2-3, 41 : 3
11 : 1	7 : 8		80 : 2, 81 : 4
11 : 3	7 : 2, 46 : 1	28 : 3	40 : 2, 7
12 : 2	51 : 5	28 : 4-5	51 : 5, 53 : 1-2
12 : 3	31 : 1, 62 : 1	29 : 2	25
13 : 1	69 : 1	29 : 3	31 : 4
14 : 2	5 : 1, 29 : 6	27 : 2	36 : 2
14 : 3-4	1 : 1, 7 : 8	29 : 4	37 : 1
16 : 1	52 : 3	29 : 5-6	25 : 2, 41 : 3
16 : 2	3 : 1, 45 : 1-2		

Gospel of Hermes	Gospel of Zarathushtra	Gospel of Hermes	Gospel of Zarathushtra
29 : 8	41 : 2	37 : 1	3 : 1, 20 : 3
29 : 9	81 : 4	37 : 2	26 : 3, 46 : 2
29 : 10	2 : 2, 28 : 3, 32 : 1	37 : 3	28 : 4, 52 : 5
	31 : 4, 46 : 2	37 : 5	51 : 5
29 : 12-13	41 : 4, 59 : 1, 79 : 4	38 : 1	31 : 2, 32 : 1
30 : 1	54 : 4	38 : 2	31 : 1, 46 : 2
30 : 3	61 : 1	38 : 3	33 : 2-3
30 : 4	37 : 3	38 : 6	69 : 5-6
30 : 5	18 : 2	39 : 1	46 : 2
30 : 6	54 : 4, 57 : 1, 74 : 2	40 : 4	60 : 3
31 : 1	51 : 5	40 : 7	37 : 3
31 : 2	29 : 4, 37 : 3, 57 : 1	41 : 1	69 : 1
31 : 5	57 : 1-2	43 : 3	53 : 1
32 : 1	39 : 1	43 : 4	61 : 3
32 : 2	38 : 3, 71 : 2	43 : 5	80 : 3
33 : 1	18 : 1, 26 : 1, 68 : 5, 74 : 3	45 : 1-2	36 : 3, 46 : 2
34 : 2, 3, 6	48 : 4	45 : 2	50 : 1
34 : 4	48 : 3	46 : 1	66 : 1
35 : 1-2	7 : 8—14—16	47 : 2	24 : 2, 69 : 4
36 : 1-3	36 : 1, 45 : 3-4, 56 : 1	47 : 4	55 : 4
36 : 5	62 : 2	49 : 1	31 : 3

PARALLELS WITH THE GOSPEL OF THE MYSTIC CHRIST

Gospel of Hermes	Gospel of the Mystic Christ	Gospel of Hermes	Gospel of the Mystic Christ
1 : 1	49 : 5, 53 : 9, 69 ; 2	18 : 1	53 : 9
1 : 2	P. 1-2	18 : 3	69 : 2
2 : 1	38 : 3-4, 53 : 8	18 : 4	30 : 3
2 : 1, 4	P. 1-2	19 : 3	29 : 5
2 : 5	32 : 7	20 : 1	P. 1
3 : 1	P. 2, 30 : 4	20 : 5-6, 10	53 : 8
3 : 3	69 : 2	22 : 1-2	40 : 1
3 : 4	69 : 1	22 : 4	P. 3
3 : 5	P. 3	23 : 12	P. 3
4 : 2	47 : 3	25 : 1	1 ; 5, 2 : 7, 3 : 2
4 : 4	P. 1-2	27 : 3	49 : 2-3
5 : 1	53 : 1, 8	28 : 1-2	48 : 3-4
5 : 3	49 : 2	28 : 1-3, 5	49 : 2-3
6 : 1-2	63 : 5	28 : 3	47 : 4
6 : 3	8 : 2, 70 : 1, 72 ; 2	28 : 4	53 : 1
6 : 4	53 : 8, 69 : 1	29 : 3, 9	54 : 5
7 : 1	53 : 9	29 : 4	32 : 7
7 : 2-3	54	29 : 9	53 : 1
8 : 1	69 : 2	29 : 11	8 : 4
8 : 2	22 : 3	30 : 1, 6	22 ; 3, 33 : 1
8 : 3	38 ; 4, 40	30 : 3	38 : 4
8 : 4	24 : 2, 35 : 3, 38 : 1	31 : 1	33 : 2
9 : 1	47 : 4	31 : 3	30 : 3
9 : 2-3	P. 3, 24 : 3, 30 : 2-3	33 : 2	58 : 3, 60 : 3
10 : 2	53 : 5	34 : 1, 7	48 : 1
11 : 3, 5	47 : 2-3	34 : 2, 6	47 : 2
12 : 3	3 : 8	34 : 3-4	43 : 2
13 : 1	P. 1, 24 : 3	34 : 6	38 : 1
14 ; 2, 4	P. 1, 3, 24 : 3	35 : 1	48 : 3
15 : 2	P. 2, 30 : 4	36 : 1, 3	30 : 4
16 : 1	24 : 3	36 : 2	53 : 9
16 : 1-2	P. 1	36 : 4	P. 1
16 : 7	54 : 4	36 : 6	53 : 1
16 : 8	P. 2, 35 : 7, 53 : 3	37 : 3, 5	21 : 3-5
17 : 2	69 : 2	38 : 1	28 : 3

Gospel of Hermes	Gospel of the Mystic Christ	Gospel of Hermes	Gospel of the Mystic Christ
38 : 2	8 : 2, 53 : 9	43 : 4	70 : 2
39 : 2	53 : 4	43 : 5	54 : 3-5
40 : 2	58 : 3	44 : 1	30 : 2, 41 : 1, 49 :
40 : 4	P. 3	44 : 2	2 : 7, 3 : 23
40 : 6	49 : 3	45 : 2-3	P. 2-3
40 : 7	47 : 4	46 : 2	53 : 9
41 : 1	30 : 3	47 : 2	P. 2, 24 : 2, 30 : 4
41 : 5	53 : 9, 71 : 6	47 : 4	39 : 5
42 : 1	69 : 2	47 : 5	54 : 1
42 : 5	48 : 2	48 : 3	53 : 5
43 : 2	24 : 3	48 : 4	53 : 3
43 : 3	54 : 2	49 : 2	47 : 4

ALSO AVAILABLE FROM THE BOOK TREE

PISTIS SOPHIA: A Gnostic Gospel, translated by G.R.S. Mead. The Gnostics were part of early Christianity and were composed of a number of mystical sects. This was one of their gospels. Virtually all Gnostic teachers were persecuted and their documents destroyed because the Church needed a uniform set of beliefs to operate under. Only now have we begun to better understand these early Christian mystics. This work remains an important milestone in Gnostic research, on par with Nag Hammadi, and should be part of any serious study. It tells the story of how we, as spiritual beings, have fallen into the world of physical creation. The soul is asleep here, bogged down in physical surroundings, unaware of our true nature. The purpose of Pistis Sophia is to awaken us, and to aid in the process of spiritual freedom. **400 pages • hardcover $55.00 • softcover $27.95**

THE BOOK OF JUBILEES, Translated by R. H. Charles. This rare and important holy book sheds new light on Judaism and early Christianity. It was written sometime between 250 BC and AD 100 by one or more Hellenistic Jews, and reflects a form of Jewish mystical thought at around the time of Christ. It retells much of the Old Testament story, but includes additional material not mentioned in the Bible. It also relies heavily on *The Book of Enoch*, which was, like this book, translated from the Ethiopic text. It covers Adam and Eve, the Fall of Man, Cain and Abel, the fall of the angels and their punishment, the deluge foretold, the ark and the flood, the tower of Babel and confusion of tongues, evil spirits, corruption of the human race, God's covenant, the Messianic Kingdom, Jacob's visions, prophetic dreams, and Moses, among other interesting topics. **224 pages • paper $18.95**

THE LOST BOOKS OF THE BIBLE OR THE APOCRYPHAL NEW TESTAMENT, assembled by William Hone. Translated by William Wake and Jeremiah Jones. First published in 1820 under the title The Apocryphal New Testement. These documents were written soon after the death of Christ, during the early days of Christianity. Yet when the Bible was compiled near the end of the fourth century, these texts were not included and were suppressed by the church. **295 pages • 6 x 9 • paper • $24.95**

THE BOOK OF ADAM AND EVE or The Conflict of Adam and Eve with Satan, Translated by Rev. S.C. Malan. This book reveals the life and times of Adam and Eve after they were expelled from the Garden of Eden, up to the time when Cain killed his brother Abel. It covers where they went, where they lived, and their various troubles and temptations, including those coming from Satan. This is an interesting book because it provides one with more information to work with beyond the standard Biblical account. The work includes a number of helpful notes by the translator, issued for clarification, and they appear consistently throughout the text. **256 pages • 6 x 9 • paper • $21.95**

To order call 1.800.700.TREE 24 hrs. OR visit www.thebooktree.com

ORDER FROM YOUR FAVORITE BOOKSELLER OR CALL FOR OUR FREE CATALOG

Sun Lore of All Ages: A Survey of Solar Mythology, Folklore, Customs, Worship, Festivals, and Superstition, by William Tyler Olcott. ISBN 1-58509-044-1 • 316 pages • 6 x 9 • trade paper • $24.95

Nature Worship: An Account of Phallic Faiths and Practices Ancient and Modern, by the Author of Phallicism with an Introduction by Tedd St. Rain. ISBN 1-58509-049-2 • 112 pages • 6 x 9 • trade paper • illustrated • $12.95

Life and Religion, by Max Muller. ISBN 1-885395-10-8 • 237 pages • 5 1/2 x 8 1/2 • trade paper • $14.95

Jesus: God, Man, or Myth? An Examination of the Evidence, by Herbert Cutner. ISBN 1-58509-072-7 • 304 pages • 6 x 9 • trade paper • $23.95

Pagan and Christian Creeds: Their Origin and Meaning, by Edward Carpenter. ISBN 1-58509-024-7 • 316 pages • 5 1/2 x 8 1/2 • trade paper • $24.95

The Christ Myth: A Study, by Elizabeth Evans. ISBN 1-58509-037-9 • 136 pages • 6 x 9 • trade paper • $13.95

Popery: Foe of the Church and the Republic, by Joseph F. Van Dyke. ISBN 1-58509-058-1 • 336 pages • 6 x 9 • trade paper • illustrated • $25.95

Career of Religious Ideas, by Hudson Tuttle. ISBN 1-58509-066-2 • 172 pages • 5 x 8 • trade paper • $15.95

Buddhist Suttas: Major Scriptural Writings from Early Buddhism, by T.W. Rhys Davids. ISBN 1-58509-079-4 • 376 pages • 6 x 9 • trade paper • $27.95

Early Buddhism, by T. W. Rhys Davids. Includes ***Buddhist Ethics: The Way to Salvation?,*** by Paul Tice. ISBN 1-58509-076-X • 112 pages • 6 x 9 • trade paper • $12.95

The Fountain-Head of Religion: A Comparative Study of the Principal Religions of the World and a Manifestation of their Common Origin from the Vedas, by Ganga Prasad. ISBN 1-58509-054-9 • 276 pages • 6 x 9 • trade paper • $22.95

India: What Can It Teach Us?, by Max Muller. ISBN 1-58509-064-6 • 284 pages • 5 1/2 x 8 1/2 • trade paper • $22.95

Matrix of Power: How the World has Been Controlled by Powerful People Without Your Knowledge, by Jordan Maxwell. ISBN 1-58509-120-0 • 104 pages • 6 x 9 • trade paper • $12.95

Cyberculture Counterconspiracy: A Steamshovel Web Reader, Volume One, edited by Kenn Thomas. ISBN 1-58509-125-1 • 180 pages • 6 x 9 • trade paper • illustrated • $16.95

Cyberculture Counterconspiracy: A Steamshovel Web Reader, Volume Two, edited by Kenn Thomas. ISBN 1-58509-126-X • 132 pages • 6 x 9 • trade paper • illustrated • $13.95

Oklahoma City Bombing: The Suppressed Truth, by Jon Rappoport. ISBN 1-885395-22-1 • 112 pages • 5 1/2 x 8 1/2 • trade paper • $12.95

The Protocols of the Learned Elders of Zion, by Victor Marsden. ISBN 1-58509-015-8 • 312 pages • 6 x 9 • trade paper • $24.95

Secret Societies and Subversive Movements, by Nesta H. Webster. ISBN 1-58509-092-1 • 432 pages • 6 x 9 • trade paper • $29.95

The Secret Doctrine of the Rosicrucians, by Magus Incognito. ISBN 1-58509-091-3 • 256 pages • 6 x 9 • trade paper • $20.95

The Origin and Evolution of Freemasonry: Connected with the Origin and Evolution of the Human Race, by Albert Churchward. ISBN 1-58509-029-8 • 240 pages • 6 x 9 • trade paper • $18.95

The Lost Key: An Explanation and Application of Masonic Symbols, by Prentiss Tucker. ISBN 1-58509-050-6 • 192 pages • 6 x 9 • trade paper • illustrated • $15.95

The Character, Claims, and Practical Workings of Freemasonry, by Rev. C.G. Finney. ISBN 1-58509-094-8 • 288 pages • 6 x 9 • trade paper • $22.95

The Secret World Government or "The Hidden Hand": The Unrevealed in History, by Maj.-Gen., Count Cherep-Spiridovich. ISBN 1-58509-093-X • 203 pages • 6 x 9 • trade paper • $17.95

The Magus, Book One: A Complete System of Occult Philosophy, by Francis Barrett. ISBN 1-58509-031-X • 200 pages • 6 x 9 • trade paper • illustrated • $16.95

The Magus, Book Two: A Complete System of Occult Philosophy, by Francis Barrett. ISBN 1-58509-032-8 • 220 pages • 6 x 9 • trade paper • illustrated • $17.95

The Magus, Book One and Two: A Complete System of Occult Philosophy, by Francis Barrett. ISBN 1-58509-033-6 • 420 pages • 6 x 9 • trade paper • illustrated • $34.90

The Key of Solomon The King, by S. Liddell MacGregor Mathers. ISBN 1-58509-022-0 • 152 pages • 6 x 9 • trade paper • illustrated • $12.95

Magic and Mystery in Tibet, by Alexandra David-Neel. ISBN 1-58509-097-2 • 352 pages • 6 x 9 • trade paper • $26.95

The Comte de St. Germain, by I. Cooper Oakley. ISBN 1-58509-068-9 • 280 pages • 6 x 9 • trade paper • illustrated • $22.95

Alchemy Rediscovered and Restored, by A. Cockren. ISBN 1-58509-028-X • 156 pages • 5 1/2 x 8 1/2 • trade paper • $13.95

The 6th and 7th Books of Moses, with an Introduction by Paul Tice. ISBN 1-58509-045-X • 188 pages • 6 x 9 • trade paper • illustrated • $16.95

ORDER FROM YOUR FAVORITE BOOKSELLER OR CALL FOR OUR FREE CATALOG

Babylonian Influence on the Bible and Popular Beliefs: A Comparative Study of Genesis I.2, by A. Smythe Palmer. ISBN 1-58509-000-X • 124 pages • 6 x 9 • trade paper • $12.95

Biography of Satan: Exposing the Origins of the Devil, by Kersey Graves. ISBN 1-885395-11-6 • 168 pages • 5 1/2 x 8 1/2 • trade paper • $13.95

The Malleus Maleficarum: The Notorious Handbook Once Used to Condemn and Punish "Witches", by Heinrich Kramer and James Sprenger. ISBN 1-58509-098-0 • 332 pages • 6 x 9 • trade paper • $25.95

Crux Ansata: An Indictment of the Roman Catholic Church, by H. G. Wells. ISBN 1-58509-210-X • 160 pages • 6 x 9 • trade paper • $14.95

Emanuel Swedenborg: The Spiritual Columbus, by U.S.E. (William Spear). ISBN 1-58509-096-4 • 208 pages • 6 x 9 • trade paper • $17.95

Dragons and Dragon Lore, by Ernest Ingersoll. ISBN 1-58509-021-2 • 228 pages • 6 x 9 • trade paper • illustrated • $17.95

The Vision of God, by Nicholas of Cusa. ISBN 1-58509-004-2 • 160 pages • 5 x 8 • trade paper • $13.95

The Historical Jesus and the Mythical Christ: Separating Fact From Fiction, by Gerald Massey. ISBN 1-58509-073-5 • 244 pages • 6 x 9 • trade paper • $18.95

Gog and Magog: The Giants in Guildhall; Their Real and Legendary History, with an Account of Other Giants at Home and Abroad, by F.W. Fairholt. ISBN 1-58509-084-0 • 172 pages • 6 x 9 • trade paper • $16.95

The Origin and Evolution of Religion, by Albert Churchward. ISBN 1-58509-078-6 • 504 pages • 6 x 9 • trade paper • $39.95

The Origin of Biblical Traditions, by Albert T. Clay. ISBN 1-58509-065-4 • 220 pages • 5 1/2 x 8 1/2 • trade paper • $17.95

Aryan Sun Myths, by Sarah Elizabeth Titcomb. Introduction by Charles Morris. ISBN 1-58509-069-7 • 192 pages • 6 x 9 • trade paper • $15.95

The Social Record of Christianity, by Joseph McCabe. Includes *The Lies and Fallacies of the Encyclopedia Britannica,* ISBN 1-58509-215-0 • 204 pages • 6 x 9 • trade paper • $17.95

The History of the Christian Religion and Church During the First Three Centuries, by Dr. Augustus Neander. ISBN 1-58509-077-8 • 112 pages • 6 x 9 • trade paper • $12.95

Ancient Symbol Worship: Influence of the Phallic Idea in the Religions of Antiquity, by Hodder M. Westropp and C. Staniland Wake. ISBN 1-58509-048-4 • 120 pages • 6 x 9 • trade paper • illustrated • $12.95

The Gnosis: Or Ancient Wisdom in the Christian Scriptures, by William Kingsland. ISBN 1-58509-047-6 • 232 pages • 6 x 9 • trade paper • $18.95

The Evolution of the Idea of God: An Inquiry into the Origin of Religions, by Grant Allen. ISBN 1-58509-074-3 • 160 pages • 6 x 9 • trade paper • $14.95

Sun Lore of All Ages: A Survey of Solar Mythology, Folklore, Customs, Worship, Festivals, and Superstition, by William Tyler Olcott. ISBN 1-58509-044-1 • 316 pages • 6 x 9 • trade paper • $24.95

Nature Worship: An Account of Phallic Faiths and Practices Ancient and Modern, by the Author of Phallicism with an Introduction by Tedd St. Rain. ISBN 1-58509-049-2 • 112 pages • 6 x 9 • trade paper • illustrated • $12.95

Life and Religion, by Max Muller. ISBN 1-885395-10-8 • 237 pages • 5 1/2 x 8 1/2 • trade paper • $14.95

Jesus: God, Man, or Myth? An Examination of the Evidence, by Herbert Cutner. ISBN 1-58509-072-7 • 304 pages • 6 x 9 • trade paper • $23.95

Pagan and Christian Creeds: Their Origin and Meaning, by Edward Carpenter. ISBN 1-58509-024-7 • 316 pages • 5 1/2 x 8 1/2 • trade paper • $24.95

The Christ Myth: A Study, by Elizabeth Evans. ISBN 1-58509-037-9 • 136 pages • 6 x 9 • trade paper • $13.95

Popery: Foe of the Church and the Republic, by Joseph F. Van Dyke. ISBN 1-58509-058-1 • 336 pages • 6 x 9 • trade paper • illustrated • $25.95

Career of Religious Ideas, by Hudson Tuttle. ISBN 1-58509-066-2 • 172 pages • 5 x 8 • trade paper • $15.95

Buddhist Suttas: Major Scriptural Writings from Early Buddhism, by T.W. Rhys Davids. ISBN 1-58509-079-4 • 376 pages • 6 x 9 • trade paper • $27.95

Early Buddhism, by T. W. Rhys Davids. Includes *Buddhist Ethics: The Way to Salvation?,* by Paul Tice. ISBN 1-58509-076-X • 112 pages • 6 x 9 • trade paper • $12.95

The Fountain-Head of Religion: A Comparative Study of the Principal Religions of the World and a Manifestation of their Common Origin from the Vedas, by Ganga Prasad. ISBN 1-58509-054-9 • 276 pages • 6 x 9 • trade paper • $22.95

India: What Can It Teach Us?, by Max Muller. ISBN 1-58509-064-6 • 284 pages • 5 1/2 x 8 1/2 • trade paper • $22.95

Matrix of Power: How the World has Been Controlled by Powerful People Without Your Knowledge, by Jordan Maxwell. ISBN 1-58509-120-0 • 104 pages • 6 x 9 • trade paper • $12.95

Cyberculture Counterconspiracy: A Steamshovel Web Reader, Volume One, edited by Kenn Thomas. ISBN 1-58509-125-1 • 180 pages • 6 x 9 • trade paper • illustrated • $16.95

Cyberculture Counterconspiracy: A Steamshovel Web Reader, Volume Two, edited by Kenn Thomas. ISBN 1-58509-126-X • 132 pages • 6 x 9 • trade paper • illustrated • $13.95

Oklahoma City Bombing: The Suppressed Truth, by Jon Rappoport. ISBN 1-885395-22-1 • 112 pages • 5 1/2 x 8 1/2 • trade paper • $12.95

The Protocols of the Learned Elders of Zion, by Victor Marsden. ISBN 1-58509-015-8 • 312 pages • 6 x 9 • trade paper • $24.95

Secret Societies and Subversive Movements, by Nesta H. Webster. ISBN 1-58509-092-1 • 432 pages • 6 x 9 • trade paper • $29.95

The Secret Doctrine of the Rosicrucians, by Magus Incognito. ISBN 1-58509-091-3 • 256 pages • 6 x 9 • trade paper • $20.95

The Origin and Evolution of Freemasonry: Connected with the Origin and Evolution of the Human Race, by Albert Churchward. ISBN 1-58509-029-8 • 240 pages • 6 x 9 • trade paper • $18.95

The Lost Key: An Explanation and Application of Masonic Symbols, by Prentiss Tucker. ISBN 1-58509-050-6 • 192 pages • 6 x 9 • trade paper • illustrated • $15.95

The Character, Claims, and Practical Workings of Freemasonry, by Rev. C.G. Finney. ISBN 1-58509-094-8 • 288 pages • 6 x 9 • trade paper • $22.95

The Secret World Government or "The Hidden Hand": The Unrevealed in History, by Maj.-Gen. Count Cherep-Spiridovich. ISBN 1-58509-093-X • 270 pages • 6 x 9 • trade paper • $21.95

The Magus, Book One: A Complete System of Occult Philosophy, by Francis Barrett. ISBN 1-58509-031-X • 200 pages • 6 x 9 • trade paper • illustrated • $16.95

The Magus, Book Two: A Complete System of Occult Philosophy, by Francis Barrett. ISBN 1-58509-032-8 • 220 pages • 6 x 9 • trade paper • illustrated • $17.95

The Magus, Book One and Two: A Complete System of Occult Philosophy, by Francis Barrett. ISBN 1-58509-033-6 • 420 pages • 6 x 9 • trade paper • illustrated • $34.90

The Key of Solomon The King, by S. Liddell MacGregor Mathers. ISBN 1-58509-022-0 • 152 pages • 6 x 9 • trade paper • illustrated • $12.95

Magic and Mystery in Tibet, by Alexandra David-Neel. ISBN 1-58509-097-2 • 352 pages • 6 x 9 • trade paper • $26.95

The Comte de St. Germain, by I. Cooper Oakley. ISBN 1-58509-068-9 • 280 pages • 6 x 9 • trade paper • illustrated • $22.95

Alchemy Rediscovered and Restored, by A. Cockren. ISBN 1-58509-028-X • 156 pages • 5 1/2 x 8 1/2 • trade paper • $13.95

The 6th and 7th Books of Moses, with an Introduction by Paul Tice. ISBN 1-58509-045-X • 188 pages • 6 x 9 • trade paper • illustrated • $16.95

www.ingramcontent.com/pod-product-compliance
Lightning Source LLC
Chambersburg PA
CBHW020737160426
43192CB00006B/229